ON THE RAILS

ON THE RAILS

Two centuries of railways

Anthony Burton

AURUM PRESS

HALFTITLE: **A Southern Railways footplate crew pose aboard their N-Class mixed traffic 2-6-0.**
TITLE PAGE: **An immense long-distance freight snaking across California.**

CONTENTS

INTRODUCTION

This book was born out of an idea for a Discovery television series to coincide with the bicentenary of the first public exhibition of a steam locomotive running on rails. It is not intended to be the film repeated in words and still images. TV has the obvious advantage of being able to bring the excitement of movement and sound into the viewer's home. It also has disadvantages. The author can sit at his desk describing, say, a scene in Britain, and write 'meanwhile in Australia' at no extra cost, whereas taking a film crew halfway round the world is a hugely expensive business. So this is not so much the 'book of the film' as a book that develops the themes of the TV series, without the constraint of being tied to a limited number of specific locations. The book has a further advantage. In filming one is constrained by what is available to be filmed: in the book one can write about people who are no longer alive, describe locomotives that have long since ended their lives in the breaker's yard and conjure up the scenes of the past. Reading the book is intended to be a very different experience from seeing the films: the one should complement the other.

As always in such works, there are debts to acknowledge. The first is to Mark Strickson of Oxford Scientific Films who, having invited me to work on one series they were making for Discovery, was kind, or foolhardy, enough to invite me back for this second series. Peter Guest, the Production Manager, had the unenviable task of bringing everything together, and he and I seem to have had almost daily talks throughout the whole of the planning and filming period. The three directors – James Castle, Clare Dornan and Chris Barker – turned the basic storylines into films which bore their own individual stamp, and we have all worked together closely over the months of production. Last, but not least, thanks to my old friend Mark Williams for his huge gift in bringing everything to life.

One of my main concerns while preparing the book was that if we could not produce the moving image on the page, then the still images should be strong and powerful. I went to the doyen of railway photographers, Colin Garratt of Milepost $92\frac{1}{2}$, who has devoted himself to recording the last days of the age of steam. His superb pictures form the pictorial backbone to the whole book. The remaining pictures are from many sources, and tracking them down has been hard work, most of which has fallen to Pip, my wife and business partner. The fact that everything has come together to look so sumptuous is the result of some inspired designing by Robert Updegraff. We have worked together on many books, and he always takes the raw material and turns it into a prizewinning dish.

In writing a book like this one is always grateful for a friend to turn to for help, advice or just cheerful encouragement. The role in this case was taken by someone who once looked after my medical problems – my friend and fellow enthusiast Dr Wayne Smith.

Anthony Burton
STROUD, 2003

OPPOSITE: **An LMS 0-6-0 Tank, an engine equally at home in the shunting yard or, as here, with a light train of empties.**

CHAPTER 1

BEGINNINGS

I N FEBRUARY 1804, former curate and amateur scientist Davies Gilbert received a letter from a friend of his, a Cornish mining engineer engaged in experiments at the Penydarren Ironworks in Merthyr Tydfil.

Last saturday we lighted the fire in the Tram Waggon and workd it without the wheels to try the engine, and monday we put it on the Tram Road. It workd very well and ran up hill and down with great ease, and very managable. We have plenty of steam and power.

The letter may seem dull and matter of fact, but the engineer was Richard Trevithick, and the experiment he described was the very first public demonstration of a steam locomotive at work on an iron railway. It was an achievement with consequences far beyond Trevithick's wildest imaginings.

To understand the background to this momentous invention we have to go back to Cornwall at the beginning of the eighteenth century. The situation there was desperate. For centuries, the area's economy had depended on mining for tin and, more importantly, copper. There was still ore in plenty under the ground, but all mines present the same problem: the deeper you go, the more likely you are to meet water. Water-powered pumps had traditionally been used to deal with the difficulty, but now the shafts had sunk to a depth at which the old pumps no longer worked. If no solution could be found the mines would have to be abandoned and the ore left undisturbed in the ground.

The answer came from a Dartmouth blacksmith, Thomas Newcomen, who knew the mining community well as he regularly supplied them with tools and implements. His machine used pump rods moving regularly up and down in the mineshaft. The down movement was no problem: gravity provided that. What he needed was something to pull them up again. So he fastened the top of his rods to an overhead beam, pivoting in the centre. Below the other end of the beam he set a giant boiler, like an overgrown kettle, providing steam to a cylinder. Inside the cylinder was a piston, suspended from the beam. When the end of the beam over the cylinder was at its highest and the piston at the top of the cylinder, steam was admitted to the cylinder, and then condensed by spraying it with cold water. This created a partial vacuum, and atmospheric pressure forced the piston down. As a result, the beam at that end also moved down, so that the opposite end rose, lifting the pump rods. Equilibrium restored, gravity went to work again, forcing the pump

OPPOSITE: **A full-scale working replica of Trevithick's London road carriage, photographed in 2003, when it returned to steam down Leather Lane, Clerkenwell where it had been assembled two centuries before.**

rods down and drawing more steam into the cylinder as the piston rose, and the whole cycle was repeated. Newcomen had built a steam engine that could work pumps to greater depths than had ever been possible before. Cornwall was saved.

There was a major problem, however, with the Newcomen engine: it was hugely inefficient. This was fine when the engine was used at coal mines, where fuel was not a problem: it was a major expense in Cornwall, where fuel had to be imported at considerable expense. There was nothing much that could be done. The Newcomen engine was essential if mines were to be kept open. Local engineers introduced improvements, including Richard Trevithick Senior, but the effects were marginal. The engine had a fundamental flaw: huge amounts of heat were wasted in alternately heating and cooling the cylinder. James Black, Professor of Chemistry at Glasgow University, had proved not just that heat was needed to raise the temperature of a liquid or gas, but also that extra heat was required to turn the former into the latter. He called it latent heat. It was a law of science, and a law that decreed that the Newcomen engine would always be profligate with fuel.

At the same time that Black was explaining his findings in the 1760s, a young man called James Watt was asked to repair a model Newcomen engine for the University. He recognized exactly where the problem lay, and set about finding a solution. He built a separate condenser, so that the steam cylinder could always be kept hot. But heat would still escape through the top of the cylinder; sealing the top of the cylinder would reduce the loss, but if this was done air pressure could not provide the force to drive the piston down. Then came the great breakthrough. Why not, he argued, forget about air pressure altogether and use the expansive power of steam itself? There would now be a partial vacuum on one side of the piston and steam pressure on the other. This idea was revolutionary. The Newcomen engine only had power on the down stroke: the James Watt engine could have power on the up stroke as well. It was a reciprocating engine, and no great mechanical ingenuity was needed to transform it from a pumping engine to one that could drive machinery. It was still a beam engine, like Newcomen's, but if the pump rods were replaced with a sweep arm it could be used to turn a wheel.

James Watt found the perfect entrepreneurial partner in the Birmingham manufacturer Matthew Boulton, and together they acquired a patent which effectively gave them a monopoly of all steam-engine development until the end of the eighteenth century. At first, the Cornish mine engineers were happy with the arrangement, for their deal was that they would pay Boulton and Watt one third of the savings that had accrued from changing from a Newcomen engine to one of the new, improved Birmingham engines. But, as time went on, attitudes began to change. Boulton and Watt were wedded to the notion of only using low-pressure steam. If more power was needed, then a bigger engine was built – and over the years Cornwall was to be home to some real steam monsters with cylinders of up to 90-inch (230cm) diameter and overhead beams weighing many tons. These needed substantial engine houses, not just as protection but to act as a support for the beam. There were those who favoured the alternative approach of using high-pressure steam, but that idea was anathema to James Watt and he had the power to prevent all experiments in that direction. This rankled with the younger engineers, and no one was more impatient than

Richard Trevithick. He crossed swords on more than one occasion with Boulton and Watt, but they had the law on their side and he had to endure years of frustration before the great day arrived and the hated patent expired. In 1800 he began a series of bold experiments that was to change the world.

Trevithick's great idea was that by using steam at high pressure, he could get small engines to do work that had previously been reserved for giants. He had a vision of versatile engines that could be wheeled out to where they were needed, not rooted to the spot. For example, he designed an engine that could be brought out to the fields to thresh corn. This was still based on Watt's already well-established idea that an engine could turn a wheel and thus drive machinery. Trevithick made a huge intellectual leap. If a machine could turn a wheel, why shouldn't it turn the wheels of the vehicle on which it was mounted? Why couldn't it move itself? There was a practical point to be considered. Would a turning wheel give enough grip on the road, or would it simply spin idly? This was answered by a simple practical experiment. A cart was set on the road and the wheels were turned by Trevithick and Gilbert pushing on the spokes: the cart moved. The question had been answered. It is hard to overestimate the importance of what was happening here. Previously, the only way to move goods on land was by using animals as beasts of burden or to pull carts. This new type of cart would pull itself.

Richard Trevithick, painted shortly before he left for his ill-fated journey to South America. He is shown pointing towards the local artist's version of the Andes.

Experiments with steam traction were not entirely new. In 1769, a Frenchman Nicolas Cugnot had designed a steam tractor which he thought could be used instead of horses to haul gun carriages. It was a clumsy device, almost impossible to steer, and, because it had no water feed pump, had to stop every twenty minutes so it could be refilled with water. A stop-start machine was not exactly ideal for battlefield conditions. After a tentative, experimental run the machine was abandoned. The steam tractor may not have had any military value, but in later years the steam railway was to prove of immense significance in moving men and material. There was one other engineer in Cornwall working on the notion of a steam carriage. William Murdoch even got as far as building an experimental, small-scale model in the 1790s. It certainly worked, but Murdoch was Boulton and Watt's representative in Cornwall, and they made it clear that he had a simple choice: continue the experiments or leave the company. He stayed, leaving development to his near neighbour, Richard Trevithick. No one can now say whether they discussed their plans or not, but it was Trevithick who moved from model to full-scale locomotive.

His first road locomotive was built in 1801, using the talents of a local blacksmith, with its more complex parts cast at the foundry of his brother-in-law, Henry Harvey of Hayle. The machine was really very simple. At its heart was a boiler mounted on a wooden frame. Inside that was a U-shaped tube, with a firebox at one end and a chimney at the other. Hot gases from the fire heated the water and then exhausted up the chimney. A steam cylinder was set vertically in the boiler, and the exhaust steam passed up the chimney to join the gases from the fire. The passage of steam was controlled by a four-way cock, providing a very basic system for letting steam in and out of the cylinder. The piston rod transmitted the drive to the wheels via crossheads. A spectator, known to us simply as 'old Stephen Williams', described the first run made by Trevithick (Captain Dick):

> In the year 1801, upon Christmas-eve, coming on evening, Captain Dick got up steam, out in the high-road, just outside the shop at the Weith. When we get see'd that Captain Dick was agoing to turn on steam, we jumped up as many as could; maybe seven or eight of us. 'Twas a stiffish hill going from the Weith up to Camborne Beacon, but she went off like a little bird.

The engine was a triumph, and a replica built to celebrate this important event proved equally capable of conquering Camborne Hill. The prototype itself was destined to have a short life. On 28 December 1801, Trevithick and his partner in the venture, Andrew

This replica of Trevithick's first road locomotive was built to celebrate the bicentenary of its first journey up Camborne Hill. It has already survived a good deal longer than the original, which lasted less than a week.

Vivian, set off to show the marvel to the local gentry, who had taken a keen interest in the proceedings. It was at this stage that one of the fundamental problems was revealed. Up to this point no one had actually needed to steer a self-propelled vehicle. If you wanted to turn a corner with a cart, you pulled at the reins to turn the horse, and the cart would follow on. Trevithick used a simple tiller to move the front wheels, but it was an ungainly device and difficult to control. In the event, it proved too difficult. The steam carriage ended in a ditch, and the party abandoned it and went off to the nearest pub. Sadly, no one had thought to put out the fire under the boiler. One loud bang, and the world's first successful steam carriage was spread around the Cornish countryside. Undeterred, Trevithick and Vivian moved on to greater things. The second carriage was to be, in effect, a steam-powered stagecoach with immense driving wheels. The passenger compartment rode high, and the large wheels theoretically made for a smoother passage on the bumpy roads of the time. Even so, a sea captain who tried it complained that he was 'more likely to suffer shipwreck on the steam-carriage than on board his vessel'. The steering problem had not been solved, and although the inventors made numerous demonstration runs in London, no one was interested.

The partnership between the two men was dissolved, with no profit to show for their efforts, but Trevithick had not yet done with steam on the move. The next part of the story is more than a little hazy. There is evidence that in 1803, Trevithick went up to Shropshire to the famous iron works at Coalbrookdale. This was one of the great innovative centres of the Industrial Revolution. The foundry had pioneered the use of coke in blast furnaces, cast the parts for the first iron bridge and solved the problem of producing steam cylinders for Watt's engines, and had a brisk business in casting iron rails for horse-drawn tramways. Trevithick had now changed his ideas, yet again, about how his locomotive might be used. Disappointed at the lack of interest in his road carriage, he went back to his earlier notion of a mobile, self-propelled power unit.

At Coalbrookdale, he found all the elements came together. Iron works at the time used water power for a number of operations, from working the bellows for the blast furnaces to powering the tilt hammers that shaped the iron. And at Coalbrookdale the works had laid out a tramway. The most efficient form of transport at this time was by water, but not all works were near a navigable river or canal. It became a common practice to lay down a simple railway to link the works to the nearest waterway. At first, these were made using wooden rails for the horse-drawn trucks. But, thanks to the work of the Coalbrookdale engineers, iron rails were becoming increasingly popular. Coalbrookdale was linked to the River Severn at Ironbridge, and sections of the simple tramway can still be seen beside the iron warehouse just upstream of the famous bridge. As all the heavy loads ran from the works to the river, gravity helped and the main job of the horses was to haul back the empty trucks. Trevithick's plan was to build an engine that could be used to work machinery at the foundry, and when it was not required for that job could be used to transport the trucks on the tramway. It was to be a versatile machine. But was it ever built?

The first evidence comes from a letter written by Trevithick in August 1802 in which he gave a long description of work on an engine, working at what was then the very high pressure of 145 pounds per square inch (psi), compared to the Boulton and Watt standard of about 10 psi. At the end he adds almost casually: 'The Dale Co have begun a carriage at their own cost for the real-roads and is forcing it with all expedition.' The man in charge at Coalbrookdale at that time was William Reynolds, who had already been considering the idea of building a steam locomotive and had a reputation for adventurous projects. The appeal for Trevithick was clear. His earlier plans had been thwarted in large measure by the problems of steering his carriage: put the carriage on rails, however, and the problem ceased to exist. There is no

ABOVE: **This is the original table-top model built by Trevithick to test his ideas about steam locomotives. It once ran on the kitchen table at his home.**

LEFT: **Trevithick's first railway locomotive was almost certainly built at Coalbrookdale, and this working replica steams at the nearby Ironbridge Gorge Museum. As with the other two replicas, it has demonstrated to a later generation just how well these simple prototypes performed.**

need to steer a railway locomotive. Reynolds' nephew, recalling those days many years later, remembered being given a wooden model of Trevithick's engine which – to his later chagrin – he dismantled for his own experiments. But he also remembered seeing parts of the old engine around the works for years to come. Even more interesting is a drawing of a tramway engine with smaller dimensions than those of the famous Penydarren locomotive. It had a 4¾in-diameter cylinder and 3ft stroke against the Penydarren 8¼in-diameter cylinder and 54-inch stroke, which would make sense as the Coalbrookdale tramway had a 3ft gauge and the Penydarren one a 4ft 4in gauge.

But if the engine was a success, why was the news not shouted from the factory rooftop so that all the world could hear of the triumph? A possible answer can be found many miles away. Trevithick had installed one of his new high-pressure pumping engines beside the Thames at Greenwich. On 8 September there was an immense explosion, so fierce that one 500lb section of the engine was found buried in the ground 100 yards away from the site. Three men were killed. It turned out that the boy in charge had gone off fishing, and in his absence a labourer, noting the engine was working faster than usual, stopped it – but did nothing to prevent the pressure rising in the boiler. It was not the engine that was at fault, but the man. Nevertheless, as Trevithick glumly noted, 'Mr.B & Watt is able to do mee every engurey [injury] in their power' by writing about the explosion to the papers. If stationary engines could explode with such devastating effect, it was not a good time to start talking about an engine that was designed to go roaming all over the countryside. If, as seems likely, the engine was built, then if nothing else it proved a useful prototype and Trevithick was ready to take the design further.

History may be unclear about just what happened at Coalbrookdale in 1803, but in recent times a replica has been built based on the drawing of that date. It now runs at the Ironbridge Gorge Museum, and works very satisfactorily. It is clearly a close cousin to the first road locomotive, but there are also important differences. The cylinder is set horizontally into the boiler and the piston rod connects with a crosshead running on a slide bar, looking very like part of a trombone. The drive is transmitted to a system of cogs on one side of the locomotive and to a flywheel on the other. The controls are comparatively simple. A regulator controls the flow of steam to the cylinder through a plug valve. There is a reversing handle, which actually performs a second and even more important function. One of the features that make driving the replica somewhat hazardous is the total absence of brakes. To stop, you need to shut off the regulator at a suitable point before the end of the run, then watch the valve motion and when the piston is at the end of a stroke pull sharply on the reversing handle. It is, to say the least, a very interesting experience the first time you try it.

If the Coalbrookdale engine did ever run, then it must have done so shortly before Richard Trevithick received an invitation from Samuel Homfray to visit him at his iron works in Merthyr Tydfil. This was one of the great boom towns of the Industrial Revolution, with four great iron works: Dowlais was established in 1759, followed by Plymouth in 1763, Cyfarthfa in 1765 and Homfray's Penydarren in 1784. The men who ran them were powerful, innovative and highly competitive. They could cooperate when there was a project that was in their mutual interest, and they did so in promoting the

Glamorganshire Canal, opened in 1794, to take their iron down to the docks in Cardiff. It was a great success, too much of a success in fact, for with 49 locks in 24 miles there were constant hold-ups as boats waited for their turn. Cooperation gave way to competition. The majority shareholder was Richard Crawshay of Cyfarthfa and he started demanding preferential treatment for his own boats. Homfray responded by building a route of his own, bypassing the worst of the obstacles. His route, however, was not a canal but a tramway, complete with passing loops to improve the two-way traffic. It ran from the works to Abercynon at a gentle gradient of 1 in 145. It survived as a horse-drawn tramway long enough to be photographed in 1862 during the construction of the Taff Vale Railway, which crossed it on a tall viaduct. The picture shows a train of five drams or wagons, drawn by two horses, heading for Abercynon. The line itself consisted of 3ft-long cast-iron plates, set on stone sleeper blocks, leaving a well-maintained roadway in between for the horses.

Homfray wanted Trevithick to build an engine that could be used both for haulage on the tramway and to work machinery at the foundry, where the main product was pig iron. Crawshay had not been at all happy when Homfray had bypassed the canal. It had certainly relieved congestion, but it had reduced the tolls paid on the canal as well — not good news for the principal shareholder. Now he heard that his rival was proposing something even more revolutionary – a tramway run with steam locomotives. His first reaction was to ridicule the whole idea: it was impossible for smooth iron wheels to grip smooth iron rails. It is uncertain who exactly turned the arguments into a wager, and not a small one either. The bet was for 500 guineas. To put this in perspective, in 1797 Richard Crawshay had reacted with astonishment and horror when his workers had asked for a wage of fifteen

This photograph of 1862 shows the Penydarren tramway still in use by horse-drawn traffic. It was on this line in 1804 that Trevithick gave the first public demonstration of a locomotive running on rails. A contractor's engine is on the viaduct, which is being constructed for the Taff Vale Railway.

shillings a week, or £39 a year. Yet here he was placing a bet equivalent to thirteen more years of wages. Homfray, on the other hand, may well have known that he was backing a winner. If successful trials had already taken place in secret at Coalbrookdale, then Trevithick would certainly have told him about them.

The Penydarren engine was, as already mentioned, a larger version of the 1803 locomotive, and that increased size enabled Trevithick to include a return-flue boiler for greater efficiency. The exhaust steam was turned up the chimney, increasing the blast to the fire, a fact which Trevithick noticed and commented on: 'The fire burns much better when the steam goes up the Chimney than what it do when the engine is Idle.' This valuable device was not to reappear in any steam locomotive until Stephenson's *Rocket*, a quarter of a century later. The new engine was fitted with a boiler feed pump, though it is uncertain how it worked. There is a hint that some form of hot-water feed was used, as Homfray in one of his accounts described a hold-up in operations. 'This was owing to the little forcing pump not being quite right to feed the Boyler & he was obligd to wait & fill with cold water.' To win the bet, the locomotive had to haul ten tons from the works to Penydarren and return with the empty trucks. The trials were in many ways a great success. By the end of February there had been a successful run with a 10-ton load supplemented by sixty or seventy people hopping on for the ride. There followed further experiments where the engine was tested at the works. The final tests took place early in March, when the versatile engine was put through its paces, first being used to pump water, then moving on to work a hammer before setting off, fully laden, for the trip to Abercynon and back. There was no question to be answered now: the engine worked.

Many railway historians have given the impression that the story of the Penydarren engine ended with the completion of the trials. In fact, the engine continued in use, but a major problem remained unsolved. The engine had a tendency to crack the short, brittle cast-iron rails and was taken off the line, but still continued for many years at the works as a stationary engine. There was one other order, from Christopher Blackett of Wylam Colliery on Tyneside. The new engine was again of basically the same design, but now Trevithick set the piston at the opposite end of the boiler from the firebox, leaving the footplate crew clear of the alarming crosshead and cranks. It was tried on a specially laid track, but it seems that the same problem of breaking rails led to the engine being used once again as a stationary engine at the foundry. Much has been made of the 'failure' of Trevithick's Gateshead engine, but it seems more than likely that it was not the engine that was at fault but the rails. Confirmation is provided by the fact that Blackett later laid improved track at his colliery, and wrote to Trevithick again in 1808 to ask if he would build a locomotive for the new rail system.

By then, however, Trevithick had moved on. That same year, he had already made what was to prove his last attempt to interest the world at large in the steam locomotive. He had built a lightweight locomotive called *Catch-me-who-can* which he had exhibited running on a circular track in London, very close to the site of the future Euston Station. Spectators were invited to view the astonishing machine, which raced round at an impressive twelve miles an hour – and which Trevithick claimed was capable of twenty miles an hour on a straight

Trevithick's final attempt to woo the public to the steam railway was to offer rides behind his engine *Catch-me-who-can*. The print by Rowlandson clearly shows that by now Trevithick had abandoned the large flywheel that was such a feature of his earlier locomotives.

track. For an admission price of one shilling the visitors could ride behind the mechanical wonder in a specially constructed carriage. But there was little interest and Trevithick had problems maintaining the track in what proved to be soggy ground. There was too much of the funfair in the demonstration, perhaps, to appeal to serious investors. The engine was sold off and sent down to the Thames where it was installed in a barge, formerly used by the Lord Mayor. Trevithick had invested a great deal of time and a not inconsiderable amount of his own money in the railway locomotive, and had nothing to show for it except a loss. He was an impatient man for whom the next good idea was always more appealing than the last. He was a brilliant innovator, but a poor developer. Had he found an entrepreneurial partner, as Watt had found Boulton, then things might have been different. But, it has to be said, Trevithick would never have made a comfortable partner. He had given the steam locomotive to the world; it was now time for others to take it on.

CHAPTER 2

THE EARLY YEARS

WHEN TREVITHICK WITHDREW from the railway scene, the stage remained empty for several years. With hindsight we can see that the work he had begun was of immense importance, but he had been one man playing to an inattentive audience. He was, in any case, not thinking of railways in terms of a new, efficient transport system, but rather as part of a much wider process. What he envisaged was really a portable engine, which could work both as a power source for machinery and a means of transporting raw matcrials and finished products. If others saw the wider picture, then they failed to come forward until circumstances combined to make the notion of a new form of transport for industry seem very desirable.

In the early nineteenth century, the main power source in the world of transport was the horse. The Napoleonic Wars sent the price of fodder rocketing to new heights. Hay was an expensive commodity, but if you happened to be in charge of a colliery, then coal was cheap. The idea of replacing the flesh-and-blood horse with an iron horse began to look very attractive. John Blenkinsop was in charge of the Middleton Colliery, then just outside Leeds, but now absorbed into its southern suburbs. Like many collieries in the North of England, the pit was linked to the nearest navigable river by means of a tramway. This one has the distinction of being the first to be authorised by an Act of Parliament, in 1758, to run from the mine for a little more than two miles through Leeds to the Aire & Calder Navigation. Blenkinsop knew of Trevithick's work – and he was also aware of the problem with broken rails. He began to think of ways in which he could increase the tractive power of a locomotive without increasing the weight and so damaging the track. His solution was to use a toothed rail, which would engage with a cog system on the locomotive – a rack-and-pinion railway, an idea that was to reappear in later years for use on mountain railways. Blenkinsop would have liked to have a central rack line, but horses were still at work on the line and they had to walk down the centre, so that was impossible. Instead he used cast-iron edge rails for use with flanged wheels, with just one of the rails having semi-circular teeth to mesh with the gear on the locomotive. Having the effective power working on just one side was not very efficient, but it was the best that could be managed at the time.

It has often been suggested that Blenkinsop did not believe that a smooth wheel would grip an iron rail. This is clearly not the case, because we know that he paid a premium to make use of the Trevithick patent for a steam locomotive, so he must have been aware of the early experiments. He was, however, cautious about how much work could be got from

OPPOSITE: **George Stephenson's _Locomotion_ was used for the opening of the Stockton & Darlington Railway, but is not so much the forerunner of a new age as a representative of the last of the old style of colliery engines.**

This diagram illustrates the operation of a slide valve. It shows (not to scale) the movement of the slide valve (above) and the piston in the cylinder (below). Purple arrows show direction of movement of valve and piston; red arrows show steam from the boiler, paler arrows show exhaust steam.

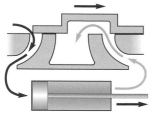

The steam port is partially open, the exhaust port is open, and the piston is on the left of the cylinder.

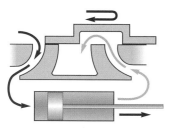

The steam port is fully open, the valve has reached the end of its travel and the piston is moving to the right.

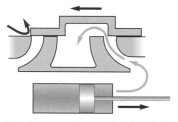

The steam port is now closed, and the steam already admitted is expanding in the cylinder, continuing to drive the piston to the right.

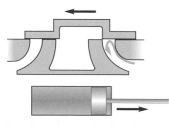

The exhaust is now closed, and the remaining steam is being compressed, slowing the piston before it stops and begins moving in the opposite direction.

a light locomotive trying to haul a heavy load, and the rack and pinion offered guaranteed traction. He went to a local engineering firm, Fenton, Murray and Wood, and it was Matthew Murray who took on the task of designing and building not one but two locomotives. This shows great confidence in what was an untried scheme. Murray's first locomotive had significant differences from Trevithick's. Firstly the boiler had a single flue producing steam at 50-55 psi and it was mounted on a separate frame. It had two cylinders, set vertically in the boiler, instead of one, with an open exhaust between them. Vertical crankshafts were connected by gears to a central drive shaft, with a cog wheel on one end. This was placed between the two pairs of road wheels. There was no feed pump, but with a track of just 2 1/2 miles there was enough water in the boiler for a return trip, and with two engines at work this was not a great problem. The first two locomotives were named *Salamanca* and *Prince Regent*. The first run was made in June 1812 and was an immediate success, with a train of eight coal wagons and as many passengers as could scramble aboard.

Matthew Murray was also responsible for one of the most important new developments in locomotive design. Trevithick's engines had plug valves in which, with the plug in one position, steam arrived at one side of the piston and was exhausted at the other. At the far end of the stroke, the positions were reversed and the other two holes opened. This provided no opportunity for the steam to expand, so a valuable source of power was lost. Murray developed a slide valve. This consisted of a D-shaped metal casting moving over a flat metal plate which had two slits or ports for steam admission and another port between them allowing waste steam to escape. The D itself was surrounded by steam, and as it moved it uncovered a port to one side of the piston, and covered the other. The piston then moved, uncovering the exhaust port. This had several advantages. It was easier to keep the valve steam-

tight than it was with the crude plug valve, the new design was simple to use and it allowed for large openings for a free flow of steam. Another even greater advantage only appeared when the valve went into regular use and improvements started to be made. The valve could then be set so that there was a period when all the ports were closed, during which time the steam could work expansively in the cylinder. This was achieved by lengthening the flat area on the D so that it overlapped the ports, and the extent to which this is done is known simply as the lap of the valve, and can be applied to both steam and exhaust ports. It sounds complex when spelled out in words, but the simplified diagram should help to make it clear. This was the first major step forward in increasing locomotive efficiency.

The Middleton Colliery line has the distinction of being the first commercially successful steam railway and the Blenkinsop-Murray system was adopted at two Tyneside collieries, and at Wigan and Whitehaven. Improvements came rapidly: a silencer was fitted over the exhaust, a safety valve was introduced and a mechanically driven feed pump added. The engines were made larger and later versions had a return flue boiler. These proved powerful workhorses and records suggest that they were able to haul a hundred tons and even more on the flat. The fame of the line spread rapidly. Grand Duke Nicholas of Russia, later to be Tsar and an enthusiastic railway promoter in his own country, was an early visitor. Industrialists from Germany called in and were sufficiently impressed to order two engines of their own, which were built in Berlin, though there is no record of their having ever done any useful work. Among the other spectators who arrived in 1813 was a twenty-one-year-old from Killingworth colliery on Tyneside, George Stephenson. The following year, he was to begin work on a locomotive of his own.

This illustration gives a more accurate idea of how the Blenkinsop-Murray engine worked, with cogs driven by crossheads from the two cylinders engaging with a larger cog that meshed with the toothed track. In other respects, it is very similar to the Trevithick engines, and a fee was paid for the use of Trevithick's patent.

OPPOSITE: **To overcome the problem of heavy locomotives breaking brittle cast-iron rails, John Blenkinsop and Matthew Murray built a rack-and-pinion railway for the Middleton Colliery Railway, near Leeds. The system was taken up by other collieries in north-east England, and this rare watercolour shows that it was even adapted for passengers.**

There is very little of the original
Middleton Colliery line left and
only models of the old locomotives
have survived. But the preserved
Middleton Railway runs on the
same site, and has another first to
its credit: the first standard-gauge
railway to be run by volunteers.

There is still a railway on the Middleton site, but it runs with conventional locomotives. Nevertheless, it has its own 'first' to its credit: it was the first standard-gauge line in Britain to be taken over and run by enthusiasts, and the illustrious past has certainly not been forgotten. The names John Blenkinsop and Matthew Murray live and steam on, attached to two modest saddle tanks. On the whole the choice seems appropriate; the locomotives are no-nonsense industrial engines, one by Peckett and the other by Bagnell, engines that could have been seen at any colliery in the middle of the twentieth century. Traces of the old line itself are harder to uncover, but those who visit the area and who search old stone walls carefully can still locate some stone blocks with a tell-tale hole in the middle, all that remains of the original tramway sleepers. A model of a Murray engine is to be found in London's Science Museum.

The success of the Middleton Colliery Railway was undoubted, but it came at a heavy price: fuel bills were high and the cost of the rail system was even higher. The latter figure came out at approximately £700 a mile, so that the construction of one mile of track cost much the same as the two locomotives. That the railway was commercially viable in spite of such drawbacks was a great argument in favour of steam. Now the hunt was on to find better ways of using the new power. William and Edward Chapman came up with their own idea for providing extra traction, which they patented in 1812. This unlikely system involved laying a chain between the tracks, which passed over a grooved wheel on the locomotive. As the wheel on the engine turned, the engine itself was dragged along the chain – in theory. In practice, the friction was enormous and the chain was in a constant tangle. The notion was abandoned. Their other idea was to prove more fruitful. They realized that the down force on the rails would be spread if there were more wheels, and thought of an eight-wheel engine. That, however, presented a different problem: getting it round corners. So they devised a system using a pair of four-wheel bogies – a genuinely useful innovation. William Brunton of the Butterley Iron Works in Derbyshire managed to score a first and last at the same time. His 1815 engine was conventional in that it had a single cylinder set into the boiler, but instead of driving wheels, it worked metal legs, complete with artificial ankle joints and iron feet. Brave but foolhardy souls were persuaded to put the mechanical beast through its paces. It blew up, and the crew were killed. The walking engine was never heard of again, though it has a macabre place in the history books as the world's first fatal railway accident.

Christopher Blackett of Wylam Colliery, who had been in the market for a Trevithick engine, now comes back into the story. When he had seen the first locomotive he had realized at once that his wooden track would never stand up under the load. So he had replaced the wooden rails by cast-iron plates, and when Trevithick showed no interest in continuing in the locomotive business he turned to his overseer, William Hedley. There could scarcely be two more different characters. Where Trevithick was mercurial, forever dashing off to try some extraordinary new idea, Hedley was slow and methodical. Trevithick had tried the one simple experiment of pushing cart wheels to see if they would grip, but no one really had

The replica of William Chapman's locomotive is known as 'The Elephant' because of its long trunk-like chimney. It is a close relation to the Middleton Colliery engines, using geared drive, but without the rack and pinion.

The collieries of north-east England were to become the great breeding grounds for early steam locomotives. In the 18th century they used steam for winding and pumping engines, and horse-drawn tramways were used to take the coal to ships on the rivers. Something of the atmosphere of those days has been recreated in this pithead scene at the Beamish Open Air Museum.

much of an idea of how much tractive power was needed to move a given load along a railed track. So Hedley set up a whole series of experiments. He arranged for a lightweight truck to be built with wheels turned manually through a crankshaft. He then proceeded to add weights to the truck and increased the number of men. It was the first time anyone had tried to determine the relationship between tractive effort and loads and to apply the results to a working railway. The result of the experiment should have proved conclusively that chains, rack rails and the like were not necessary to help a locomotive work to pull considerable loads, providing the track was strong enough. But that did not stop him taking out a patent in 1813 for various devices using complex systems of cogs, chains and whatever else he could think up to increase traction. He was not a man to rush headlong towards new ideas. He had proved to his own satisfaction that the combination of smooth wheel and smooth rail would work: but, just in case something went wrong, he had all the alternatives covered. His first locomotive was built at the same time, very much to the Trevithick pattern, with a single cylinder and a flywheel, and Hedley himself was as critical as anyone. 'It went badly,' he wrote, 'the obvious defect being want of steam.' The significant thing, however, is that it did work, though Hedley could see that there was considerable room for improvement, and applied himself to the task. He began by designing a much larger boiler, the first to be made from wrought iron, with a bigger firebox and a return flue. That sorted out the steam problem. Now he began to look for more efficient ways of using the steam.

The first change was to use two cylinders instead of one and to set them outside the boiler. We now know that this was an important move forward, but the same could not be said about all the innovations. The locomotive had what appears to modern eyes to have been an alarmingly cumbersome drive mechanism. It seems to look back to the stationary beam engines which had dominated the world of steam throughout the previous century.

The force is transmitted from the piston rod, through a beam, pivoting at one end which is fixed to a frame near the chimney. Connecting rods from the centre of the beam join a drive shaft and the actual drive was through gearing, as on earlier engines. A familiar problem soon appeared: the heavy engine broke the tramway plates. Hedley's first answer was to borrow an idea from Chapman and lift the whole boiler and frame system onto a new eight-wheeled frame. An illustration, dating back to 1825, shows a remarkable-looking object with cogs supplying drive to all four axles. That it was not a great success in this form is made very clear by the fact that as soon as the track was improved, the engine reverted to a four-wheel version. One of these early engines, *Puffing Billy*, is now in the Science Museum in London and a second, *Wylam Dilly*, has a home in Edinburgh. The Wylam track was a 5ft gauge, and *Puffing Billy* went on doing stalwart work until the conversion to what had become the standard gauge in the 1860s. These were robust machines, and the eight-wheelers were recorded as making over 800 journeys a year, even though the gear wheels had to be replaced annually. Hedley's name has been largely forgotten by the public at large, but these were successful locomotives, the first using conventional traction to go into regular service and to prove their worth over a number of years.

Hedley's engines had scarcely been introduced to the colliery world than another engineer appeared on the railway scene. The Wylam Colliery was a very profitable concern, but by no means the only one in the north east. A consortium known as the Grand Allies had existed since the seventeenth century, and their colliery at Killingworth was every bit as wealthy as Wylam. It was inevitable that the engineer who had been appointed in 1812 to oversee all the machinery would be encouraged to build and design a locomotive to match their rivals at Wylam. Quite apart from the fact that the locomotive was beginning to prove its worth, the Grand Allies needed to keep up with the mining Joneses.

William Hedley was among the pioneers who began building locomotives which dispensed with the rack and pinion. *Wylam Dilly*, built for the Wylam Colliery in 1813, survived to be photographed half a century later, with Hedley's top-hatted sons admiring their father's workmanship.

The engineer was, of course, George Stephenson. He set to work in 1813 and by 1814 his first engine, *Blucher*, was out on the tracks. The locomotive itself had very little new to offer over the Hedley engines, but there was one important difference. The Killingworth track was laid with edge rails instead of a plateway, so the locomotive had flanged wheels. There are no records to show that anyone considered this to be a possible problem, though it had not been tried before and the surface area in contact between wheel and rail was smaller in the new system than in the old. There was said to be some sort of system for heating the boiler feed water, and there was a chain drive to the tender, which was supposed to give extra adhesion. The latter device was found to be quite unnecessary and was rapidly dropped. The first decade of the railway age ended with a number of different locomotives at work, but all were rough, crude and slow. They were very much tied to the workaday world of the collieries: new machines to help out with the everyday work of shifting coal from pit head to waiting ship. No one was looking at a bigger transport system that would cover the whole county, let alone the country. In any case, the different lines could not be connected together, even if anyone had thought the idea worth trying. Each colliery had its own gauge, decided on a more or less arbitrary basis. Killingworth was 4ft 8½in and Stephenson, when he came to think about a more extensive rail system, simply stuck with that when he began to build more lines, not because it was ideal but simply because he never saw any good reason to change. It became the Stephenson gauge, and in time the standard gauge that was to be used all over Britain and even further afield. Equally no one was thinking of passengers: there would have been very little comfort in being towed along behind those early engines. But others had at least considered the possibility of using railed track as part of a passenger system.

The Swansea and Oystermouth Railway was opened in 1804, using horse-drawn wagons to haul stone. In 1807, it began a new life as a seaside passenger line, but still used horses to pull the carriages – probably the first railway passenger service.

In 1804 an Act was passed authorising the construction of a tramway from the stone quarries at Oystermouth to Swansea, and although it had a few name changes through the years, it became generally known as the Swansea & Mumbles Railway. The Act specified that wagons and carriages were to be pulled by men, horses or 'otherwise'. Bearing in mind that this is South Wales and 1804, that 'otherwise' is interesting, and the mention of 'carriages' proved significant. In 1807 a local man, Benjamin French, paid the company a fee of £20 per annum for the privilege of running a passenger service on the line. The attraction of leaving smoky Swansea with its banks of copper smelters for the clean air of Oystermouth and Mumbles Head was obvious. A Miss Spence recorded taking the trip in 1808 and declared that she 'had never spent an afternoon with more delight'. Richard Ayton, who wrote up his voyage round Britain in 1813, was made of less stern material. He described the carriage as being a sixteen-seater, made of iron with iron wheels running over a typically rough tramway track to the accompaniment of 'the noise of twenty sledge

hammers in full play'. The unfortunate passenger, Ayton said, emerged from the experience 'in a state of dizziness and confusion of the sense that it is well if he recovers from in a week'. It may have got off to a rough start, but the tramway survived as a popular tourist attraction, converting first to steam and then to electricity before finally closing down in 1960. There is no record that the little line had any direct bearing on later developments, but it was the first railway to run a regular passenger service, and it was a success. Who knows, perhaps the serious men of the north east, looking for ways to improve their colliery lines, heard of it – and a seed was sown.

In the decade following Trevithick's first experiments with steam on rails, considerable progress had been made. Yet, somehow, the initial momentum was lost. A lot has been said and written about George Stephenson being the 'father of the railways', but it should be clear by now that the claim cannot be upheld, for he was only one of a number of men working in the field – and certainly not the first. What he did have, however, was a stern determination to stay with the new invention. When Richard Trevithick died the obituarist in the *Civil Engineers' and Architects' Journal* of 1833 wrote scathingly of the Cornishman that 'he ought not to have left Stephenson to work out the locomotive engine and the railway'. It is a view of Trevithick that has persisted, the impetuous man who lacked the patience to

In later years, the Swansea line was extended to Mumbles, but steam was not introduced until the 1870s. The opening of Mumbles Pier brought a huge increase in traffic, with as many as 40,000 crowding the little trains on Bank Holidays.

see the job through, slipshod and careless. There is just enough truth to make the charge seem viable, for no one ever called Trevithick a patient man. But the man cannot be divorced from his circumstances. He took the vast, low-pressure steam engine and shrank it to the point where it could move itself with high-pressure steam. He tried it on the roads, and when that did not work he made experiments on rails. Men such as Hedley and Murray used his ideas and added to them, but the basics were Trevithick's. And one factor must always be kept in mind: Trevithick financed his own experiments in those early years. He risked his own cash, earned by his own efforts, to build locomotives. His prototypes worked remarkably well, and further progress was only halted in the early days by the unsatisfactory state of the track. There can be no doubt that if Trevithick's boldness had not paid off, if his machines had not worked, then he would have lost a great deal of time and money. No one can say who would then have had the temerity to try again, and the whole of railway development could have been put back for years and even decades. Stephenson, on the other hand, had the backing of a powerful group of mine owners who were prepared to put their money into this experimental system. Life is a great deal easier for the inventor when someone else is paying the bills, not to mention the wages. He had the huge advantage of knowing that locomotives did work, and the opportunity to study them at first hand before starting on his own experiments. This is not to denigrate Stephenson's immense achievements, but simply to put them in context: he was a developer of locomotives, not the initiator.

Stephenson's great claim to fame lies in events that occurred in the years immediately after the first burst of experimentation. He persisted, never lost faith in the steam locomotive and for a number of years was the only man in the world working away at building and improving locomotives. There were, however, others who were pursuing the idea of creating a genuine railway network that would serve more than merely local interests. The most influential was William James of Henley-in-Arden in Warwickshire, one of the sadder characters in the railway story. He was a wealthy and successful land agent, who had been involved in canal work locally but then got bitten by the railway bug. He actively promoted a modest tramway, the Stratford & Moreton Railway, which was duly authorised in 1820. It was a somewhat unlikely venture, linking the modest market town of Moreton-in-Marsh to the not very successful Stratford Canal, but James had his own reasons for promoting the line. He wanted to see it built as an up-to-the-minute modern railway, with wrought-iron rails and steam locomotives. For him this was just a beginning, a proving ground. It was to be the first stage in a much more ambitious plan that would see lines spread out from the Midlands to London and on down to the south coast. If the little line worked, then greater things were sure to follow. He wrote to Stephenson asking for details on performances and got back one of the first detailed notes of what the Killingworth engines could perform. Speeds varied from a mere crawl at just over 2mph on an upward slope of the modest gradient of 1 in 144, or as the report put it one quarter inch per yard. On the descent they could reach a giddy 10mph, all this with a modest load of 50 tons. Stephenson recommended that any line to be worked by locomotives should not have a gradient greater than 1 in 192.

William James of Henley-in-Arden was one of the first and most enthusiastic advocates of steam railways. Sadly, he proved rather too enthusiastic, neglected his other business interests and fell into bankruptcy.

The figures convinced James that locomotives were just the thing for the Stratford & Moreton Railway, but the Board of Directors did not share his optimism. Their gaze was not on distant horizons, but on their own modest venture. They raised a whole range of objections: bridges would have to be stronger for locomotives than for horses; locomotives needed wrought-iron rails, which were more liable to rust than cast iron; track maintenance would be more expensive with locomotives than with horses; and locomotives could not work in the snow or in very heavy rain. Other arguments were less sound: they considered that the extra cost incurred by overcoming friction would cancel out any savings, and lastly and rather charmingly they cited 'the frightening appearance of locomotives in action'. The arguments had some validity and the tramway was built – the typically flat-topped bridge can still be seen crossing the Avon at Stratford today – and it was never worked by locomotives. James, however, was not discouraged. He wrote and published pamphlets, surveyed possible lines and after a meeting with George Stephenson in 1821 added the promotion of Killingworth-type locomotives to his enthusiasms. 'The Locomotive engine of Mr. Stephenson is superior beyond all comparison to all the other Engines I have ever seen.' He also began recommending the new type of cast-iron rail developed by William Losh with Stephenson's help. Certainly he did more than his share to make the world at large aware of the wonder that was the steam railway. And he also spread the notion that if anyone was serious about building railways and locomotives to run on them, then Stephenson was the man. Stephenson could not have hired a more efficient P.R. man. What James had not anticipated was that Stephenson's success would ultimately be bought at the price of his own downfall. James prepared the way for the decisive years which took railways from the narrow confines of a local industry and brought them out into the world as a revolutionary form of transport for all.

One of William James's most important projects was a tramway linking Stratford-upon-Avon to Moreton-in-Marsh. The bridge over the Avon at Stratford still survives; it now only carries pedestrians, but one can see just how well the line was built.

CHAPTER 3

THE STEPHENSON YEARS

I T WAS OBVIOUS to the business community throughout north-east England that railways were already having an effect on the fortunes of the Tyneside collieries. Further south in County Durham, things were not progressing as rapidly, and transport was one of the key factors. The huge coalfield centred on Bishop Auckland was an inconveniently long distance from the nearest port, Stockton-on-Tees. There had been a great deal of talk about improving transport, but very little action. Canal plans had appeared and disappeared, and the only practical work had been the improvement of the River Tees under an Act of 1808. When work was completed, the problem of how to get the coal to the new navigation remained unresolved. The canal enthusiasts popped up again and the horse tramway supporters made their case. A meeting was called at Stockton town hall in 1810, which did nothing whatsoever to resolve the argument but agreed, in the best British tradition, to form a committee to investigate the problem. It took them two years to agree to call in John Rennie, one of the most eminent engineers of the day, to survey a possible route. He proved even less speedy than the committee, producing a report in 1815. The timing was, to say the least, unfortunate. The local bank had just collapsed and no one had much enthusiasm for investment. The report was put on a shelf and forgotten for a further three years.

In 1818, financial life was looking brighter on Teesside and the report was dusted off, but by now opinion had swung firmly towards the railway as opposed to the canal. Rennie was approached again and asked to carry out a survey with another engineer, Robert Stevenson. Rennie replied in high dudgeon that he had always acted in the past without collaborators on works, 'many of them of infinitely greater magnitude and importance than the Darlington railway'. Mutually offended, the committee and Rennie went their separate ways. Another engineer was now called in, George Overton, who had been the engineer for the Penydarren tramway, and he promptly found himself in the middle of a local row. The Stockton members of the committee wanted a line that would go by the shortest possible route to the coalfield, in effect heading due north, bypassing Darlington. The Darlington members were understandably opposed, and eventually they won the day. In 1821 an Act was passed for 'making and maintaining a Railway or Tramroad from the River Tees, at Stockton'. Options were still being left open.

OPPOSITE: **Thomas Bury's 1833 view of the Olive Mount cutting on the Liverpool & Manchester Railway shows a very dramatic scene. In later years the cutting has been widened out so that the effect has been lost.**

One of the most important men on the committee was the Darlington businessman Edward Pease. As a Quaker, he was barred from public office, and instead applied his considerable energy and expertise to commerce and industry. Now fact and mythology become intertwined. Samuel Smiles, the famous biographer of engineers, wrote a typically dramatic account of the first meeting between Pease and George Stephenson. Stephenson, he said, arrived at Pease's door with his friend and colleague Nicholas Wood and instantly converted an astonished Pease by declaring that his Killingworth engine was doing the work of fifty horses. Pease was apparently totally charmed by this modest man, who described himself as 'only the engine-wright at Killingworth'. The picture Smiles paints is of an honest workman walking to distant Darlington in the hopes of making a case for the locomotive. Wood's own account is rather different. He and Stephenson rode to Newcastle, where they took the coach to Stockton. From there they walked to Darlington, not because they could not afford the fare but in order to see the likely line of the railway for themselves. They then went on to a pre-arranged appointment with Pease. This sounds altogether more likely. Stephenson was already a man with a considerable reputation and as the only engineer actively working at improving steam locomotives would have been listened to with considerable interest. What all agree is that Pease was convinced that the Stockton & Darlington Railway should be worked with steam locomotives, and that the best man to put in charge of both the civil engineering, the construction of the line, and the mechanical engineering, designing the locomotives, was George Stephenson.

George Stephenson's birthplace beside the track of the former Wylam Colliery tramway. It is a modest building of which the Stephensons only occupied a single room. In those days a collier had to have at least four children before being allowed the luxury of a second room

In October 1821 Stephenson began surveying the line with his eighteen-year-old son Robert. The young man was still officially an apprentice at the colliery, working under Nicholas Wood, but his health was poor, and Wood released him from the heat and dust of the mine to the open-air life of a surveyor. It was the beginning of one of the most famous and important partnerships in railway history. Father and son were very different in many respects. George received almost no formal education, and was scarcely literate when he started work as a boy. What he knew he had learned on the job, not in the classroom, and he grew up with a deep distrust of theoreticians, who he lumped together as London men. This distrust was deepened in the events that followed a disastrous explosion at the Felling Colliery in which ninety-two miners lost their lives. It was caused by the lethal combination of methane gas and naked flames, and a reward was offered for anyone who could invent a safety lamp for use in the mines. One winner was the scientist Sir Humphry Davy who was awarded 2000 guineas (£2100), a huge sum but small considering the lives saved by the Davy safety lamp. George Stephenson, working independently at the same time, produced his own safety lamp, which he characteristically put to the test by taking the lamp down a pit to the point where there was a massive escape of gas. It was effective, but Stephenson was only offered 100 guineas. The mine owners of the north east were incensed, and the committee upped Stephenson's award to 1000 guineas. Now it was Davy's turn to get into a rage, refusing to believe that an illiterate pitman could devise something as useful as an invention based on the best scientific principles. He demanded that the payment to Stephenson be stopped, but the mine owners stood firm. It is a story that may seem to have little relevance to railways, but it confirmed for Stephenson that practical experience was as valuable as theory any day, and that experts were not to be trusted, especially if they came from the capital. It was an attitude that was to colour his dealings for the rest of his life.

George Stephenson

George may have been wary of the educated, but he was well aware that, in a changing world, the men of the future would need more than a little reading, writing and arithmetic. So when Robert left the local school, he did not head off to the pit but went off daily on a little donkey to a private school in Newcastle. At home in the evening, the boy gave the father lessons, helping him to achieve the education he had never had the opportunity to enjoy in his own childhood. Now they were working together on what was to prove one of the most important projects of the age. Had Rennie known its significance, he might have been less scathing about the Stockton & Darlington Railway.

The Stephensons set out on their survey and chose a route that differed considerably from that of the original tramway plan. Now, Stephenson had to decide on the type of rail to use. He and Losh had done very well with their cast-iron rails, but another local ironmaster, John Birkenshaw, was producing rolled, wrought-iron rails in 16-foot (4.9m) lengths. Stephenson saw at once that they were far superior and opted to use them, to the considerable annoyance of Losh. Stephenson's honesty had lost him a partner and created a problem. He would normally have turned to Losh to manufacture the locomotives for the line, but now he was forced to look elsewhere. He turned to Murray in Leeds, but he had moved away from railway construction. No one else seemed interested, so a decision

The replica of *Locomotion* now gives passenger rides at the Beamish Open Air Museum.

was taken: the family would start a company of their own. In 1823 Robert Stephenson and Company went into business from new premises at the Forth Street Works, Newcastle-upon-Tyne. Edward Pease was the principal shareholder with £1600 of shares; the two Stephensons had £800 each and Michael Longridge, owner of the Bedlington iron works where Birkenshaw had developed his rails, was the fourth.

After the survey Robert Stephenson had gone to Edinburgh University, and was unimpressed. 'Natural historians', he declared, 'spend a great deal of time in enquiring whether Adam was a black or white man. Now I really cannot see what better we should be, if we could even determine this with satisfaction.' Robert was, in this at least, very much his father's son – unconcerned with knowledge that had no practical application. The sort of knowledge he required was to be gained on the shop floor and out in the field. The line that was laid down still bore the marks of its origins in the old tramway systems, which in turn owed a great deal to the thinking of the canal engineers. The track was kept on the level as far as possible, keeping heavy engineering works to a minimum. When changes in level were needed, then the trucks would be hauled up and lowered down inclines by means of stationary engines at the top. An excellent example of this type of system, restored to working order, can be seen on the Bowes Railway at Springwell in Tyne and Wear and perhaps even more clearly on the Cromford & High Peak Railway in Derbyshire. On the latter, the whole line can be traced and at Middleton Top the magnificent steam winding engine is regularly demonstrated. Here, the trucks were attached to a continuous cable, and the system began work in 1825, the year of the opening of the Stockton & Darlington. Although everyone thinks of the Stockton & Darlington as a conventional steam railway, no one yet trusted the entire task of moving goods and people to locomotives.

In 1824 Robert left his father and the works that bore his name and set off to find his fortune as a mining engineer in South America. His reasons have never been clear, but it cannot have been easy trying to work with a man of such strong personality as George, even for a non-relation. For a son looking to make his own mark on the world it must have been near impossible. Somehow the company carried on without him and produced four locomotives to open the service on the new line. They were originally simply numbered, but later named, and plain Number 1 became *Locomotion*, followed by *Hope, Black Diamond* and *Diligence*. A replica of *Locomotion* was built to celebrate the 150th anniversary of the 1825 opening of the line. It can now be seen at the North of England Open Air Museum at Beamish, where it works in an appropriate colliery setting.

Contemporary illustrations of *Locomotion* give it all the appearance of an animated sewing machine. Seeing the replica at work does nothing to dispel the image, and it was certainly no advance on previous engines. It has two vertical cylinders embedded in the boiler, each set above an axle and driving through crossheads. The boiler itself is a single flue, with the firebox created by a firebrick wall near the middle. The wheels are coupled and the slide valves are operated off a single eccentric. Reversing is an interesting exercise. The driver works from a somewhat alarming platform beside the boiler and has to check the wheel position to see which way the locomotive will go as steam is admitted. If, which is as likely as not, the valves are in the wrong position, then the connecting rods have to be unclipped and moved manually so that steam will appear on the correct side of the piston. Once under way, everything has to be recoupled, a job which would be unlikely to pass any modern safety at work regulations. At this time, wheels were solid and the engine was totally unsprung.

A Stockton & Darlington Railway share, showing the bridge over the River Sherna near Darlington.

Although the S&DR has always been written of as a triumph, the first public railway to be operated by steam, things did not go as well as history presumes. Steaming was a problem, and Timothy Hackworth, who was put in charge of mechanical engineering, returned to the idea first used by Trevithick of turning exhaust steam up the chimney. This was all right insofar as it improved the steaming, but with a single wide flue there was a strong tendency for the extra blast to tear at the fire and hurl red-hot ashes and chunks of burning fuel up the chimney. This was so bad that beaters had to be employed along the trackside to put out the flames, which must have made a trip down the S&DR an alarmingly colourful experience. There were boiler explosions on *Locomotion* and *Hope* in 1828, killing the footplate crew on both occasions. Contemporaries blamed this on the crew fiddling with the safety valve to get better performance; an accusation that the crew were not in a position to refute. The other problem was knowing when the boiler needed refilling. The only gauges were test cocks in the boiler end. The crew had to open a cock very gingerly and try to see what was coming out, steam or water.

The dangers are obvious. It was only in 1829 that John Rastrick of Stourbridge introduced the familiar water gauge, set outside the boiler. None of these problems, however, marred the grandeur of the opening on 27 September 1825. Stephenson was at the controls, joined by his brother James on the footplate with Timothy Hackworth as guard. The organizers had issued tickets for three hundred passengers, but no one could control the numbers, and anyone who could clamber aboard the train did so. It was all a great success and attracted an enormous amount of attention. To many it seemed that the steam railway had finally come of age, but it was not quite that simple.

Once the excitement was over and the S&DR went into regular operation then the true nature of the line was revealed. The locomotives had nowhere near a monopoly over freight movements. Horses still did a great deal of the work, and the inclines worked by stationary engines were no less important. In essence, this was still a colliery line to which passengers were admitted, much as they had been on the little Swansea and Mumbles Railway. And in those first years the passengers did not even get to enjoy the thrill of steam. They were carried in what was simply a conventional stagecoach, but with flanged iron wheels. Flesh-and-blood horses not iron horses hauled them up and down the track. But if it was not quite the revolution in transport that it seemed to later generations, it was recognized by contemporaries as offering something quite new. Perhaps railways would not be limited to moving coal after all.

The poster advertising passenger services on the Stockton & Darlington fails to mention that they will be travelling in an old-fashioned stagecoach, pulled by horses, but which has flanged wheels to run on rails.

At the dinner following the grand opening, numerous toasts were drunk. One of these was to wish success to another new project, the proposed line that would link two of the most important towns of the industrial age, Liverpool and Manchester. The Industrial Revolution, and the cotton industry in particular, had transformed Lancashire in the eighteenth century. The links between the commercial and manufacturing heart at

Manchester and the principal port of Liverpool depended mainly on canals such as the Duke of Bridgewater's, begun right back in 1760. It was a system that was proving increasingly inadequate at meeting the growing demand for fast, efficient movement of people and goods. Among those who came to view the scene was William James, fresh from his promotion of the Stratford & Moreton Railway. This was just the opportunity he had been waiting for to push his plans for a network of steam railways. He met a local merchant, Joseph Sandars, who had been loud in his complaints about the inefficiency and excessive charges of the canals, and in 1822 Sandars agreed to pay for a survey of the line. James turned to his friends the Stephensons and Robert, fresh from his surveying in Durham, was recruited to help with the work.

In the coalfields of the north east there was great enthusiasm for railways. Even the grandest of landowners derived a good deal of their income from mineral rights. Tramways had been a commonplace for years. Things in Lancashire turned out very differently. Landowners were not in the least keen on railways, and indeed many of them had invested heavily in canals – such as the Duke of Bridgewater, who famously remarked that canals would do very well, provided they could be clear of those damned railways. So the surveyors were turned off the land by the mighty and were likely to be pelted on their way through villages by locals fearing the advent of the fire-breathing monsters. The land the line was to cross presented fearsome difficulties, not least a vast peat bog, Chat Moss. Even James struggled under the weight of problems, and to make matters far worse his own finances were in a mess. In his enthusiasm for railway promotion he had neglected his main business and was being sued by his brother-in-law. He was bankrupt, with only the railway interest to cling to for support. Then that was pulled away. The Committee were unimpressed by the man and his troubles and in 1824 he received a letter telling him that he no longer had the confidence of the subscribers and was out of work. The job of chief engineer was being offered to George Stephenson and when he wrote to inform the unhappy James, Joseph Sandars seems to have been more than a little ingenuous: 'I am quite sure that the appointment of Stephenson will, under all circumstances, be agreeable to you.' It was nothing of the sort. James spoke bitterly of his former friend's duplicity, but there was nothing to be done. He may not have been alone in finding Stephenson's treatment of a man who had done so much for him somewhat shabby. Robert had been taken under James's wing and he may well have regretted his father's actions. It was perhaps no coincidence that it was shortly after this that he announced his departure for a new life in South America.

George Stephenson soon found the work of surveying every bit as difficult as James had done. The fierce opposition was led by a Mr Bradshaw who managed the Bridgewater estates. He even went so far as to have staff firing guns at random during the night to ensure that no surveyor crept onto the land under the cover of darkness. Lord Sefton, another landowner with powerful canal interests, threatened to have a hundred men on hand to turn back the surveyors. Stephenson declared roundly that great men have no right to stop a survey, which was true in law, but they could make life very difficult. Stephenson was still busy on the Stockton & Darlington and much of the work went to assistants who were less willing to stand up against the mighty of the land. The survey was rushed and patchy, and even though William Cubitt was called in to do a few spot checks, no one could really vouch for its accuracy. But it was on the basis of this survey that the promoters had to go to Parliament for cross-questioning by a Select Committee.

The canal and river navigation companies had had plenty of time to marshal their forces and their lawyer Edward Alderson must have featured in Stephenson's nightmares for years to come. The experience might not have been too bad had Stephenson taken more time to go through the botched survey, but he soon showed himself woefully ignorant when it came to details. Alderson played him like a matador tormenting a bull and all Stephenson could do was grunt and snort. He had quoted a price of £375 for a bridge, but under questioning he turned out to know neither how high it was nor what the materials would cost. A bridge over the Irwell was described as having an arch at ten to fifteen feet above the water, which would have made the river barely navigable at the best and seen it covered in floodwater at the worst. He had to stand and listen to Alderson demolish his professional respectability.

> Did any ignorance ever arrive at such a pitch as this? Was there ever any ignorance exhibited like it? Is Mr. Stephenson to be the person upon whose faith this Committee is to pass this bill, involving property to the extent of 400,000£ or 500,000£, when he is so ignorant of his profession, as to propose to build a bridge not sufficient to carry off the flood water of the river, or to permit any of the vessels to pass which of necessity must pass under it, and to leave his own Railroad liable to be several feet under water.

Not surprisingly, the bill was rejected and the London men had given Stephenson a thorough roasting. They had laughed at his accent, and asked him if he was a foreigner, and one lawyer had tried to suggest he was mad. It was the low point of his career, and he had to suffer the ignominy of seeing new engineers called in to take his place. George and John Rennie, sons of the famous canal and bridge engineer, came north. They were experienced not just in the work of engineering, but in the equally important task of facing Parliamentary Committees. They brought with them a young, upcoming engineer to do much of the work, Charles Vignoles. The new route was to include a deep cutting through solid rock at Olive Mount, Liverpool and a direct route across Chat Moss, though there was little clue as to how this was to be achieved. Work went well and in 1826 the bill was passed, and work on the Liverpool & Manchester Railway could begin. The Rennies were invited to take over the work of construction, with the help of an 'operative engineer'. Two names were put forward to the Rennies: George Stephenson and John Urpeth Rastrick. It is hard to imagine a more desperate scenario than having Stephenson reporting for orders to the Rennies, who sensibly turned him down. They also turned down Rastrick, though he was a first-rate man, and announced cheekily that they would be happy to employ Thomas Telford. As Telford was the grand old man of civil engineering with infinitely more experience than the two Rennies this was never going to happen. So the Rennies vanished from the scene, leaving young Vignoles to carry on as best he could. In the event, Josias Jessop, another son of a great canal engineer, William Jessop, was called in and Stephenson had the subsidiary role of working engineer alongside Vignoles. It was never going to last. Jessop and Vignoles soon found that Stephenson was impossible to deal with, and Vignoles in particular soon became tired of the constant denigration of anyone with a London connection. Jessop went and Vignoles followed, though the directors sympathized with his having fallen foul of Stephenson's 'queer temper'. George was back where he wanted to be: in sole control of the construction of the most important engineering project in the world at that time.

It is easy to forget in the excitement of designing locomotives that the civil engineering of the railway is also of the greatest importance. A train is only as good as the track it runs on, a point which is as true today as it was then: which is why, until recently, in France the Eurostar flew at speed to the Channel Tunnel, whereas on the English side the trains staggered along antique tracks. At least the railway engineers had the experience of the canal engineers to draw upon. By the time the first railways were being built, the canal men had dug immense tunnels and invented such vital techniques as 'cut and fill', in which deep cuttings were dug through the rising ground of a hill and the spoil then carted away to be built up as embankments in the next valley. They even had a workforce, ready and experienced to do the hard graft. In canal days they had been known as navigators, the men who dug the navigations, but that seemed a little too grand for the quarrelsome, hard-living gangs. They became plain navvies. It is always worth remembering that the railways were built by thousands of men using tools little more sophisticated than pickaxe, shovel and barrow. Great cuttings such as Olive Mount were constructed by drilling the rock with hand drills and shattering it with plain black powder. The men were mainly employed by contractors. One of the most powerful of these in later years was Thomas Brassey, who described employing former canal navvies. He also recorded the amount of work they could do, and it was prodigious. A two-man team was expected to fill a fourteen-set train of wagons in a day. That is the equivalent of digging a hole 3ft deep, 3ft wide and 45ft long, and then hurling the rock and earth over the sides of the wagons. We may talk of the Liverpool & Manchester Railway as Stephenson's, but we should never forget the anonymous army who made it all possible.

The big difference between this railway and the earlier canals was the method in which the work was organized. Stephenson had brought in new assistants, including Joseph Locke who was to go on to make a considerable reputation for himself as a railway engineer, and the last of the London men had left. But instead of the assistants handing out work to contractors, they employed direct labour, each responsible for some 200 men. Telford, the old canal hand, was asked to report on progress and was horrified by what he found. He pointed out that under the Stephenson system, the company had to pay for all the equipment themselves, and pay rates seemed to be totally arbitrary: '3½d (1.5p) per yard to 5s (25p) as they think it deserves'. No doubt Stephenson had reached the point where he felt it necessary to have personal control of everything, and it has to be said that arguments between company engineers and outside contractors were a recur-

This remarkable picture of 1831 shows visitors wandering down Edge Hill tunnel, admiring the new gas lighting. It is a little safer than it might appear, as locomotives were not permitted in the tunnel, and trains were hauled by cable to overcome the 1 in 48 slope.

ring theme of the canal days and one that was to continue through to the railway age. So, the Liverpool & Manchester Railway was something of the odd one out in terms of organization, and that was to lead to problems later.

Stephenson was not an experienced civil engineer, and one sometimes feels that he spent a good deal of time reinventing the wheel. Until the eighteenth century, bridges had generally been built at right angles to whatever they had to cross. This made construction simple. At Rainhill, however, a bridge had to be built to carry an existing road that lay at an angle to the line of the tracks. There were two alternatives: one was to build a straight-across bridge and alter the road by putting in a kink at either end; the other was to build a bridge on the skew. Stephenson, it has been written, pondered long and hard over the problem, attempting to solve the skew problem by carving shapes out of turnips. All he needed to do was look at the work of canal engineers who had solved the problem, which involved laying the stones or bricks forming the arch in diagonal instead of horizontal courses.

Again tunnel construction problems had been solved in the canal age, and the surveying techniques needed to get a straight bore had been well worked out. At the Liverpool end of the railway the Edge Hill tunnel caused great problems. Tunnel working involved sinking shafts down to a level determined in the survey, then working out on pre-set headings from the bottoms of the shafts. If the work was done well, the different sections would all meet in a straight line. This did not happen at Edge Hill. The shaft alignment was so far out that in places short tunnels had to be dug out at right angles to reach the actual agreed line. One misalignment was only just caught in time, for otherwise the two sets of workmen would have gone right past each other, burrowing away in their very own tunnels. Things became even worse when one section collapsed, and the company asked Joseph Locke to send in a report. This was a bit awkward, as Locke was employed by Stephenson, but he did his job honestly – and was sacked by the engineer for his pains. It is true that tunnelling was difficult and often dangerous work. The only light for the workers at the face was supplied by candles. Geology was a science in its very infancy, so that the nature of the different strata was little understood. Water was a constant threat, and more than once men were driven from the workings by floods. Visitors were curious to see the great work, and the more adventurous were lowered down the shafts in buckets to see for themselves. To one of the intrepid, the scene gave 'no contemptible idea of some infernal operation in

J. C. Bourne was one of the few artists to take an interest in railway construction, and to record what he saw with accuracy. Here a cutting is being driven through a hill near Linslade to take the line of the London & Birmingham Railway. In the foreground a rock is being blasted apart, with no one seeming to take any great interest in safety precautions.

The canal interest were bitter opponents of the early railways. Here a barge on the Sankey Canal is approaching the viaduct carrying the Liverpool & Manchester Railway. The waterways men were right to be worried: the viaduct still carries traffic; the canal is derelict.

the region of Pluto'. It seems an inescapable fact that Stephenson lacked the experience to see such major engineering works through. If the judgement seems harsh, then it is worth pointing out that just a few years later when Isambard Kingdom Brunel started on the Great Western Railway, he faced an even greater tunnel challenge than Edge Hill at Box. Not only is his tunnel straight, but the morning sun shines straight through on the engineer's birthday. Brunel was never a man to miss the flamboyant gesture.

Stephenson probably thought that his greatest difficulty would be the blasting away of a deep cutting at Olive Mount, and contemporary illustrations show a dramatic rock canyon. The effect has been reduced by widening over the years. But the real problem was Chat Moss, and whatever Stephenson's shortcomings he had no match when it came to dogged determination. The Moss was a swamp-like mass of black, oozing earth resting on clay. The navvies had to tie planks to their feet to stop themselves sinking, and when one of the engineering staff slipped off a walkway he was in real danger of disappearing for ever if he was not hauled out by navvies. The obvious first step was to dig drainage ditches, but as fast as they were dug they filled up again. That problem was solved by making a crude drain out of bottomless barrels laid end to end. Stephenson noted how some plants had knit together to form miniature rafts floating on the bog, and the idea came to him to try something similar. He made his own 'rafts' of heather and brushwood which eventually reached a point where the line could be laid on top. The bizarre idea worked.

Elsewhere the only answer was to build an embankment. Soil was tipped in and disappeared under the surface, but logic decreed that eventually it would hit a solid foundation. There was no shortage of doubters, but the tipping went on and the soil kept vanishing until the day was reached when a load actually stayed above the level of the peat. Eventually the great bank would rise some five feet above the wasteland. It was a triumph. The other great work of civil engineering was the Sankey viaduct, 70ft (21m) high, its nine brick arches clad in stone. At the end of the labours, the engineers could look proudly on a modern railway linking two great centres of population, even if neither was yet dignified by the name of city.

The civil engineers had done their work, but as the end of their labours came into sight, one great question remained to be answered. How were the trains to be moved? The locomotive men were certain they had the solution, but there was a big difference between a colliery line, which the Stockton & Darlington still was, and a railway on which passenger transport was expected to play an important part. Over in Durham, the passengers were still rattling along in their stagecoach on rails: the rough, rumbling locomotives were ungainly and had never been required to work over such a long distance. There were, however, some grounds for optimism. A Gateshead engineer, Robert Wilson, had built a curious locomotive with four cylinders, so that each cylinder drove just one wheel. It was not a success, but rather than waste it altogether, it was sent to Shildon, the locomotive works for

Timothy Hackworth was put in charge of locomotives for the S&DR and *Royal George* was one of his most powerful engines, with three pairs of coupled wheels. It contained a number of innovations, including a spring safety valve.

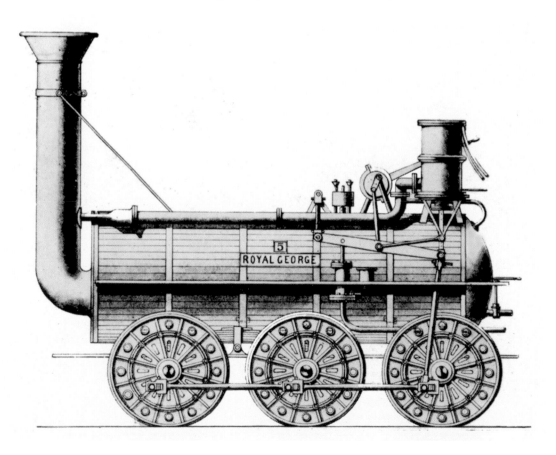

the S&DR, where Timothy Hackworth was now in charge. He rebuilt the whole engine and introduced some very new ideas. For a start, he was dissatisfied with the steaming of the early S&DR engines, so he reverted to the older idea of a return flue boiler, and used steam blast exhaust. He had two cylinders set outside the boiler, but he changed the wheel arrangement. The engine was given six wheels, with one pair being driven directly and the other two pairs coupled to them. It was the first 0-6-0 and proved a great success. He designed a new type of wheel made up of two parts and covered by a wrought-iron tyre, and he increased safety by replacing the old weighted safety valve with a spring valve, much less easy to tamper with. The engine was named *Royal George* and was the most powerful locomotive yet built. Even so not everyone was convinced. A faction in the company wanted to use a different system altogether, a variation on the devices in use on inclines. Stationary engines would be set at intervals all along the line and would haul the trains from one to the other by cable.

A delegation of engineers was sent out to examine the alternatives as they were then in use. They came back with the very unsatisfactory answer that both worked, and shilly-shallied over which was actually the best. The company decided to settle things for themselves. The arguments in favour of locomotives were strong, but could the engines match up to the performance necessary for continuous running on the new line? The only way to find out was by a trial. In 1829 they offered a premium for any engine that could haul a train along a length equivalent to a return journey on the railway at a speed of ten miles an hour. It was all to be decided at Rainhill in 1829.

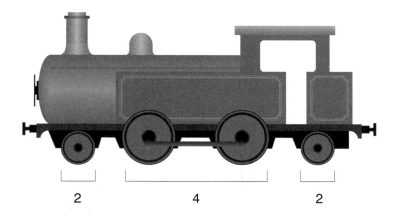

2   4   2

Wheel arrangements for locomotives are usually given by three digits. The first represents the number of leading wheels, the second the drive wheels connected together and the third the trailing wheels. The example shown is thus a 2-4-2.

Three serious contestants emerged, one not very serious and a fifth which was bizarre, if not frivolous – a rough carriage worked by a horse on a treadmill. The other non-starter was built in Scotland but the cart on which it was being carried overturned and caused irreparable damage. There were two obvious candidates who came forward immediately. Timothy Hackworth had just built the most powerful locomotive ever constructed and must have been quite confident that he would carry the day. The Stephenson camp was also now in a better shape, for Robert had returned from what had turned out to be a less than happy venture in South America. His story did, however, have an absolutely extraordinary ending. He was in Cartagena, waiting for a boat for New York, when he heard about an Englishman who had also arrived in the port, but had lost all his possessions and money in a gruelling journey from the gold mines of Costa Rica. The man turned out not to be a stranger, but the first builder of a railway locomotive, Richard Trevithick. Robert, who was on his way home to play a crucial part in the development of the railways, gave the man who had started it all the fare to get him back to England. It is a meeting of great poignancy, for Trevithick's life would soon be over, his achievements denied by his contemporaries, while Robert was to become one of the most successful engineers of the age.

Hackworth's engine, *Sans Pareil,* was essentially a scaled-down version of *Royal George* with four coupled wheels instead of six. The competition rules called for the engines to be sprung, but with vertical cylinders the springing was as likely to resonate as to dampen the motion, and lead to a loss of power. That, however, was not to be Hackworth's major problem. He had no manufacturing facilities of his own, had no private income and could only work on *Sans Pareil* in the time left over from his main work on the S&DR. He had to rely on others to realize his plans, and the critical casting of the cylinders was entrusted to his main rival, Robert Stephenson. This was to prove the subject of a controversy which has lasted right down to the present day.

TIMOTHY HACKWORTH, *Manufacturer of* LOCOMOTIVE, MARINE, HIGH PRESSURE, AND OTHER STEAM ENGINES, MILLS, &c. *On the most approved Plans.* New Shildon, NEAR Bᵖ Auckland.

LEFT: **Hackworth's business card. He left the S&DR to set up as an independent locomotive engineer. He had considerable success, and even supplied locomotives to Russia.**

BELOW: **Hackworth's most famous locomotive was *Sans Pareil,* built for the Rainhill trial of 1829, which was set up to find a locomotive that could run a regular, fast service on the new Liverpool & Manchester Railway. It did not win, but the replica has proved a sturdy and reliable engine.**

Robert Stephenson

Robert Stephenson's locomotive was to be altogether different. From the start, Robert was aware that the old colliery engines were not going to be suitable for a mainline service. There is a general principle in science and technology that can never be quantified but which seems to work in practice: the elegant works better than the ugly. In January 1828, Robert had written to Michael Longridge at the works to say that he had been talking to his father 'about endeavouring to reduce the size and ugliness of our travelling engines'. The first step was to place cylinders angled at approximately 45° on either side of the boiler. This was valuable in reducing the hammer-blow effect on the track of vertical cylinders, and was successfully tried in an earlier locomotive, *Lancashire Witch*. The real problem, however, was still that of ensuring a good supply of steam. Here the idea came not from the Stephensons themselves but from the Liverpool & Manchester treasurer, Henry Booth. He proposed a revolutionary system. The firebox was no longer to be part of the flue, but was to be separate and jacketed, surrounded by water. The hot gases were led out through twenty-five copper tubes which would heat the water in the boiler. Steam blast was used to ensure a good fire. Earlier engines using steam blast had found that it was, if anything, too powerful, so that the fire became a miniature volcano hurling red-hot lumps of fuel up the chimney. In the new engine, the multi-tube boiler ensured that the heat was used where it was needed, to raise steam. The pistons drove the uncoupled front wheels, giving an 0-2-2 arrangement. By now Britain no longer had a complete monopoly of locomotive development. Working quite independently in France, Marc Seguin had also come up with the idea of the multi-tubular boiler. He was engineer on the Etienne & Lyon Railway, officially opened in 1828, but still relying on horses. Seguin was, it seems, a true visionary, already thinking of improvements to the steam locomotive in a country which had yet to try them. For some time, the Stephenson locomotive was simply known as the Premium Engine, because it was built to win the premium prize. By the time it reached Rainhill it had a more romantic name – *Rocket*.

The third entry was the work of two engineers, John Braithwaite and John Ericsson. Braithwaite had inherited a successful engineering business in St Albans from his father, himself an inventor of a diving bell, with which he had salvaged goods valued at £130,000. Ericsson had been a captain in the Swedish army and had proved himself an ingenious inventor. They only heard about the trials because a friend had sent them a cutting from a Liverpool paper, and by then there were just seven weeks left before the trial. It seems extraordinary that two men who had never designed a railway locomotive in their lives could come up with a revolutionary new design and build it in so short a time. The engine was aptly named *Novelty*, and if nothing quite like it had ever been seen before on the railways, it was not altogether unknown in London. It had its origins in a fire engine that had turned out to blazes in both the House of Commons and the Opera House in London, but had been attacked by the hoses of the regular firefighters, who feared for their jobs. It consisted of a lightweight body with spoked wheels and a water tank slung underneath. It had a vertical boiler surrounding the firebox and pipe work. Fuel was fed in from the top. The steam was delivered to two cylinders, driving a cranked axle,

ABOVE: **The three main contenders at the Rainhill trial of 1829. We can now see that *Rocket* was by far the most important, with design features that would be developed over the next century and more. Contemporaries favoured the racy *Novelty*, but it failed to complete the course.**

RIGHT: ***Rocket* is one of the most famous locomotives in railway history. Designed by Robert Stephenson, it was an easy winner at the Rainhill trial and its success ensured the future of the steam railway. The original is in the Science Museum, and this replica is regularly steamed at the National Railway Museum, York.**

the first to be used on a locomotive. John Dixon of the Stephenson camp described it as a tea urn, but less biased spectators loved its sporty appearance. It was a racing car set against a pair of sedate family saloons. When the trials began it was the popular favourite.

The trials began on 6 October 1829 and, as everyone knows, *Rocket* triumphed: fast, reliable and powerful, it had a glorious series of runs, more than passing the tests laid down for the competition. To Hackworth's dismay, *Sans Pareil* had to be withdrawn because of a cracked cylinder. This was, of course, the cylinder cast by his rivals, Robert Stephenson of Newcastle. Had he been nobbled? No one will ever know. To the crowd's great disappointment, the favourite *Novelty* quite failed to live up to its reputation, proving, as George Stephenson had predicted, to lack staying power. Many claimed that the fault was not intrinsic in the design, but was a result of the haste in which everything had been done. In the end there was no contest; *Rocket* was the only locomotive that passed the test, and was duly declared the winner.

To celebrate the 150th anniversary of the Rainhill Trials in 1979, replicas of the three locomotives were built, and I was fortunate enough to be able to follow their progress from drawing board to steam trials. *Sans Pareil* was, like the original, built in Shildon and when the fire was lit and the engine chuffed out of its shed it was obvious to everyone that this was a powerful locomotive which worked remarkably smoothly. Timothy Hackworth's great-great-grand-daughter, Jane, was on hand, and as a true Hackworth she came away convinced that but for the perfidious Stephensons the family would have carried off the trophy. *Novelty* was no more successful than it had been on the first outing. The fragile engine puffed a short way out along the track before derailing. The best efforts of the builders failed to get it to work properly, and at the grand cavalcade held at Rainhill on the anniversary the little engine was reduced to the ignominy of being carried in front of the crowd on a flat truck. *Rocket* proved highly successful, performing well and, it seemed, vindicating the verdict passed 150 years previously. That, however, was not quite the end of the story. In 2002 the decision was taken to trundle out the three engines again, and put them through their trials. *Novelty* failed again, but this time the cause was clear. There was a fundamental design problem. The fireman had to feed in the fuel from the top of the vertical boiler. He had no means of testing the state of the fire, and in a very short time the build up of clinker brought everything to a halt. *Sans Pareil*, on the other hand, turned in a splendid performance, more than justifying the old Hackworth family claims that, given the chance, the locomotive could well have beaten *Rocket*. But it didn't: *Rocket* still turned in the best performance, but only by a whisker. We now know how fortunate it was that the result came out as it did, for the Hackworth engine, no matter how good it was, represented the ultimate development of old designs. *Rocket* was the future. The Stephensons had built a prototype capable of development, a locomotive containing all the main features that were to be incorporated in the steam engines that were to follow.

One of the judges at Rainhill, John Urpeth Rastrick, took his notebook along and sketched important features. This page shows the firebox and the multi-tubular boiler on *Rocket*.

Rainhill represented one of the great turning points in railway history. The steam loco-motive had won the day; the devotees of cable haulage were defeated. Now the Liverpool & Manchester emerged as a genuine, modern railway. It would not be a freight line on to which passengers would reluctantly be admitted. The Company built stations where passen-gers could wait in comfort for their trains to arrive, and the original Manchester terminus still survives as part of the Museum of Science and Industry. Outwardly, it is a stylish country house of the period, but behind that were all the elements that were to become familiar in stations around the world – booking office, waiting rooms and covered platforms. Nearby, across the tracks, the other side of the rail industry is represented by early goods sheds. The line gave a huge boost to innovation, not least in locomotive development.

The Liverpool & Manchester was not the first railway to see passenger coaches pulled by steam locomotives: it was just beaten to the honour by a comparatively minor line, the Canterbury & Whitstable. Even that was a Stephenson triumph, with a line surveyed by George, construction superintended by Robert and a locomotive, *Invicta*, built by Robert Stephenson & Co. The engine was of the *Rocket* type, but already the design was being recon-sidered. In the next generation of locomotives, the angle of the cylinders was lowered nearer

Following the success of *Rocket*, locomotive design moved forward at a great pace. It is clear that *Rocket* was a prototype, but Robert Stephenson soon followed this with the *Planet*. This replica runs at Manchester, and is recognizably a forerunner of later steam locomotives.

to the horizontal and the weight of the engines was greatly increased. *Rocket* had deliberately been built on the light side to ensure success in the trials, for which speed was more important than drawing power. This phase of development culminated in Robert's development of the *Planet*, delivered to the Liverpool & Manchester in 1830. The firebox was set in the end of the boiler barrel and the cylinders continued their downward progress, ending up horizontal and in line with the drive wheels below the chimney. They were now neatly tucked away inside the wheels. This gave a new wheel arrangement of 0-2-2, which could readily be adapted to 0-4-0 by linking the wheels. The new engines no longer used the boiler as the main frame; instead a separate outside frame was built consisting of timber baulks to either side, each timber sandwiched between metal plates. Springs and bearings were now outside the wheels, and the final change came with the use of a cranked axle, as first seen on *Novelty*. The wheels, like *Rocket*'s, were wood with iron tyres. In the Planet class of locomotives one can finally see the steam engine as it was to develop over the next hundred years.

There was one other outstanding development on the mechanical engineering side which was to emerge from the Stephenson works. Considerable progress had been made in valve gear design since Trevithick's day. In the 1830s, a system of Y- or X- shaped 'gabs' had been used, which could be moved to engage with pins on a rocking arm that would reverse the action. The big advantage of the system was that the locomotive could be easily reversed on the move, thus providing an efficient braking system. The use of lap and lead had improved the efficiency in the use of steam, but there was one other factor that could be brought into play with good effect. So far valves had only allowed for a set cut-off point when steam stopped entering the cylinders. There were huge gains to be made by having this cut-off point variable to meet different running conditions. The answer was found by William Williams of Robert Stephenson & Co in 1841. In the old systems, the reversing lever had to be firmly set in place or the drive was disengaged: there was no intermediate position. Williams realized that the problem could be overcome by allowing the piston rod to slide in a slotted link. Now the movement could be smoothed out, and intermediate positions could be used to vary the point at which live steam was admitted. Variable cut-off was at last possible. Robert Stephenson was delighted when he heard the news, and declared that 'the contriver of it should be rewarded'. Nevertheless, the patent was taken out in the name of Robert Stephenson & Co, not Williams.

Robert Stephenson was now about to come into his own as one of the foremost engineers of the age. His great chance came when in 1830 the job of surveying for the proposed London & Birmingham Railway was given to George Stephenson & Son. It was the son who undertook the work, and it was the son who in spite of considerable opposition was given the task of completing the line as chief engineer. When work started in 1833, he was a married man, but still only thirty years old. If some complained of his youth and lack of experience, he could at least argue that he had as much experience of railway engineering as any man, with the possible exception of his own father. The line was a triumph but not without its difficulties. The Chilterns formed a barrier across the route, but the answer was already there to see. The Grand Junction Canal, built in the 1790s, had come this way, piercing the hills in a deep cutting, with spoil being used for embanking. The canal, however, had been able to climb to its summit level at Tring through locks, and more locks could lead it down the other side. The railway equivalent would have been inclines as used on the S&DR and at the Liverpool end of the L&MR. Stephenson wanted no such interruptions to mainline travel, so his only option was to go through at a lower level. The approach from the south was through a tunnel, then, as with the canal, there was a deep cutting at Tring.

The construction of cuttings involved blasting through rock or excavating clay and soil. Channels were cut down the face of the cutting, leaving supporting pillars of earth. When everything was ready, the supporting pillars were cut away and the whole section levered out. Ideally it would fall as a piece, but it was just as likely to crumble. It was not unknown for the whole to collapse before the final stage was reached, falling on men working below. The technique used for getting the spoil up to the top of the bank was that of the canal age, using barrow runs. Planks were laid up the steep side of the cutting, at the top of which was a pulley system. One end of the rope was fastened to a horse at the top, the other to the barrow. Once the barrow was filled the horse walked on and the navvy balanced the barrow in front of him as he walked up the greasy planks. Frederick S. Williams wrote a book about railway construction in 1852 and described the barrow runs.

The man rather hangs to than supports the barrow, which is at once rendered unmanageable by any irregularity in the motion of the horse. If he finds himself unable to control it, he endeavours, by a sudden jerk, to raise himself erect; then throwing the barrow over one side of the board, or 'run' he swings himself round and runs back to the bottom. Should both fall on the same side, there is a great risk of the barrow with its contents falling on him before he can escape.

Railway construction involved huge armies of men, but very little in the way of machinery. This scene by Bourne shows Tring cutting on the London & Birmingham and its barrow runs. Horses haul barrows up the side of the cutting while the men guide them, hoping not to fall off the greasy, slippery planks.

Going down was no better for the navvy, who had to run down the planks with the barrow at his heels. The nature of the work can clearly be seen in the lithograph by J. C. Bourne, who visited Tring during construction.

Another major work was the mile-and-a-half-long Kilsby tunnel. When questioned by the Parliamentary Committee Robert had confidently answered that it would be 'Very easy indeed: in all clays it is very easy to tunnel, unless they be a great deal mixed with sand'. By the time the tunnel was opened he must have wished never to hear the word 'sand' again. It was not just sand that he met but quicksand, sand mixed with spring water so that as fast as it was dug out more flowed in to fill the space. The only answer was to use pumping engines to get the water out, and as the work dragged on, Kilsby was renamed 'Quicksand Hill', and seven pumps were at work night and day. It took eighteen months to complete less than 600 yards, but the remainder, away from the quicksand, over a mile of it, was finished in another six.

Another of Bourne's illustrations captures the dramatic atmosphere of a construction shaft at Kilsby tunnel on the London & Birmingham. Robert Stephenson sank sixteen of these shafts, and the men dug in both directions from the foot. Twenty-six of them lost their lives in the four years it took to complete.

One of the railway schemes Robert Stephenson was involved with was the Newcastle & Berwick Railway, which was to be linked with Darlington and the S&DR in the south. By this time, in the 1840s, another engineering star had appeared upon the railway stage: Isambard Kingdom Brunel. A man of extravagant ambitions, and occasionally wild ideas, Brunel was then advocating a novel system, the atmospheric railway. This dispensed with a locomotive altogether. Instead, rolling stock was attached to a piston inside a tube with a slot in the top closed by a valve. Air was sucked out of the tube by a steam engine, drawing the piston and train along the track. The north-eastern promoters heard of the notion, and declared it very interesting. George Stephenson announced it to be humbug and that was that, but Robert investigated the idea thoroughly. It was, as he said, no different in principle from the old idea of haulage by cable between stationary engines, except that the rope was made out of air. He doubted it would work, but even if it did it still suffered from a major disadvantage: any fault anywhere in the system would bring the whole to a halt. His arguments were convincing, and Newcastle would be served by locomotives. Brunel, however, went ahead with his system in Devon, and all Stephenson's reservations proved well founded. The slit in the pipe was closed by a leather valve, and even the least crack resulted in a huge power loss. In winter the leather froze solid and the system was scarcely usable, and in no time at all the leather began to rot. The atmospheric railway was kept on for a year then abandoned, and Brunel rejoined the world of steam locomotives.

Brunel tried an alternative to steam locomotives on the South Devon Railway: an atmospheric railway, with the train attached to a piston sucked down the pipes by a vacuum created by pumping engines. This scene shows the pipes and Dawlish pumping station. The process was not a success.

Robert Stephenson had to construct two major bridges on the line to Holyhead, and he devised a novel system, in which the tracks ran in hollow, box girders. This illustration shows one of the tubes being floated into place at Conwy, where it would be jacked up by hydraulic presses.

Meanwhile, although Robert Stephenson was uninterested in atmospheric experiments he was preparing an equally bold plan for the Newcastle & Berwick. The Tyne was to be crossed on a high-level bridge, but one which was to carry both road and rail traffic. There were to be two decks, the upper one carrying three lines of rails, the lower the roadway. Work began in 1845 with the construction of coffer dams on the river bed. Here another new invention was put to use, James Nasmyth's steam hammer for pile-driving. Inside the dams the five piers of local sandstone were built, the highest rising 146ft. The superstructure was of the bow-and-string form, with the cast-iron arch or bow tied by the wrought-iron strings. Everything about this bridge was innovative and it still stands today, carrying a weight of traffic that Stephenson could never have envisaged. The idea of a combined rail and road bridge had obvious advantages, and it is perhaps surprising that it was not more widely adopted. One interesting example can be seen crossing the Spree in Berlin. It differs greatly from the Stephenson bridge. Where the former shouts its modernism, the latter is built of red brick, with tall towers at either end giving it a strangely medieval appearance when viewed from a distance.

The other great challenge for Stephenson came on the line from Chester to Holyhead, where bridges had to be built at Conwy and across the Menai Straits. Telford had already crossed both using suspension bridges for the Holyhead road, but the suspension bridge was ruled out for railways. So Stephenson had to come up with a fresh solution, the biggest problem being that the wide Menai Straits had to be kept open for shipping. There could only be two intermediary piers, and the bridge had to be high enough for tall-masted ships to pass underneath. His solution was the box girder, but an enormous box girder. The trains would not run on top, but inside the immense hollow girders. These were to be tubular bridges. Even so, he was deeply worried about the practicality of the scheme, so he went to see the experienced builder of iron ships, William Fairbairn. He received just the encouragement he needed, for Fairbairn was able to show him a 220ft-long ship, propped up at bow and stern, but unsupported in the middle. Robert Stephenson took a much more scientific approach than earlier generations of engineers. He needed to get the right cross-section for the tubes, so he set up laboratory experiments using models.

Stephenson wisely decided to start with the shorter Conwy bridge, 425ft long compared with the daunting 1800ft at Menai. The tube was riveted together on site, floated out on a pontoon and raised into position by hydraulic jacks. On 6 March 1847 the Conwy tube was set on the pontoon, a nerve-racking exercise. It was floated out on the high tide, and everything went with astonishing smoothness.

> The tube, being lifted by the pontoons, began to move off, snapping the small ropes that kept it back; it glided quietly and majestically across the water in about twenty minutes ... At eleven o'clock the deep and rapid Conway was an impassable gulf, and in less than half an hour it was spanned by an iron bridge.

And there it still stands today. The Britannia Bridge across the Menai Straits has fared less well, the tubes having been severely damaged by a fire in the twentieth century.

Stephenson built an even grander tubular bridge across the Menai Straits. The Britannia Bridge was one of his greatest achievements, but sadly the tubes were destroyed in an accident, though its original grandeur is captured in this early photograph.

A great deal has been made of the competition between Brunel and the Stephensons, and it is true that the rivalry was keen. Brunel saw no reason why a nationwide rail system should be built to a gauge that happened to suit one colliery owner, and felt that far smoother, faster running would be possible with a wider gauge. He opted for 7 feet and that prevailed throughout his Great Western Railway empire. There was nothing wrong with his argument. Had he begun at the same time as the Stephensons his views might have prevailed, but by the time he came on the scene there was simply too much track built to the Stephenson gauge for the rest of the country to be converted to Brunel's grand scheme. But rivalry did not prevent Robert Stephenson and Brunel becoming friends and helping each other out with advice. Brunel had offered his assistance in the planning of the Holyhead Railway bridges, and he was there to provide support to his friend on the great day when the Conwy tube was raised.

The success of the Stephenson schemes in Britain brought them to the attention of everyone who was contemplating building railways. Leopold I of Belgium, who came to the throne in 1831, turned out to be a railway enthusiast and was soon promoting a line that was to be government run. It opened in July 1835 with two Newcastle locomotives, one of which was named simply *Stephenson*. Father and son were invited to the opening, and to George's delight the king declared himself honoured to meet the famous engineer. He was made Knight of the Order of Leopold, not quite what the ten-year-old boy heading down the pit might have expected for his old age. Robert was given a similar honour.

Stephenson locomotives were now being sent all over the place: Germany soon followed Belgium and in 1836 a Stephenson engine had crossed the Atlantic to Canada. But in Canada, Robert had rather more to do than supply the motive power. He was later asked to advise on a bridge to cross the mighty St Lawrence. The plan was to use a tubular bridge again, and at least the river was shallow and running over a rock bed. Piers could be constructed without too many problems, but even so it was an immense 6512ft long. The plans were agreed, but Stephenson had to allow for Canadian weather. In winter everything froze, but when spring came it only brought more problems. The swollen river flowed along at high speed, bringing giant ice floes crashing into the piers. Stephenson had to build immense cutwaters at the foot of each pier to withstand the battering of the ice. There were problems acquiring stone, which turned out to be on Indian land. Thirteen chiefs arrived in full regalia and head-dresses but were unwilling to discuss matters with James Hodges the railway negotiator, whom they saw as too young to be taken seriously – he was only just over forty years old! Agreement was eventually reached and quarries were opened. The iron sections were made in Birkenhead and prepared for assembly on site under the supervision of another Stephenson, George Robert, Robert's nephew. The work conditions were appalling, with the weather being a major problem. Men suffered from frostbite in winter and in summer the endless glare of the sun could produce temporary blindness, while cholera was a scourge of the navvy camps. In spite of it all the work was completed, but far behind schedule, and rising prices resulted in a severe loss for the Stephensons.

Building railways overseas was never dull, whatever countries the engineers visited. As a young man Nicholas I had been impressed by his visit to the Middleton Railway; now as Tsar he

Robert Stephenson's locomotive works in Newcastle built engines for the world. *Der Adler* (The Eagle) was built for the opening of the Nuremberg-Fürt Railway in 1835. Parts of the original were incorporated into a reconstruction which is on show in the Nuremberg Museum. This later replica was built in 1952 and is taken on regular outings.

was keen to promote the new means of transport in Russia. After a few failed attempts to build a system using Russia's own engineers, it was finally agreed that the British should provide both rails and locomotives. It says a great deal about the state of Russian transport at that time, that, although there was an iron works in the Urals able to supply rails to St Petersburg, it was cheaper to have them shipped out from Merthyr Tydfil in Wales. Locomotives were supplied by both the Stephenson Newcastle works and by Hackworth at Shildon. Timothy Hackworth's seventeen-year old son John was sent to Russia with the Shildon foreman and a team of fitters. It must have been an extraordinary experience for the young man, though he described his adventures in the best stiff-upper-lip tradition. The overland journey was by sleigh, during which the whisky in their flasks froze solid and they were pursued by a pack of wolves. On arrival they had to try and explain the wonders of the steam locomotives to the local engineers, without the advantage of anything approaching a common language. It was all a success and the Tsar appeared in person to wonder at how far the locomotive had progressed since his visit to England.

Indeed it had, and now railways were being built across the world and spanning whole continents. Having tried his hand in North America, Robert Stephenson turned to Africa in 1851 as chief engineer for a railway from Alexandria to Cairo. Once again he had to cross waterways, the Karrinneen Canal and the Nile. Now he had a new problem to face, for both were navigable with low banks. He turned to the box girder again, but this time with the lines on top, and arranged for the centre sections to be swung open for river traffic. A ferry service was introduced while the bridges were under construction, and it was soon adapted by having rails laid on the deck to take locomotives from side to side – the world's first genuine rail ferry. The Stephensons were in huge demand by countries just entering the new world of steam railways, but some soon broke loose and took over management of their own affairs.

CHAPTER 4

THE TRIUMPH OF THE ENGINEERS

OPPOSITE: **The trestle bridge was a great favourite with American engineers. This example carries the Boone and Scenic Valley across the Des Moines valley. The locomotive, however, is a foreigner, a 2-8-2 built in China.**

PERHAPS THE MOST ASTONISHING aspect of the railway story is the speed with which railway construction spread around the world. There were just over twenty years between Trevithick's first successful running of a steam locomotive on rails and the opening of the first public railway to be worked regularly by steam. Within the next quarter century, railway builders were at work on all five continents. The engineers acquired a boldness that made almost any obstacle seem trifling. New techniques were developed and new materials employed. Equally importantly, a system was developed which encouraged the efficient use of an immense labour force. Because all the developments of the first two decades had taken place in Britain, it was inevitable that Britain would set a standard and that British skills would be widely in demand. But what exactly did the British do that so impressed the world in those early years? One of the best ways to answer the question is to look at one of the very first trunk routes, the Great Western Railway, and its charismatic engineer, Isambard Kingdom Brunel.

There has never been an engineer who has grasped the popular imagination as Brunel has done, which is not at all the same thing as saying that he was the greatest of engineers. What set him apart was his vision. Who else but Brunel, when challenged over the possibility of building a railway from London to Bristol, would have replied by asking why they should stop there? Why not go on to New York? And what really set him apart was that he matched actions to his words by designing the first successful transatlantic steamship. His friend Robert Stephenson certainly did more to advance both branches of railway development, civil and mechanical engineering, than Brunel and he certainly got fewer things catastrophically wrong. We admire Stephenson, but it is Brunel we love for his passion. Something of the man's character seems to come through in all his works, and that certainly includes the Great Western Railway.

That Brunel got the job of chief engineer for the proposed railway in the first place was all down to his precocity and daring. As a twenty-four-year-old whose only qualification was having worked with his father Marc, himself an engineer of distinction, Brunel submitted a design for a bridge to cross the Avon gorge at Clifton, Bristol. The design was for the longest suspension bridge yet attempted, and he put himself in direct opposition to the grand old man of British engineering, Thomas Telford. It was Telford who declared that Brunel's design was too ambitious to work and who put forward his own plans for a Gothic

Isambard Kingdom Brunel

alternative, based on elaborate towers rising to the tops of the cliffs on either side. It was Brunel's far superior design that won the day, though it was never to be completed in his lifetime. But if the bridge was to be a disappointment, it gave him the right introductions to the right people at the right time. He got the GWR, a far bigger prize than the Clifton bridge. And from the start he showed that when it came to railways, as with bridge building, he would not be tied by precedent.

The GWR was a line designed to link what was still one of Britain's greatest ports, Bristol, to the capital. Brunel started by asking himself what were the main requirements for a good railway and the answer he came up with was a level track, with rails firmly secured and with generous dimensions to allow for comfortable travel. It was the latter part of the requirements that caused the most trouble. Famously, Brunel opted for a broad gauge with rails 7 feet apart, though an extra half inch was to creep in when it came to actual construction. He has been roundly condemned for the decision. One must, however, see it in terms of what was happening in the rest of the country. Robert Stephenson was already committed to the standard gauge of 4ft 8 ½ in for the route to London from Birmingham, and Brunel admitted that if the two systems were to be joined, then he would have to give way and build to the Stephenson gauge. But the companies did not envisage, let alone agree to any junction; each was to have its own, quite separate London terminus. So, if they were never to meet, then Brunel felt he had carte blanche to create his own, as he thought, superior system in the West of England and then take it on up into Wales.

LEFT: **The Battle of the Gauges: the replica of the Great Western *Iron Duke* dwarfs Stephenson's *Rocket*.**

Having decided on the broad gauge, Brunel landed himself with far greater engineering works: everything had to be on a much bigger scale, which meant wider tunnels, bridges and cuttings. All this effort would be wasted unless he could also achieve the rigid level track that he considered essential for smooth, fast running. So, once again, he came up with his own solution for track laying, based on longitudinal sleepers under the rails, instead of the familiar transverse sleepers used today. Again, his decision to build what was called at the time 'the baulk railway' has been criticized. But George Stephenson was still using stone sleeper blocks as in the tramway days, when he built the Liverpool & Manchester Railway, and even Robert used them in cuttings on the London & Birmingham. This was looking back to the past, not thinking about the future. Brunel's system was designed for great rigidity, which he thought was the key to smooth travel. We now know that this was a mistake, as a certain amount of flexibility improves running characteristics for the trains. The rails themselves were inverted Us and were set on to longitudinal pine baulks, the tops of which were faced with hardwood. These were braced along the way by transoms, which ran across the full width of both tracks and were spiked into the ground. The final touch was the addition of heavy ballasting. It was expensive to build but contemporaries thought it well worth it. In 1838, *Herepath's Railway Journal* described what happened with stone sleepers where, after every train, 'a gang of workmen appears, whose task it is to raise and adjust the blocks over which the engine has just passed, lest the succeeding train should be thrown off the track, or otherwise damaged. Nothing of this kind, I apprehend, can happen on the Great Western Railway.' The writer concluded that the GWR would save money in the long term by reducing the maintenance and replacement costs.

OPPOSITE: **One of Daniel Gooch's locomotives with 8ft single drivers near Reading in a painting by an anonymous artist. It shows the line with a third rail for use by standard-gauge trains, and a South Eastern Railway standard-gauge can be seen in the background.**

Perhaps the most important decision any engineer ever makes comes when he chooses the line he is to follow to get from one end of the route to the other. Brunel now brought his other criterion into the reckoning. The line was to be as flat as possible for as much of the route as possible. He would follow the Thames valley out from London, after which there was a precedent to follow – should he care to follow it. In the canal age, communication westward from the Thames had been down the River Kennet, after which the artificial Kennet & Avon Canal led to Bath and the Avon valley route to Bristol. Brunel had other ideas. He was to continue up the Thames valley to a point just short of Abingdon, at Didcot, and only then swing westward in a great curve through the Vale of the White Horse, before turning back towards Bath. It was such an extravagant curve that the joke at the time was that the initials GWR stood for the Great Way Round. But Brunel had exactly what he wanted. Well over half the route was at an average gradient of less than 1 in 1000, most of the rest was at 1 in 750 and even the steepest section of all was still only a modest 1 in 100. The result was exactly as the engineer had predicted: the GWR trains ran faster than their rivals on other lines. It was typical of Brunel that when he decided to appoint a Locomotive Superintendent, who was to have the job of designing appropriate engines for the broad gauge, he ignored the veterans and went for Daniel Gooch, who was to celebrate his twenty-first birthday six days after taking over! Once again daring decisions paid off, and Gooch went on to become one of the great locomotive engineers. On 11 May 1848, a Gooch express made the journey from London to Didcot in 47½ minutes, at an average speed of 67mph. To put that in perspective, the modern timetable shows a journey time of 42 minutes, not much of an advance after a century and a half of development. But to achieve his billiard-table railway Brunel had to produce some major engineering works, and again his ingenuity and originality are obvious.

In order to keep his levels, Brunel had to construct a tunnel through Box Hill, and to make a complex task even more difficult, he decided that the track through it should be at a steady 1 in 100 gradient. This set the surveyors and engineers an interesting exercise in three-dimensional geometry. The tunnel was to be of immense size, and as the GWR was from the first a great publicist, an *Illustrated Guide* to the line was published for the opening, giving statistics that are still impressive, leaving no doubt that this was a heroic undertaking. Box tunnel is 3195 yards long, ventilated by six 25ft-diameter shafts varying from 70 to 300ft deep. 414,000 cubic yards of earth and stone were excavated and because only a short portion was through rock that would stand unsupported, 54,000 cubic yards of masonry and brickwork were needed. Thirty million bricks had to be made, and every week a ton of gunpowder was used and a ton of candles lit to illuminate the work. A visitor to the workings wrote a somewhat romantic account of work in the tunnel during construction. There were more shafts sunk for construction than were retained for ventilation, and he was lowered down Number 7 shaft. He noted, with admiration, 'the rock face and every now and then a beautiful rill as clear as crystal issuing from some fissure', a sight that would have been less welcome to the engineers, for whom water was one of the great obstacles to progress. As he got nearer to the workings, he no longer had to rely on his own solitary candle for light, as he found candles set all round the walls. He had been going through an area where the tunnel had already opened up to its full dimensions, but now he had to struggle up fallen rock to the narrow heading. He waited while a shot was fired.

Daniel Gooch in 1845, with a model of one of his locomotives

The match is applied, the explosion follows and a concussion such as probably you never felt before takes place; the solid rock appears to shake and the reverberation of the sound and shock is sensibly and fearfully experienced; another and another follow; and with a slight stretch of the imagination you may fancy yourself in the middle of a thunder cloud with heaven's artillery booming around.

What the visitor did not report was the danger faced by the thousand workers who laboured for two and a half years in the dark. During the work, the Bristol Infirmary reported 'unusually high' figures for casualties, but was no more precise. On a later tunnel at Woodhead on the Sheffield & Manchester Railway, the company surgeon reported dealing with 97 fractures and 140 other injuries, but when asked about fatalities he merely replied that as the dead had no need of his services he had not kept notes. Something of the contemporary attitude towards the navvies can be gauged from an interview with an engineer on the same tunnel, who explained why he did not use the safety fuse instead of the common fuse. He agreed it was indeed safer 'but it is attended with such a loss of time and the difference is so very small, I would not recommend the loss of time for the sake of all the extra lives it would save'. There is no reason to suppose that Brunel shared the same callous attitude, but the loss of life at Box was still considerable, certainly more than a hundred. At times there is even a certain gallows humour in the situation. One unhappy man fell down one of the shafts, and according to an eyewitness, his last words as he plummeted to his death were 'Oh dear!' Somehow it is hard to reconcile the words with any image of a railway navvy. The main danger, however, was not from falls but from the blasting itself. A hole would be drilled in the rock and it would be packed with black powder, which was 'stemmed' (packed) into place with a rod. Iron rods were commonly used in spite of the dangers from sparks. When things

Watford tunnel on the London & Birmingham by J. C. Bourne. The illustration shows shear legs for lifting above the tunnel mouth and horse-drawn wagons removing spoil from the workings.

did go wrong the effect was disastrous. One workman was stemming when the powder ignited and the stemming rod was driven straight through his head.

On its completion in 1841 Box tunnel was considered one of the wonders of the railways. Not everyone was enthusiastic. One of the individuals who keeps popping up in the Brunel story, rather like one of those comic characters who appear from time to time to enliven a serious drama, was Dr Dionysius Lardner. He was a man of supreme pomposity matched with wonderful ignorance. His carefully considered view of engineers was that they were 'merely judicial men, who do not have the extensive powers of generalization, which is a matter of Arithmetic'. He used his arithmetic to 'prove' that no one could survive a journey through Box on the downhill gradient as the train would reach a speed of 120mph, a speed at which no one would be able to breathe. Even if they survived that horror, the train would 'deposit 3090lb of noxious gases incapable of supporting life'. One can only be impressed by the accuracy of the calculations. Brunel, the engineer unqualified in mathematics, pointed out to Lardner that his scientific calculations had failed to take into account the effect of either friction or air resistance, but the splendid Doctor was happy to ignore comments from such an uneducated man. In spite of the absurdity of Lardner's arguments, some passengers refused to go through the tunnel, and the company felt obliged to lay on a stagecoach between Box and Corsham for the nervous.

Brunel may have been irritated by his critics, but he also seemed amused by some of their absurdities, and he was not above teasing them for his own amusement. The other wholly original structure on the line is the bridge across the Thames at Maidenhead, famously depicted in Turner's painting *Rain, Steam and Speed*. Brunel was continuing his steady westward progress along the Thames valley up towards Maidenhead, but here the river turns sharply to the north and continues in that direction for about five miles. The bridge was needed to ensure the smooth progress that was so essential to the overall plan. It emphasizes the virtues of the line, crossing the river on two semi-elliptical brick arches. No one had ever built a bridge with arches so flat and wide, and the critics inevitably declared it to be impossible. When the arches were completed in 1838 a slight subsidence was noticed at the eastern end. Brunel came to investigate and discovered that the timber centring had been removed before the cement had properly set and the fault was easily corrected. As a sop to his critics, he said he would keep all the timber supports in place right through to 1840. The critics continued to have a good time at Brunel's expense, convincing anyone prepared to listen that the bridge would collapse. What they did not know was that it was Brunel who was laughing at them, for he had secretly arranged to have the centring eased away from the brickwork and the timbers were no longer even touching the arches. All was revealed in the autumn of 1839 when a storm blew all the woodwork away. The arches have stood ever since, and it remains one of the most elegant of all brick railway bridges.

Other engineering works along the line, such as the cuttings and embankments, were built in much the same way as those on other lines, but the Great Western was one of the first of the new inter-city lines to follow on from the success of the Liverpool & Manchester. For the first time, railway companies appreciated that passenger traffic was as important as freight. Passengers needed facilities: they needed places where they could buy tickets and

shelter from the elements while they waited for their trains. They needed stations. And a line joining the two great cities of Bristol and London needed terminal stations that matched the grandeur of their settings. Of the two, Paddington was by far the more important, not just because it served the capital, but also because it was clear that Bristol would be a terminus only until the lines moved westward again.

Paddington is especially interesting because it introduced a new element into the railway world, for it is the result of a collaboration between the engineer, Brunel, and an architect, Matthew Digby Wyatt. The original station had been a rough and ready affair at the little village of Paddington on the outskirts of London, but Brunel was always thinking in terms of something grander. The lines came into London in a cutting, and his idea was to use this to create a dramatic effect, inspired by Paxton's building for the Great Exhibition of 1851. That had been a Crystal Palace: this was to be a railway cathedral. The vast train shed would consist of a central nave, flanked by two narrower aisles, and to complete the analogy there were even transepts. Decorative cast-iron pillars support the three hugely impressive roofs of wrought iron and glass. The central span is 102ft across, the aisles 70 and 68ft. Other stations depend on an elaborate or striking facade to create an effect of majesty, but Paddington has nothing of the sort. Instead, there are simply two ramps to either side of the train shed, one for passenger arrivals, the other for departures: a neat and practical arrangement. In spite of

Paddington Station shown in an engraving of 1854. The illustrator has captured the cathedral-like atmosphere of the station with the cast-iron colonnades and arched roofs strongly reminiscent of nave and aisles.

The goods shed at Bristol in 1846 by Bourne. Unlike the mock-medieval passenger station, this is a purely functional building. An interesting feature is the covered wagon in the foreground, which has sheeting drawn over a series of iron hoops, a device commonly used on road wagons of the period.

later additions to accommodate a growing network, the original design survives, and it is still a place of marvels and quirky details. Just look up, for example, at the oriel window that allows the occupants of the offices to look out across Platform 1. Behind the terminus was an area known as The Lawn, which has recently been developed into a third-rate shopping mall, wholly devoid of character. There is a statue of Brunel, who seems to be averting his gaze from the mediocrity tacked on to his masterpiece.

At Bristol, Brunel allowed himself to indulge in architectural fantasies. It is interesting to note that the man who had scoffed at Telford's design for a Gothic bridge at Clifton was prepared to produce his own mock-medieval station. The facade is castellated and vaguely Jacobethan, but the real surprise is the train shed. At Paddington, structural considerations lead the design; here architectural conceits rule. The train shed is a fair imitation of a medieval great hall, complete with hammer-beam roof. But the hammer beams have no real function. The widely splayed beams have the thrust taken up by iron columns, which form arcades outside the line of the main building. The extension of the GWR westward, eventually reaching the tip of Cornwall, led to the abandonment of the old terminus in favour of the present through station. Much of the old building survives and is full of interesting details. The lines came in at what is, in effect, first-floor level, so that there is an area beneath the tracks, which made it easy for locomotives to be ashed out.

Stations were not the only requirements of the new line. Freight movement was equally important to the prosperity of the line, so a series of goods sheds were built for storage and loading and unloading in the dry. These were practical structures, not needing to impress customers with anything other than their practicality. Few survive intact, but there is a good example at Stroud, on the GWR line from Swindon to Gloucester. It is notably well built of local stone, which has been dressed to give a smooth finish that is very appealing.

An early decision was taken to end reliance on other companies for locomotives and rolling stock. Results in the early days of the line had not been successful, largely because Brunel himself had imposed impossible conditions on the builders, particularly by limiting piston speed to 280ft per minute, little more than half the speed then to be found on some other locomotives. This meant that engines had to have huge drive wheels to compensate. If ever evidence was needed that Brunel was far less successful as a locomotive engineer than he was as a builder of tracks, then these early years provided it. He was lucky that with the appointment of Daniel Gooch all the early difficulties were resolved. Now the company needed its own works. It was Brunel himself who chose the spot, roughly halfway between

The engine house at Swindon by Bourne. This was an immense structure with accommodation for up to 36 locomotives. They can be seen in the side stalls, while one engine is being wheeled out onto the moveable platform above the pit for maintenance work or repair.

London and Bristol, at the little village of Swindon. The new works opened with a staff of over 400 men, but they were almost a mile from the original village. Accommodation was needed, so the GWR gave a contract to the London builders J. and C. Rigby and it is generally believed that the overall design was once again the work of Digby Wyatt. The New Town is an early example of Victorian town planning, with neat streets arranged on a regular grid around a central square. The houses are pleasant rather than ostentatious, built of local limestone, with privies and washhouses in the small backyards. They may not be spectacular but they provided a standard of accommodation far better than that of the jerry-built slums of the mushrooming industrial towns. Later facilities included a church, school and Mechanics Institution. The workshops were equally utilitarian and developed steadily over the years before they were closed in the 1980s. Today, the quality of the buildings has ensured that some at least have survived, and one section has now become an excellent museum, Steam, devoted to the story of the Swindon works and the GWR.

There is an interesting corollary to the story. As part of the deal, the Rigbys were given a ninety-nine-year lease for the refreshment rooms at Swindon station, which they promptly sold on. In the days of corridor-less trains, stops were essential for passenger comfort, and a compulsory ten-minute stop was built into the timetables. The new proprietors of the refreshment concession saw no need to worry greatly about the quality of what they sold. Everything looked grand enough, including a coffee urn in the shape of a broad-gauge locomotive. It was what the urn produced that was rather more questionable. The owners were greatly offended to hear that Brunel himself had complained about the coffee, and he promptly denied the charge.

> I assure you Mr Player was wrong in supposing that I thought you purchased inferior coffee. I thought I said to him I was surprised that you should buy such bad roasted corn. I did not believe you had such a thing as coffee in the place; I am certain I never tasted any. I have long ceased to make complaints at Swindon. I avoid taking anything there when I can help it.

It seems that the reputation of the railway buffet was formed in the earliest years – and still lingers on.

Mention of the timetable brings up one of those interesting sidelines of railway history. Before the coming of the railway, nobody minded very much if the time in London was the same as the time in Penzance. Even travellers were not particularly concerned. Indeed, for anyone travelling between north and south, times were unlikely to vary much at all, as they were travelling up the same meridian. But when travelling between east and west there would be a definite variation in local time. It might not be as great as that between, say, London and New York, but it would be real and measurable. As a result a watch carried by a passenger at Penzance would not show the same time as the watch of the guard on the train from London. Someone had to decide which time should be used on the timetable. So a new time was introduced, Railway Time. Railway clocks were set against the standard time, based on the guard's watch, and could be substantially different from other clocks in the town, until time was officially standardized throughout the country.

These remain the main features of the line, but it is very far from an exhaustive list. And the GWR did not end with the construction of the first mainline: it spread throughout the West Country and into Wales. There were to be other great structures, including the last great engineering work designed by Brunel, the Royal Albert Bridge across the Tamar at Saltash. He borrowed an idea from Robert Stephenson, but adapted it to produce something altogether more graceful and, as time has proved, more durable. He took advantage of the structural strength of wrought-iron tubes, but used them in a quite different way. Here the tubes have an oval cross-section and form arches across the river, and from these the plates carrying the track are suspended. It is as if he had looked at the work of two great engineers at the Menai Straits, Telford and Stephenson, and taken ideas from the best of both to create his own unique solution to the problem of building a long, high-level bridge. The bridge is still in use today, but forms a bottleneck, being only single track. Nevertheless, with its two arched spans, each 461ft long, it is as impressive as it was when it was opened by Prince Albert in 1859. Brunel was then too ill to come to the ceremony, but was later taken across on a bed mounted on a flat cart. By the end of the year he was dead, and in recognition of his great works his name was inscribed on the portals of the arch.

Brunel was a great individualist, and it showed in everything that he did. He recruited young men who nominally owed their allegiance to the Great Western Railway, but first and foremost they were Brunel men. Where others were prepared to delegate, Brunel was always

Brunel's last engineering masterpiece, the Royal Albert Bridge, crossing the Tamar at Saltash. It is an extraordinary construction with the girders that carry the tracks suspended from immense hollow, wrought-iron tubes.

The viaduct at Ivy Bridge, Devon in c. 1850. As the Great Western empire expanded westward from Bristol, Brunel began to build a new type of viaduct, with timber spans above stone piers. They have been replaced, but the stone stumps can still be seen.

at the centre of the action. He designed his own coach, known to his associates as the 'Flying Hearse', not inappropriately for a man who worked himself to death. It was both mobile office and temporary home, with a couch that could be made into a bed on the many occasions when he worked late into the night. But although he concerned himself with all aspects of the work, he left the actual organization of the labour force to independent contractors. This was a pattern that was to be followed by railway engineers throughout the world.

The Great Western is just one line among thousands built in the nineteenth century, but the elements that make for a great railway remain the same, regardless of international boundaries. Being the pioneer has its advantages: as the first in the field there is a huge demand for your expertise. The early British engineers certainly never had to complain of lack of work. In December 1845 *Felix Farley's Bristol Journal* listed the works on which the leading men were then engaged.

> Mr Brunel is connected with 14, Mr Robert Stephenson with 34 Sir John MacNeil with 37 Mr Locke with 31 Mr Vignolles [sic] with 22 Sir John Rennie with 20 Mr Rastrick with 17 Mr Miller with 10 Mr Gravatt with 10 Mr S. Hughes with 9 Mr W. Cubitt with 11 Mr Gibbs with 12 Messrs Birch with 7 Mr Blunt with 8 and Mr Braithwaite with 9.

Not all of these works were in Britain. And what was true of the engineers was equally true of the contractors and even the navvies.

One of the early French lines was first surveyed by Vignoles in 1833. It was to run from Paris to Dieppe, where it would be linked by ferry to a line from London to Southampton. The French proved reluctant to invest, and it was not until 1839 that agreement was reached with the help of finance from the French government. The chief engineer was Joseph Locke, who had learned his trade with the Stephensons on the Liverpool & Manchester, but had like so many others fallen out with George (p. 41). He was to go on to become one of the greats of the railway world. One of his most important, if not most romantic, achievements was the development of a new type of rail, the double-headed or bull-head rail, which made it possible for faster and heavier trains than before to use the track. He had first introduced the rails onto the Grand Junction, which linked Birmingham to the Liverpool & Manchester via a short branch from Warrington. Locke was also a great believer in using big contractors employing massive work forces, rather than spreading the work out around a number of small firms. One major structure on the Grand Junction was the Penkridge viaduct, and the contract went to another young man, Thomas Brassey, who had begun his working life as a surveyor, but had been encouraged to move into the railway business by George Stephenson. It is said that Brassey's wife also encouraged him in the new venture. She was not to know that Brassey was to become perhaps the greatest contractor of them all, constantly travelling as the work demanded. (The appendix on page 200 lists the many lines he worked on.) When Mrs Brassey found herself moving house for the eleventh time in thirteen years she might have regretted her earlier enthusiasm.

Thomas Brassey, one of the greatest of all railway contractors

When Locke was put in charge of the line from Paris to Rouen, his first thought was to use local men, but he found their prices exorbitant and turned to Brassey, who went into partnership with another big contractor, William Mackenzie. The Brasseys moved to Rouen, and at least Mrs Brassey had the advantage of speaking fluent French, which was more than could be said of the army of 5000 navvies brought over with them. Local labour was also recruited, and the navvies found their own way of communicating.

> They pointed to the earth to be moved, or the wagon to be filled, said the word 'd-n' emphatically, stamped their feet, and somehow or other instructions, thus conveyed, were generally comprehended by the foreigner.

This was at least an improvement over the method used by a man described as 'a big brawny navvy' in charge of a local workforce on the Great Indian Peninsula Railway. He was interviewed by Sir Bartle Frere of the East India Company.

> Well, my good man, you appear to be the manager here.
> Yes Sir, was the reply
> And how are you getting on?
> Oh, Sir, we are getting on very well.
> How many natives have you got under your orders?
> Well Sir, about 500 on 'em altogether.
> Do you speak their language?
> No Sir I don't.
> Well then, how do you manage to let these natives understand what they are to do?
> Oh Sir I'll tell you. I tell these chaps three times in good plain English, and then if they don't understand that, I takes the lukri [stick] and we get on very well.

At the start of work, the British navvies earned twice the pay of the locals, but thanks to their experience they were able to do twice as much work. One of Brassey's timekeepers saw a party of French gentlemen viewing the navvies with amazement, and heard one remark: 'Mon Dieu! Les Anglais, comme ils travaillent!' The French workers were happy at first, for although they got less than the English, they were still making twice as much as they had before the railways came. Such a situation could not last for ever. European navvies were eventually able to compete on equal terms with the British, and French contractors gained the confidence to bid for major contracts against the might of Brassey and Mackenzie.

The Paris-Rouen line was extended to Le Havre by the same team. The engineers had one major obstacle to overcome, the deep valley cut by the Ste Austreberthe, a tributary of the Seine. The crossing was made at the little town of Barentin and visiting it today one can only imagine the excitement that was caused when the construction of the immense viaduct began. Even now it dominates everything, soaring over the main street and a little bandstand, where perhaps the opening day was celebrated by one of those French bands which seem to appear to enliven any notable event. It is an immense structure, a third of a mile long, rising a full hundred feet above the main street and spreading out to either side on twenty-seven arches. It is very handsome, the height emphasized by extending the piers as pilasters reaching to the full height of the balustrade. It also has a reassuring air of solidity, for the central piers in the town are braced by intermediary arches halfway up the columns. Appearances, however, can be deceptive.

In 1844, Brassey and Mackenzie won the contract for the viaduct, underbidding their French competitors by ten per cent. William Mackenzie was well pleased, but noted that 'we

Crimple viaduct carries the line between Harrogate and Leeds across the track of the disused Leeds to Thirsk line. Built in the 1840s, it has a reassuringly massive solidity.

in reality are 6 per cent too low – our estimate is 2,008,635Fr.' Were dangerous savings made to keep down the costs? Mackenzie wrote to Locke to tell him that the mortar they were using was not of good enough quality, and he was prepared to use hydraulic mortar instead, if the company would pay half the extra cost. Locke refused, and the work went ahead. It was a bad economy. In 1846, the entire viaduct collapsed, and the suspect mortar appears to have been to blame. It is to the great credit of Brassey and Mackenzie that they did not even pause to apportion blame, but simply announced that they would rebuild it at their own expense. They were as good as their word and the entire majestic structure was completed in only six months. This involved not just the actual construction, but finding another eight million bricks, and this in an age when bricks were still hand-made, one at a time in moulds.

The only comparable brick viaduct, the Göltzschtal between Reichenbach and Plauen, was built in 1851. This is one of the great feats of German engineering and is strongly reminiscent of Roman aqueducts such as the Pont du Gard in France. The approaches to the valley are carried on triple arches, even more spectacular than the double arches at Barentin. But the wide, central span is built as an immense double arch.

In 1850 the Mackenzie-Brassey partnership came to an end, and Brassey went on to contract for lines all around the world. The only contractor who could match Brassey was Morton Peto and patriotism was to bring the two men together in a heroic venture in the 1850s. In 1854, the Crimean War had ground to a halt with the British army camped above Sevastopol, their only supply route a foul track, so deep in mud that it killed off even captured Russian oxen. Cavalrymen had to look on as their chargers were pressed into service as pack animals, and the work was so heavy that they died at the rate of three or four a day. *The Times* correspondent William Howard Russell summed up the situation succinctly: 'There is nothing to eat, nothing to drink, no roads, no commissariat, no medicine, no clothes, no arrangements; the only thing in abundance is cholera.'

Peto wrote to the government offering his services in building a railway to supply the troops at the siege. Brassey quickly joined him and they persuaded various railway companies to part with equipment of all kinds. The word went out that navvies were needed and they turned up in their hundreds. The contractors made one stipulation: the navvies were civilians answerable only to them. They were not to be subject to military discipline, nor were they to do any military work. They were to build a railway and that was it. When the first batch of 500 was ready to depart, the Duke of Newcastle came to see them off. He was astonished by how well equipped they were, but could not imagine what all the tarpaulins were for. Peto explained that they were for the use of the men until wooden huts were ready. The Duke thought this was a wonderful idea, and said that he wished the soldiers who slept on the ground could be as well provided. Peto promptly offered to make similar tarpaulins available. The Ordnance Department was horrified at the notion of such irregularity and refused the offer. In the Crimea, the soldiers continued to suffer as the bureaucracy ground its way through endless paperwork.

The Army in the Crimea was not immediately impressed by the unruly navvy army that had joined them. One officer, Captain Clifford, wrote in his diary on 8 February 1855 that they were 'unutterable things'. Three days later and everything had changed: he had seen

RIGHT: **This photograph by Roger Fenton shows a group of navvies at the Railway Yard at Balaklava during the Crimean War. They amazed the military authorities by the speed with which they built the railway.**

BELOW: **Bramhope tunnel was one of the most important works on the line between Leeds and Thirsk. At one time there were 7000 workers on the site, but not all survived. This memorial, in the form of a miniature tunnel, stands in Otley churchyard as a remembrance of 23 men who died in its construction.**

just what the unutterable things could do. He declared that 'They do more work in a day than a Regiment of English Soldiers do in a week' – and all that without the benefits of beef and beer. The rate of work was phenomenal. A pile driver was landed from a ship in the afternoon. In the evening it was taken to pieces and taken up to a stream. Within twenty-four hours, the piles had been driven, the bridge built and the tracks had moved on another hundred yards. In seven weeks thirty-nine miles of track had been laid, and it was time to hand it back to the army. Presented with a first-rate transport system, the first act was to draw up regulations for the use of the railway. With supplies desperately needed, the commissariat decreed that nothing should be sent before 8 a.m. and all transport had to stop by 5.30 p.m. The comments of the navvies who had worked night and day to do the work are not recorded. At least these men who had been vilified for so long as drunken brawlers came back to England as national heroes.

The British domination of the early years of construction lasted for many years in the Empire. Elsewhere, new engineers appeared with new ideas, one of whom was Gustav Eiffel. One area where the French were well ahead of British practice was in providing formal education for their engineers. Eiffel graduated from the École Centrale des Arts et Manufactures in 1855 and soon set up his own business, specialising in iron construction.

Long before he built the famous tower which bears his name he had produced some spectacular structures, including magnificent railway bridges, two of which are outstanding. In 1877 he designed a bridge over the Douro at Oporto which soared over the river in a single 530-foot span. Compared with the mighty bridges of brick and stone being built elsewhere it looks alarmingly skeletal and fragile, but Eiffel followed it with another, even bigger, iron arch at Truyère in southern France, which rose to a height of 400ft, making it the highest bridge in the world at that time. But the age of iron in bridge construction was drawing to a close, hastened by a tragedy in Scotland.

Thomas Bouch, an engineer with a sound reputation, was given the task of building a bridge across the two-mile-wide River Tay near Dundee. The design was conventional for the day, and although the bridge itself was long, the spans seemed reasonable, with fifty piers joined by iron lattice girders. Bouch prided himself on keeping costs down, but there is a narrow divide between economy and negligence. All might have been well, but a design with very little latitude for error was executed by careless contractors. At the end of 1879, just a year after opening, the bridge collapsed in a storm and 75 lives were lost. The bridge was replaced and the successor is still a remarkable sight as it snakes away from one shore to the other. But Bouch had no hand in the new; he died in disgrace. He had already prepared ambitious plans for another immense bridge in Scotland, across the Firth of Forth. He had planned a suspension bridge, with two spans based on a central pier on the island of Inch Garvie. No one was going to go ahead with that scheme now.

ABOVE: **This 160-metre steel arch spanning the Douro at Oporto, designed by Gustav Eiffel, is dual-purpose, taking both rail and road traffic.**

BELOW: **An alternative version of a dual-purpose bridge crosses the River Ain in the Jura region of France near Cize-Bolozon.**

ABOVE: **One of the best known of all railway bridge crosses the Firth of Forth. Following the collapse of the Tay Bridge, the original plans were scrapped and the viaduct was redesigned as three double cantilevers for the main spans. The engineers were Sir John Fowler and Benjamin Baker, and it was completed in 1890.**

OPPOSITE: **Newcastle Central Station was begun in 1848 and used what was then a new structural technique of iron arched trusses to create wide spans without intermediate supports. Even more remarkably, this pioneering building was also built with a pronounced curve.**

Two engineers, John Fowler and Benjamin Baker, came up with a revolutionary new proposal, a cantilever bridge, built not from iron but from steel. It was based on sound scientific principles. The cantilevers had central diamond-shaped structures, extended by arms out to either side, and were linked by short girders. The effects of sun, wind and cold were all calculated and allowed for by means of expansion joints and sliding bed plates. The steel tubes used in construction were huge, up to 12ft in diameter. The men who worked on the bridge, the 'briggers', were mainly Scots, well used to working in steel, even if they were less accustomed to doing so a couple of hundred feet up in the air. To give some idea of the effort involved, the steel was held together by 4000 tons of rivets, all of which had to be heated in furnaces just where they were needed, whether down at ground level or at the end of an advancing girder. It is greatly admired, and Baker explained just what it was that appealed to him in the design.

They made the compression members strong tubes, and the tension members lattice work, so that to any intelligent eye the nature of the stresses and the sufficiency of the members of the structure to resist them were emphasised at all points. It would have been futile to attempt to ornament the great cantilevers, and so, to keep the whole work in harmony, they studiously avoided any attempt at ornamentation of the piers, and people would search in vain for even a moulded capping, or cornice throughout the whole work. The object had been so to arrange the leading lines of the structure as to convey an idea of strength and stability. This, in such a structure, seemed at once the truest and highest art.

There speaks the voice of the engineer, and in many ways the Forth bridge was to set important precedents. Steel was the new material, and with its use came a new aesthetic: the idea that beauty need not be derived from ornamentation, but appears when structures most clearly define their function. The same aesthetic was to rule in the twentieth century when other new materials came into use, notably reinforced concrete. Steel and reinforced concrete were both used in one of the most recent of major developments, the line designed to take France's high-speed trains, the TGVs, between Paris and Marseille. Baker would have approved the lack of frippery, and the simple elegance of the designs. The 1080ft (330m) long Garde-Adhémar viaduct uses a well-tried engineering technique, a double bow-string, but its modernity is never in question.

Simplicity was not always considered desirable, however, in nineteenth-century railway architecture, and was certainly not much in favour when it came to major stations. Stations often seem to divide into two quite separate elements; the practical engineering side and the architectural embellishment. The happiest results seem to come when the two are perfectly matched. In other cases, the engineering, which can be spectacular in its own right, can be overwhelmed by the additions. There is no better example than St Pancras, the London terminus of the Midland Railway. The station was designed by William Barlow, with a single cast

iron and glass roof soaring above the tracks with a 240ft span, which was to be the largest of its kind for a hundred years. The supports scarcely seem capable of holding up such a vast expanse and the walls hardly capable of withstanding the outward thrust of the arch. What is not obvious is that the train shed is, in effect, at the first-floor level of the building as a whole. Underneath are vast vaults, specially designed to take beer barrels from Burton-upon-Trent and beneath these the whole structure is held by horizontal iron ties.

The end of the station is closed off by a glass screen, resting on Gothic arches. From the start, however, the plans called for a station hotel that would represent the public face of St Pancras to the world. It is into this masterpiece of the Gothic revival that the pointed arches lead. Hotel and station are integrated physically, but are a world apart in style. The architect, Sir George Gilbert Scott, was still smarting from having his grand Gothic design for the Foreign Office rejected in 1856, and he was determined to show Whitehall what they had missed. In spirit the hotel is very similar to the Foreign Office design, though significantly adapted for the new site. The station was completed in 1868 and work at once began on the hotel. It is Gothic at its most exuberant, and the interior is as impressive as the famous exterior. It was not, however, without its modern touches such as electric bells and hydraulic lifts, then grandly referred to as 'ascending rooms'.

This watercolour of Welwyn viaduct, painted by W. Humber in 1850, gives a good idea of the impact railways had on the traditional British countryside. Built of brick, it strides across the valley of the Mimram for almost a mile on forty arches.

Victoria Station, Bombay is one of the most extravagant to be found anywhere in the world, a bizarre cross between the Gothic of St Pancras and the Moghul architecture of northern India.

It is difficult to imagine any railway structure matching St Pancras for Victorian exuberance and elaboration, but the Victoria Terminus, Bombay succeeds so well that it is often referred to as the St Pancras of India. The effect of discovering a curiously English station in the heart of an Indian city is heightened by the familiar double-decker buses passing to and fro on the road outside. The station was also the headquarters for the Great Indian Peninsula Railway, and was opened in the year of Victoria's Golden Jubilee, 1887. At first sight it seems to have the familiar Gothic elements, but then one sees that they have been mixed with other devices borrowed from Moghul architecture, in a profusion of domes and turrets. The carved faces that look down from the facade are as likely to be turbanned as top-hatted. It could be taken as an architectural metaphor for the contrasts and inconsistencies of the British Raj.

That great stations really are great buildings by any standards is well demonstrated in Paris. The Gare d'Orsay by Victor Laloux has something of St. Pancras in the splendour of its grand, curved main hall, but the ornamentation is very much of its period. And there is one notable difference here: there was no need to worry about glass being blackened by smoke, as the trains would be electric. The tracks have gone, but it has a new life as the Musée d'Orsay. It is interesting how much more one is aware of the building itself in its new role as an art gallery than one normally is when visiting a station. It was the inspiration of a new generation of station in the early twentieth century best exemplified by Hamburg, Copenhagen Central and Grand Central, New York. Stations come in all shapes and varieties, often reflecting current architectural trends. At San Diego, California in 1915, the chosen style was Spanish Colonial, and the station could easily be mistaken for a church strayed over the border from Mexico. At Kuala Lumpur, built at a similar date, in place of the colonial church there is a cross between a mosque and a temple, with even less of a hint to suggest that it might be possible to catch a train there. Every style of European architecture was called into service for a station somewhere in the world. The most modern stations have generally reverted to seemly, functional simplicity. Berlin's new central station, for example, is strongly reminiscent of the great Victorian train sheds, little more than two tunnels of glass and steel.

The technology of railway construction changed surprisingly little in the nineteenth century, apart from one crucial area – tunnelling. One of Isambard Brunel's first engineering works was as assistant to his father, Marc Brunel, in constructing a tunnel under the Thames. It was designed as a road tunnel, but now carries the London Underground tracks. It was an immense undertaking, but seems almost modest compared with the plan to cut a railway tunnel under the Severn to provide a shorter route to Cardiff from

Opened in 1931, Milan Central Station is comparatively modern, and is notable for the immense expanse of its huge central bay, based on steel arches with a 320-metre span. Even more modern is the train, the new Cisalpino, linking Italy to Switzerland and Germany. It tilts to deal with the tight curves on this mountainous route.

England. In October 1879, Sir Daniel Gooch took a party underground to see the workings, but warned them to bring umbrellas as it might be a little wet. This turned out to be a huge understatement. Before the end of the year, the tunnellers hit an underground spring, which burst through into the workings and set the work force running for their lives. Huge steam pumps were ordered from Harveys of Hayle, one with a 72-inch diameter, the other a 70-inch, that between them could raise 3000 gallons a minute. But even they could not conquer the Great Spring. The only answer was to try and seal it off using divers. The first man had to abandon the task as he made his way thirty feet down the shaft and off down the dark, flooded tunnel. His air line floated to the top and the drag became too great for him to proceed. The job was eventually done, and work went ahead. It was not to be the last alarm. In 1883, vile weather sent a tidal wave rushing down the Severn. It swept over the workings and sent water cascading down a shaft. Three men then climbing to the surface were washed away to their deaths, while the 83 men trapped by the water reached a wooden staging from which they were eventually rescued by boat. Finally, in 1886 the work was complete.

Perhaps the greatest challenge of the nineteenth century was the construction of the Simplon tunnel through the Alps, linking Switzerland to Italy. Not only was it the longest tunnel in the world, at 12 miles, but in places the peaks stood over 4000 feet above the tracks. There was no question here of sinking shafts from the surface! The engineers planned two tunnels: the wide main tunnel, and a smaller service tunnel alongside, which could eventually be widened. Hydraulic drills were used, and aqueducts had to be built at either end of the tunnel to provide a sufficient head of water. They also had to use air compressors to compensate for the lack of ventilation, but even so temperatures in the workings were recorded as high as 55°C. The work was relentless and even the modern drills were worn away faster than the rock. A 60cm bit was soon reduced to an unusable length and had to be replaced – and this might be done as often as four hundred times a day. Drilling and blasting carried on to the triumphant opening in 1906.

It is easy to trace a direct line of development from the days of the pioneers through to railway workings all round the world. What one would expect to find is an ability to learn from the lessons of the early lines, and an avoidance of some of the more obvious mistakes. One of the first things to be decided in a country starting off on the railway adventure was the gauge at which to build the track. In India, there was considerable debate over whether to opt for the Stephenson gauge or to go with the broad Brunel tracks. Eventually a decision was taken to go for neither but opt for something in between, 5ft 6in. There was nothing wrong with the decision had it been adhered to, but it was later thought to be too expensive and a second version appeared, the metre gauge. This was used mainly for State Railways, run by individual states within their own boundaries, so there was not the same difficulty of gauge breaks that was to plague the British system.

There was a logic to the Indian system: the same could not be said about the early years of railway development in Australia. This was still a very young country as far as European settlement was concerned and the first settlers were not exactly eager colonists. The first had arrived by convict ship at what was to become Sydney, New South Wales, as recently as

1788. It was only with the circumnavigation of 1802-3 that it became known that they were actually set down at one end of a whole continent. The convict settlement soon developed into a more conventional community that began to push into the interior. In 1813, three explorers crossed the Blue Mountains and discovered a fertile grassland, which was to provide Australia with one of its great sources of wealth – sheep. The South Australian Land Company was formed, and in 1834 South Australia became a second province with a capital at Adelaide. At once a movement eager for a rail connection began to develop.

In 1848 the two legislatures got together and sensibly agreed to build their lines to the Stephenson gauge. Australia had no manufacturing industry of its own, and there was a great deal to be said for being able to order locomotives and rolling stock straight off the shelf, as it were. Then the Sydney Railway Company appointed F. W. Shields, an Irishman who had worked with Vignoles. He argued that a narrow gauge might be suitable for a cramped little island, but Australia with its vast open spaces could afford to be more generous. They need look no further for a model than his native Ireland, and should set the rails 5ft 3in apart. South Australia had no objections, and everything seemed settled. The Sydney Company, however, discovered that they had rather less funds than they needed, and decided that one useful economy would be to cut Shields's salary. The Irishman would have none of that: he left and his place was taken by James Wallace. He now returned to the first arguments of the advantage of conforming to the main gauge then employed in Britain, including his native land, Scotland. The Sydney directors were as easily convinced by Wallace as they had once been by Shields and reverted to their original plan. Work was promptly begun. Unfortunately, South Australia, having agreed to follow Sydney, had also begun at what they still thought was the mutually agreed Irish gauge. They, not unreasonably, refused to make any more concessions, and that was that. As settlements in Australia spread, new provinces were formed, wanting their own railways. Queensland was keen to join in, but cash was short, the terrain was difficult and they opted for their own 3ft 6in gauge. The country that had started out in the railway business in agreement that the one essential was that there should be a uniform gauge had ended up with three.

The spread of railways was rapid throughout densely populated Europe, but the nineteenth century was also an age of expanding frontiers. In Britain, for example, the rail system was an addition to an already complex system of railways, rivers and canals, which made the job of getting men and materials to construction sites comparatively simple. When constructing the tunnel under Standedge Fell, between Manchester and Huddersfield, the railway men simply struck side passages out into the earlier tunnel on the Huddersfield Canal. Material could then be brought in and spoil taken out by boat. There were no such luxuries available to the men who were to build a railway across a whole continent to unite the New World.

CHAPTER 5

TRANSCONTINENTAL

BY THE TIME the railway age had begun, the new American republic was well set on the road to self-sufficiency. This movement was speeded up by the British Orders of Council of the Napoleonic Wars, which were intended to stop all trade with France and French ports overseas, but which acted against the interests of America's rapidly growing merchant fleet. Some saw where this was leading, and a Parliamentary commission in London reported that unless the interruptions to trade were ended, 'the United States will be able to manufacture for their own consumption'. Indeed they were, and soon showed inventive talents to match those of the old world, with entrepreneurs such as Samuel Colt and Eli Whitney setting out on the road to mass manufacture using 'interchangeable parts'. In the world of transport, the Americans were already showing that they were going to go their own way. They even preferred their own language: the British railway was to become the American railroad.

The system grew up, as it had in Britain, as an extension of the canal system with rails coping with the sections that were beyond the sensible limits of conventional locks. But in America, engineers went far beyond anything contemplated in the Old World. In 1825 in England, an Act was passed for the Cromford & High Peak Railway. It was to join the Cromford Canal at one end to the Peak Forest Canal at the other, forming a link between the two centres of the cotton industry in Derbyshire and Lancashire. The hills were conquered by inclined planes and horses would pull the rolling stock along the level sections in between. There were trans-shipment points at the two termini. At Marple, there was a warehouse into which boats from the Peak Forest could float at one end, while trucks could leave on rails at the other. It was not the most convenient way of moving goods across country. In the same year that the Cromford & High Peak Act was passed, a mass meeting in Philadelphia approved the idea of a canal to Pittsburgh. Again there was a range of hills in between, the Alleghenies, which rose to a height of 2291 feet. The engineers, James Geddes and Nathan Roberts, realized that the only answer was to build canals out from Pittsburgh and Philadelphia and to cross the 26½ miles of hill country by means of a railway and steam-worked inclines. But passengers on their system would not have to go to all the trouble of getting their luggage out of boats, into carriages and back into boats again. They were going to go the whole way by boat, but these would not be ordinary boats. The special packet boats were built so that they could be split into two sections and each section could be mounted on wheeled trucks for the journey through the Alleghenies.

OPPOSITE: *Tom Thumb* is a small, vertically boilered locomotive built in 1830 by a New Yorker, Peter Cooper, to convince the proprietors of the Baltimore & Ohio Railroad that they had no need to look overseas for engine builders. Americans could do the job themselves.

When a canal was built to join Philadelphia to Pittsburgh it had to cross the Alleghenies. The hills were conquered by building railways over the summit, and special sectioned packet boats were built for the job. This is the start of the journey for one half of a boat in Broad Street, Philadelphia (ABOVE). On the railed sections, the packet boats were split in half, hauled up and down inclines by cable and pulled on the level by horses (BELOW).

Charles Dickens used this remarkable system, but was not greatly impressed by the boat, which he described as 'a barge with a little house in it'. He was even less taken with the sleeping arrangements. He found

suspended on either side of the cabin three long tiers of hanging book-shelves, designed apparently for volumes of the small octavo size. Looking with great attention at these contrivances (wondering to find such literary preparations in such a place), I descried on each shelf a sort of microscopic sheet and blanket; then I began dimly to comprehend that the passengers were the library, and that they were to be arranged, edge-wise, on these shelves, till morning.

Other canals were more conventional, but a few interesting facts can be gleaned that were to have a bearing on the railway future. The Delaware & Hudson was built with a navvy workforce that was largely Irish. One of the engineers, interviewed for a local paper, described the working conditions as being particularly easy and the weather good. 'But that doesn't mean a thing to these club-swinging Irish. I don't know what they've got to fight about. They don't need a reason: they fight just for the hell of fighting.' The work went on and by 1828 over a hundred miles of canal had been completed, including a unique suspension aqueduct across the Delaware. The fifteen miles between the aqueduct and the Pennsylvania coalfield were to be covered by a railroad. At that point an important decision was taken. One of the company's engineers, Horatio Allen, was sent off to England to purchase four steam locomotives from, inevitably, Robert Stephenson.

When Allen returned, he had only ordered one Stephenson engine, the other three coming from the Foster, Rastrick works at Stourbridge. It was one of the Rastrick engines, named the *Stourbridge Lion*, that was taken over to the Delaware & Hudson for a trial. Allen, having brought the locomotive from England, took it upon himself to put the engine through its paces. He had, he said 'never run a locomotive nor any other engine before' but then neither had anyone else in America at that time. The route for the trial was a three-mile stretch of track, laid with strap-iron rails, which were essentially wooden rails, their top surfaces protected by an iron strip. They were cheap to make, but not very strong. Allen had imported examples of British iron rails, but it does not appear that they had yet been brought into use. To add to the problems of the route, the line crossed a creek on a trestle bridge, followed by a sharp bend. Allen described the experience:

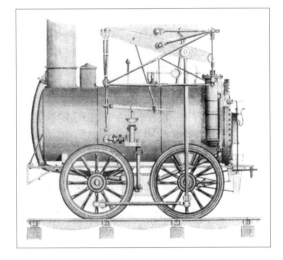

> I took my position on the platform of the locomotive alone, and with my hand on the throttle-valve said 'If there is any danger in this ride, it is not necessary that more than one should be subjected to it.' The locomotive having no train behind it answered at once to the movement of the valve; soon the straight line was run over, the curve (and trestle) was reached and passed before there was time to think ... and soon I was out of sight in the three miles' ride alone in the woods of Pennsylvania.

The *Stourbridge Lion* was built by the Stourbridge manufacturers Foster, Rastrick to work the railed section of the Delaware & Hudson Canal. At its trial in 1829 it proved too heavy for the light tracks, but had the honour of being the first steam locomotive to work in America.

That all sounds fine, but there were immediate problems. The engine weighed in at over seven tons and was built very much to the *Puffing Billy* pattern with external cylinders, overhead beams and a drive to coupled wheels in an 0-4-0 arrangement. With the heavy downward force, an unsprung frame and a fragile track the outcome was much as it would have been during the first experiments on British colliery tramways. The rails were knocked out of line, the trestle bridge swayed alarmingly and the pioneering engine was hauled off to a shed, never to run again. Eventually it was scrapped. The first experiment with a steam railway had ended in failure, but Horatio Allen was undeterred. He went off to take up a post as superintendent of the Charleston & Hamburg Railroad in South Carolina and, unimpressed by what he had seen of British imports, he designed a locomotive of his own, *Best Friend of Charleston*, which was built in New York and sent round the coast by steamer. Unlike the *Stourbridge Lion* it had a vertical boiler. In December 1830, with the intrepid Allen once more in control, it proved its worth and a month later went into passenger service. The triumph was short-lived, for soon afterwards the boiler exploded and the fireman was killed. America had suffered its first railway fatality. The fault seems, once again, to have resulted from a footplate crew tampering with the safety valve in the hope of improving performance. The engine was repaired and went back into service, but this time with a buffer car set between the locomotive and the passenger coaches.

Other pioneers were also at work. In 1830, work began on the little Camden & Amboy, a line which was to link New York to Philadelphia. The prime mover behind the scheme was Colonel John Stevens, one of the first enthusiasts for steam power in America. As early as 1812 he had published a pamphlet arguing 'the superior advantages of railways and steam carriages over canal navigations'. He first proposed the Camden & Amboy in 1815 and reinforced his argument by building a rather primitive locomotive which he demonstrated on his Hoboken estate. America had not up till then been ready for the steam railway, but now matters had changed. The president of the Railroad was Colonel Stevens' son Robert, who went across to Britain to check on new developments. He arrived at just the right time and was able to order a Planet class locomotive, *John Bull*, from Robert Stephenson. He also saw the latest development in rail technology, fish-belly rails, but was less convinced of the need for such an expensive technology in America. As a result he designed the T-rail, which was simple and economical to produce. Even so, things did not go well and there were problems keeping the engine stable on the rough track. A mechanic on the railroad, Isaac Dripps, thought the problem could be eased by putting a pair of guide or pilot wheels in front of the locomotive. These were tacked on rather than being an integral part of the design, but they proved very successful, and it could be said that they converted *John Bull* into a brand new type of locomotive, a 2-4-0. Leading wheels became a regular feature on American locomotives.

Among the other rail pioneers were two brothers, Evan and Phillip E. Thomas of Baltimore. In 1826 Thomas made a visit to England to see the newly opened Stockton & Darlington Railway and was sufficiently impressed to promote the Baltimore & Ohio Railroad. The B&O was incorporated in February 1827 and can reasonably claim to be America's very first, purpose-built public railway. Initially, however, the haulage was entirely down to horses, and the first attempt to import a locomotive from Britain literally foundered when the ship bringing it over sank. This was not altogether a disaster for the company, as it gave local engineers the opportunity to try out their ideas. Track on the early British railways was bad, but America's was if anything even worse, lightweight and uneven.

First Enclosed Car on B&O 1830

The first horse-drawn passenger coach of the Baltimore & Ohio had all the grace of a mobile garden shed.

The alternative to improving the running of the heavy Planets was building lighter locomotives. A New York inventor Peter Cooper built a one-ton experimental machine, which was later christened *Tom Thumb*. At first sight, with its vertical boiler set on a simple frame, it resembled the Rainhill *Novelty*, but in reality it was very different. The most important difference was the way in which the drive was transmitted through gears. In its first runs in 1830 it pushed a cart with passengers along a 13-mile stretch of track in an hour. That was enough to convince the company to develop their own locomotives. They decided to stage their equivalent of the Rainhill Trials, with the proviso that entries had to rely on American technology.

Cooper passed the development of his ideas to Phineas Davis, who came up with the winner, *York*, an obvious descendant of *Tom Thumb*. The design was rapidly improved and in its final version the engines still had a vertical boiler, but now there were two vertical cylinders each attached to overhead beams, fixed at one end. The motion of the beams and connecting rods gave the engines the name of Grasshoppers. The spur-and-pinion driveshafts were connected to gears, giving drive to all four wheels. The advantage of the design was that it combined a lightweight frame with short wheel base and good traction, and the little engines soon became familiar on the line. Tragically Davis was killed during the development of the Grasshoppers, and the work was passed to Ross Winans. As a result of his improvements, the Grasshoppers remained in service almost to the end of the nineteenth century. It was the first major success for an American locomotive design.

There were other promoters keen to develop railways. The Mohawk & Hudson was planned to run from Albany to Schenectady, but when the shares appeared on the market in 1826 they could not even be given away. But the other early successes had their effect and in 1834 the simple strap rails were being laid and thoughts turned to locomotives. The first was built at the Cooper Iron Works, New York. It was named *De Witt Clinton*, which is an interesting choice as Clinton's principal claim to fame was as a doughty fighter for canals, and his greatest achievement was the promotion of the mighty Erie Canal. The locomotive is an extraordinary, clumsy-looking affair, with a remarkably high dome. Equally remarkable are the coaches, which, like those of the Stockton & Darlington in the early years, are simply stagecoaches with flanged wheels. Passengers, it seems, were just as happy to ride on the outside as on the inside, and they did not necessarily spend all the time there in any case. The engine could manage a modest 15mph on the flat, but when it came to an uphill gradient it was liable to give up altogether and everyone had to get out and push. In time the rails were to stretch from Albany to Buffalo and an express service was introduced, promising a journey time for the 290-mile journey of about fourteen hours. This could never have been realistic, and one unhappy traveller found that the actual time was nearly three times as long. The nights were the worst, with the only illumination in the carriages supplied by a pair of candles. Those who travelled on the first American railroads needed every bit as much pioneer spirit as those who built them.

America learned rapidly, and although the vertical boiler engines did well enough, the real future lay with the locomotives that had been developed from *Rocket* and the later Planets. One man who appreciated this was Matthias Baldwin and his first locomotive, *Old Ironsides*, unashamedly borrowed ideas from the Stephenson works. He was wise to do so and he soon developed an important manufacturing business that was to prove one of the most successful in America – and indeed the world. In later years the company was to produce some immense and immensely successful locomotives. In the 1890s they began to turn out huge 2-8-2 engines, many of which were made for Japan, and the name Mikado was eventually applied to all engines with this wheel arrangement. The great days of Baldwin steam culminated in the 4-8-4 Northerns. They looked and were hugely powerful, but combined this with great efficiency. Contented owners who bought these majestic giants were delighted to discover that not only could they haul more than their rivals, but they also used less fuel in doing so – an irresistible combination. Matthias Baldwin would have been both amazed and delighted if he could have seen such power spreading across the continents from the works he had started in Philadelphia.

American railways in the early years developed as a profusion of small companies, many of which built their own locomotives, though a general pattern soon emerged. Although the essential elements had been developed in Britain, there were adaptations needed to fit the locomotives to American conditions. Track tended to be lighter than in Europe, and the civil engineers usually took the route that involved the minimum of engineering. Whereas in Europe engineers would make extensive use of cut and fill, construct long tunnels and build massive viaducts in brick or stone, in America lines tended to go round obstacles in often extravagant curves, go over hills in steep gradients and use timber trestles for viaducts. The locomotives needed good suspension, excellent track-holding ability and a high tractive effort.

The great workhorse of the early years was the 4-4-0, which was first developed in the 1830s and became known as the 'American Standard'. The two pairs of coupled drive wheels provided the power, and the four smaller pilot wheels mounted on a separate bogie brought stability and the ability to cope with tight curves. These locomotives look vastly different from their British cousins. From the first, they had covered cabins, a luxury unknown to British footplate crews who stood in the open regardless of the weather. It was believed by the owners that keeping the crew uncomfortable also kept them alert: needless to say, those owners rarely travelled that way themselves. The American extremes of climate at least made it essential that their crews had protection. Another difference was the bulbous chimney, a necessity for keeping sparks under control in locomotives that mainly relied on wood as a fuel. Instead of passing through neat fields, American railroads ran through open country, where even the cattle roamed free, so at the front of the engine was the 'cow catcher'. Other details are minor, but added to the general effect of American locomotives being a distinct class: the warning bell instead of the steam whistle, the immense headlamp. The British designers liked neat, tidy engines, with inside cylinders and connecting rods, and as many of the working parts tucked away out of sight as possible. The Americans reasoned that having cylinders, connecting rods and pipework on the outside of the engine might make it look slightly cluttered, but that that was a price worth paying to achieve easy accessibility for maintenance. The designers also worked on the 'if you've got it flaunt it' principle. Elaborate brass work gleamed on boiler and dome, painted decoration was colourful, and sign writers were kept busy adding company name, locomotive name and number to both locomotive and tender. The other vital difference is less obvious. The suspension was very much better than on earlier engines. An equalising beam was fixed on the drive wheels, providing an acceptable ride on the often rough tracks.

Railroad construction moved ahead rapidly in the eastern United States, but by the middle of the nineteenth century Americans were steadily moving west and the tracks followed. On 22 February 1854 a new railway was opened stretching from Chicago to Rock Island, Illinois. The Rock Island line made it into popular song, but its opening was an event of immense significance. The railroads of the east were joined to the Mississippi with

its immense fleets of rafts, barges and steamboats taking cargo all the way down to New Orleans and the Gulf of Mexico. The arrival of Chicago & Rock Island Locomotive No. 10 with six coaches of passengers was greeted with bands, banners and a salvo of cannons. According to the enthusiastic reporter of the scene there was 'a multitude that no man could number' there to welcome the newcomer, though if the entire population of Rock Island and Davenport on the opposite bank had turned out there could hardly have been more than 20,000. But what made the arrival so much more than just another small railroad opening was the fact that although the Mississippi had brought the tracks to a halt, they were pointing west. It was no accident that the line had reached the Mississippi at just this point, for the town was named after an actual rocky island in the middle of the river. The promoters were already thinking ahead: the island would be just the thing to supply a sound footing for a railway bridge. The company name was about to change: it would become not just Rock Island & Chicago, but the Rock Island, Chicago & Pacific Railroad.

The chief promoter of rails to the west was Henry Farnam, and he was the man who set in motion the project of bridging the Mississippi. All historians of railway history soon become aware that the same stories repeat themselves over and over again. The early opposition to railways in Britain came from the river and canal navigations, and the Mississippi rivermen were equally vociferous in declaring that railroads would destroy their trade and bring them to ruin. In this case, Farnam's Railroad Bridge Company triumphed and the work was duly

Central Pacific Locomotive No.1, the _Governor Stanford_, built in 1862. This type of 4-4-0 became known as the American Standard, with a pilot bogie to even out the ride on the rough track and two pairs of coupled driving wheels for power. The bulbous chimney helps to suppress sparks from the wood-burning fire.

completed. A reporter injected all the excitement of the occasion into his hectic prose. The date was 22 April 1856, when the first train moved on from Rock Island and set off for Iowa.

> There was a pause – a hush, as it were, preparatory to the fierceness of a tornado. The cars moved on – the bridge was reached – 'We're on the bridge – see the mighty Mississippi rolling on beneath' – and all eyes were fastened on the mighty parapets of the magnificent bridge, over which we glided in solemn silence. A few minutes and the suspended breath was let loose. 'We're over,' was the cry. 'We have crossed the Mississippi in a railroad car'.

The triumph was to last no more than a few days. On May 6, a packet boat out of New Orleans crashed into the bridge and fire spread to the bridge timbers, destroying one whole section. Suspicion fell on the rivermen, and the idea that this was a deliberate act of sabotage was only heightened when the next riverboat to appear carried a banner inscribed 'Mississippi Bridge Destroyed. Let All Rejoice'. The vessel that had done the damage, the *Effie Afton*, had never been seen that high up the river before, but that didn't prevent the owners from suing the bridge company, claiming that their structure had made navigation impossible. The case came to court, and the railwaymen had the services of a young, up-and-coming lawyer who had done his homework well and made out a sound defence. He proved to have a thorough knowledge of the river and its ways, and showed that the steamboat had been operating with just one paddle, which had swept it into the bridge at high speed. His name was Abraham Lincoln. The river interest failed to win their case, but proceedings moved up the legal ladder until in 1858 the Supreme Court supported the legal right of railroad companies to build bridges across navigable rivers. The way west was open.

Even before the legal position was clear, Farnam drove the tracks onwards. The citizens of Iowa City offered a premium of $50,000 if the line arrived before 1 January 1856. It looked as if the task was beyond him, but with bonfires lit along the line to provide warmth and light, the men worked on through day and night. On Christmas Eve he was still three miles short, the temperature had plummeted, men were complaining of frostbite, but the work went on. The job was done with only hours to spare, and much of the prize money went into one of the city's biggest ever parties, to which all the citizens were invited. It seemed that nothing could stop the westward march.

In 1859 a civil engineer, Theodore Judah, came to Sacramento to build a short line from the town to the local goldfield. It was here that an infinitely more daring plan came to him. He had come from the east where railroad building was resulting in an intricate spread of lines, and he realized the huge advantages to be had from linking up to that system. He convened a conference and set out his proposals for a line from California that would cross the Sierras and finally follow the line of the Platte valley to Missouri and Council Bluffs, near Omaha, Nebraska. Not many thought that a line could be built over the mountains, particularly as it was to climb to a height of around 7000 feet, but the delegates agreed that Judah would be authorised to travel to Washington to lobby for the line. He was not the only man to be thinking of a transcontinental line. A line had already been built right across the state of Missouri from Hannibal on the Mississippi to St Joseph on the

Missouri. On a memorable day in April 1860 the railroad showed what could be done in providing a service to the west. A messenger from the east arrived at Hannibal with mail, which was then transferred to a special train. It set off at full speed for St Joseph, a journey of almost 200 miles that was completed in five hours which, in those days, was genuine express travel. That just left 2000 miles to go to California, and this time the mail went by a very different express, the short-lived but famous Pony Express. The railroad directors predicted that soon the iron horse would take over from the ponies, and to prove their confidence they ordered a specially designed mail van, though not a mile of track had yet been laid. But all the schemes came to a halt in 1861 with the outbreak of the Civil War.

The railroads were to play an important part in the war. The well-developed system in the North meant that Union forces could be easily supplied as they advanced into the South. The Confederacy was comparatively poorly served with track, and the lines that had been built had not yet been joined to create a usable network. The southern lines were regularly attacked and in one daring raid a group of Union soldiers stole a Confederate locomotive and proceeded to drive it north, destroying track and the telegraph system as they went. They were pursued by Confederate forces on another engine, and were eventually caught and executed as spies. The stolen locomotive was to have a starring role in, and give its name to, one of the greatest movie comedies of all time, Buster Keaton's *The General*. The locomotive itself, belonging to the Western & Atlantic, was a typical American Standard engine. Confederate forces did their best to disrupt the railway system of the North, but the only line to be seriously affected was the Baltimore & Ohio. The South was to end the war with virtually all its rail infrastructure in ruins, while in the North, well away from the war zone, not only were lines left untouched, but plans for the future were still being actively considered.

Even before the war ended, Judah began surveying the route through the mountains. The discovery of gold in Nevada encouraged potential investors to believe that the railroad could be more than a dream, and in June 1861 the Central Pacific Railroad was duly incorporated. Judah was aware of the competition from the Hannibal & St Joseph, but they were soon joined by an energetic and unscrupulous newcomer, the Leavenworth, Pawnee & Western. With the connivance of the local Indian agent, they had already swindled the native Americans out of land officially made over to them, declaring it was 'surplus', whatever that may have meant. It was certainly not surplus to the people who lived there. The directors appeared in Boston boasting that they represented the first major route to head west, though neglecting to mention that they had not actually built any track heading in any direction. Judah decided that they would be good partners, and the alliance could well have worked but for the outbreak of war. The proposed route was far too close to the contested land between North and South for anyone to consider building there in the time of the border raiders. Nevertheless a new company was authorised in 1862 to build rails starting in the east: the Union Pacific.

So it was that two companies were authorised to build the transcontinental railroad, the Central Pacific to start at Sacramento and make its way across the Sierras, the Union Pacific at Omaha, heading down the Platte valley. There was an incentive to move at speed as the Act

A construction crew crossing a trestle bridge on the Union Pacific. The picture shows very clearly that rough timbers have been used in the haste to push the line forward, yet fragile as they seem such structures survived well. The locomotive has a straight chimney, indicating that it is coal burning, so that there is not the same danger from sparks as with wood burners.

authorising construction specified that as well as receiving United States Bonds whenever forty miles of track was completed, the companies would also get land grants to either side of the line. Someone must have remembered that the land was populated, so a rider was added stating that the government would 'extinguish as rapidly as may be the Indian titles to all lands falling under the operation of this act'. The two other contenders who had dropped out of the race were given a sop: they too would have land grants provided they built lines to meet the new Pacific Railroad at the 100th meridian, an empty stretch of land in the Platte valley. The railroad companies managed to negotiate even bigger concessions out of the government. Thomas Durant of the Union Pacific brought $437,000 to Washington to back his lobbying and lavish entertainment of congressmen; a little, but not very discreet, bribery and some persuasion resulted in the land grant being doubled. The rewards for the railway companies could be immense, and their owners wanted to make sure that the profits were as big as possible. Those who built the most miles got the most money: every mile built by one company was a mile lost by the other. It was a contest with a great deal at stake.

The story of the transcontinental railway is a curious mixture of the noble and ignoble. The work done by the men on the spot, from engineers to navvies, was incredible: the chicanery of the moneymen was on an almost equally unbelievable scale. An example of the latter appeared right at the beginning of work in the east. Peter Dey, the chief engineer, had made his estimates and surveyed what he thought was the best line. Durant had upped the estimates to increase company profits and brought in a new chief engineer called Seymour, who promptly recommended a much more circuitous line out of Omaha. It increased the length of track from Dey's 23 miles to 32. There were no obvious engineering advantages, but the new route brought in an extra hundred thousand acres, and not just any land but the land that would be needed as Omaha expanded with the prosperity brought by the railroad. Dey resigned, but although Seymour was compliant enough to do his masters' bidding, he was not a good engineer. His economies proved worthless. He used cheap wood for the sleepers, ties as they are known in America, and used them longitudinally instead of transversely. In the latter he at least had a good antecedent, for Brunel had used the same system on the Great Western Railway – but not with poor-quality softwood. Seymour then tried an expensive preservative on the wood, which was totally ineffective. In the end the 'cheap' ties cost more than the more expensive, durable wood he should have ordered in the first place. He was a bizarre character, who insisted on wearing a silk hat when visiting the track and sheltering under an umbrella. At least he proved a source of amusement to the dispossessed Pawnees who turned up to watch and laugh.

The work should have been easy, involving as it did laying track over level open ground, but the workforce never managed more than a mile a week. Durant woke up to the fact that in trying for short-term gains he was now in serious danger of losing the long-term profits. The Leavenworth, Pawnee & Western was now the Union Pacific, Eastern Division and their men were advancing at a rate of a mile a day. If they reached the 100th meridian first, then they would have the right to keep on laying track west. Seymour's days were done, and a new chief engineer, former Union General Grenville Dodge, took over. New contractors were also employed: John S. Casement was brought in with his brother Daniel. They were not very imposing figures – John, the taller of the two, was only five foot four – but they revolutionised the work programme. Dodge's organizational skills together with the Casement brothers' boundless energy was to make an immense difference.

The biggest change was the way in which work was put in hand. Everything followed in a logical pattern. In the vanguard were the surveying parties, marking out the line of the track. Then followed the graders, laying down the track bed and building bridges, cuttings and embankments. As the track advanced, special trains kept the supplies coming in a steady stream. These trains had box cars where men could sleep and eat, but most importantly they brought the raw material of ties, rails and spikes. The line, unlike those in Europe, dispensed with chairs for holding the rail, making the work that much faster. The gangs manhandled rails out of the cars and loaded them onto horse-drawn carts which then carried the supplies to the railhead. According to a contemporary account everything then advanced with total precision. Two gangs worked in unison, one to each side of the track. They lifted the rails, set them in place and moved on, taking just half a minute for each rail. The next gang followed behind, spiking the rails in position, with three hammer blows for each spike, ten spikes to the rail and 400 rails to a mile. And the objective was to complete a mile a day.

The workforce was a mixture of soldiers back from the war, and the Irish navvies once again played a major part. The Casements promised them extra pay to increase the rate of track laying, first to two then three miles a day, and more and more men were brought in.

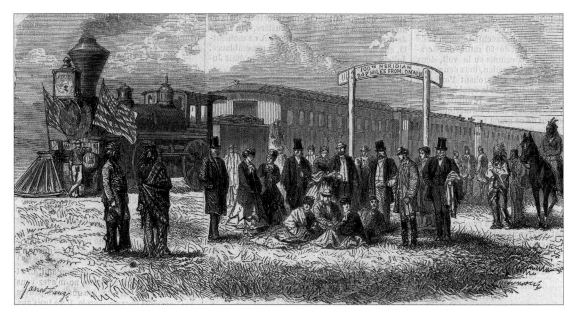

When the Union Pacific reached the 100th meridian, special excursions were laid on for tourists, though by the time they got there the tracks had already moved on westward.

On October 5 1866 the tracks reached the all-important 100th meridian and the Union Pacific could carry on west. A special excursion train was laid on with brand-new coaches but by the time they reached the meridian, 247 miles from Omaha, all they found was a board in the wilderness: the gangs had already moved on. Local Indians had entertained the visitors with mock battles, but there were real battles to be fought as the iron rails snaked out across the age-old hunting grounds of the plains. With other things on their minds, the railroad builders had little interest in Indian rights. The Central Pacific was also building its lines out from Sacramento. No one knew where the two companies would finally meet, but whoever built the longest line got the most land.

Even the Casements could not defeat the winter blizzards, so in November, with the track having covered over forty miles from the meridian, a camp was made at the point where the North and South Platte Rivers meet. It consisted of no more than a rough and ready station and the tents of the workers, but it was dignified with the name of North Platte, though dignity was just about the last thing anyone found there. As the temporary railhead it became the jumping-off point for anyone heading west, and a town grew up to meet the needs of the travellers. It was in just such places as this that the legend of the Wild West was born. Travellers needed food and supplies, but there was an equally brisk trade carried out in the brothels and gambling halls that were thrown up alongside the stores. Visitors reported a town that was truly lawless, and among the visitors was a reporter who was to become famous for his meeting with David Livingstone in Africa, Henry Morton Stanley. His account was colourful.

Every house is a saloon, and every saloon is a gambling den. Revolvers are in great requisition. Beardless youths imitate to the life the peculiar swagger of the devil-may-care bull-whacker and blackleg.

A little work was done, but mostly the men were kept busy losing the money they had made sweating through the summer months.

As the Union Pacific raced across the Plains, the Central Pacific battled its way across the mountains. The physical problems were bad enough, but matters were made worse by the lack of a suitable workforce. Those with the get-up-and-go spirit that had brought them west were not likely to sign up as labourers on the railroad. The ones who were prepared to sign up tended to be drifters who having drifted into the work were just as likely to drift out again. Charles Crocker, the general superintendent of works, had a brainwave. Why not employ Chinese workers? James Harvey Strobridge, who was directly in charge of the workforce, was horrified by the notion. He was a professional railwayman and an Irishman: navvies were giant beef-chewing men, not tiny rice-eaters. They could not be up to major construction work. Crocker pointed out that a nation that could build the Great Wall of China might just possibly be up to railroad construction. In any case they would accept low wages and little would be lost by trying fifty of them on the line as an experiment. Strobridge agreed and was completely won over. They were the best workers he had ever encountered. They argued a lot and noisily but seldom actually fought and did not go on strike – and they were cheap. Soon every Chinese worker in California had been taken on by the railroad and ships were sent to China to bring back more. The company were delighted, but many of the other men on site refused to work with the Chinese and left. Eventually there were to be nearly 10,000 Chinese working for the Central Pacific, representing 95 percent of the entire workforce.

The Central Pacific relied almost entirely on Chinese labourers and this photograph shows their camp at Brown's Station.

It must have been exasperating for the Central Pacific to hear the news of the speedy advance of their rivals dashing across the plains as they made slow and painful progress up the mountains. By November 1866 the lines had advanced almost a hundred miles, but more importantly they had climbed nearly 6000 feet. Although this was the second half of the nineteenth century, the work was still done by hand, using the same technology that had been used in the gentler landscapes of Britain at the start of the railway age. Only the scale was different. The Central Pacific did have one advantage over their rivals. They had no need to stop for winter. The greatest works of all were the tunnels, twelve of them in all, that would take the lines across the mountains. The railhead had been established at Cisco, now best known as a ski resort – a fact that gives some idea of the conditions there. Altogether 8000 men were brought up the tracks and set to work in three eight-hour shifts through the day and night. Although they were working underground, protected from the weather, conditions were still extreme and the work of drilling by hand into the solid rock for blasting was arduous. Heavy snowfalls made it difficult to get men and equipment to the sites in the Donner Pass, which was to be the railroad summit.

The company was determined to keep the railroad heading east so, while they were waiting for the winter snow to melt on the Sierras, equipment, even including locomotives, was hauled on sledges down the eastern slopes. Those left behind faced an exceptionally bad winter, with blizzards and avalanches that continually covered the track that had been laid. If the line was to be usable, something had to be done and the job of protecting the track went to a Scots engineer, Arthur Brown, who constructed forty miles of timber snowsheds. These were simple structures, rather like open barns, with pitched roofs supported on rough frames. But though crude they were effective, which is just as well since the final bill came in at over two million dollars. Now, at last, the Central Pacific could lay track at speed, heading out from Reno across the Nevada desert. Once the pass was open, the men returned to the Sierras to finish the work on the tunnels and to complete the line from Sacramento to Reno and beyond. When the first train made the journey, a reporter described the line as being 'one of the most beautiful, smooth and solid roads on the continent'.

The Central Pacific were well aware that the Eastern Division of the Union Pacific, later known as the Kansas Pacific, had been building track across the Plains and had met fierce resistance from the Indians. Cheyenne, Sioux and Arapaho all sent raiding parties in an attempt to stop the tracks crossing their traditional hunting grounds and driving away the game on which their lives depended. There were genuine incidents very like those that were to feature in a thousand Westerns, with young engineers riding for their lives pursued by bands of Indians. One worker, William Thompson, was wounded in a skirmish and to preserve his life he pretended to be dead. The ruse worked – but he had to lie motionless and endure scalping. The reprisals of the US military were ferocious, and the official word was sent out that all Indians were to be assumed hostile. One of the most hated and ruthless of the military leaders was George Armstrong Custer, who was himself to fall at the famous Battle of the Little Big Horn.

The war with the Indians was long and costly, and the Central Pacific had no intention of repeating the pattern. They made deals with the Indians, offered the chiefs passes to ride on the trains and even employed Indian workers on the track. The women, they noted, proved tougher than the men at hard physical labour. The work went on at great speed. The Central Pacific had seen enough of heavy engineering works in their climb across the mountains. Now everything would be kept on the flat as far as possible, even if that meant immense curves following the natural contours rather than a more direct route. In other circumstances, this would have seemed wasteful, but not when the government were paying out $30,000 a mile in subsidy, far more than the actual construction costs. In time, money would have to be paid out again to have the line straightened, but none of that mattered in the race towards Utah, which it was soon obvious that the Union Pacific would be the first to reach. It was equally clear that it was here that the rivals were eventually to meet. Common sense suggested that the time had arrived to agree on a junction for the completion of the transcontinental railway. But common sense was in shorter supply than greed. The two companies continued grading, laying down their routes, as if the other did not exist. The farcical position was reached where they had teams at work on parallel lines, and a deep enmity soon developed between the Chinese working from the west and the Irish from the east. At one point, the Irish were carrying out blasting without giving a warning to the rival gangs working close by, but on a higher level. After a few of these explosions, the Chinese retaliated and the debris cascaded down onto the Irish workers, burying several of them. The two sides called a truce on the spot, showing more sense than their superiors who continued the race. Perhaps the ultimate absurdity came in the Promontory Range, where the Central Pacific had crossed a deep valley using a substantial embankment. The Union Pacific then arrived on the scene and built a precarious, flimsy trestle bridge no more than fifty yards away.

The government finally realized that the nonsense had to be brought to a halt. A final meeting point was agreed at Promontory Point. There was, however, still one matter to be decided between the two sides. Crocker of the Central Pacific had bet Durant of the Union Pacific that his men could lay ten miles of track in one day. On 28 April 1869 eight men were chosen to do the work of carrying and spiking the rails: Dailey, Elliott, Joyce, Kennedy, Killeen, McNamara, Shay and Sullivan – names which suggest that the Union Pacific did not have a monopoly of Irish navvies. Working twelve hours with just a brief stop for lunch, these eight men reached the ten-mile mark and passed it. Then on 10 May the link was completed at a lonely spot in Utah, Promontory. The last rail was spiked in place with a gold spike, and the two locomotives, *Jupiter* from the west and Union Pacific No. 119, faced each other head to head. In a symbolic gesture first one backed off to allow the other to cross onto the rival company's tracks, then the position was reversed. The continent had been crossed by rails.

The building of the transcontinental railway was remarkable and the engineering works were a triumph, but there was a heavy price. For the men who built the lines, the greatest danger was not from Indian attacks nor accidents at work. It came from the so-called Hell on Wheels towns that sprang up along the line as temporary homes for the gangs. They swarmed with gamblers, prostitutes and outlaws and were as lurid as they ever appeared in fiction. Some became permanent towns and cities, but the lawlessness did not always end when the rails moved on. At Laramie, for example, four hundred building lots

An artist's impression of the ceremony at Promontory, Utah when the Central Pacific and Union Pacific were finally joined in 1869. The painter included all the worthies who had contributed to the enterprise, whether they were there or not, even including some who had died before the event.

were sold within a week and a makeshift town mushroomed and established a reputation for violence that was unmatched in the west. Gun battles were a routine reality, and one saloon fight ended up with five dead and fifteen injured. The railway navvies were as likely to be caught up in the violence as any. Nevertheless the work was completed, east and west were joined, and Promontory earned its place in railway history, now remembered in the Golden Spike Park, where *Jupiter* and No. 119 steam again.

This was not the only transcontinental line in North America. Canada in the middle of the nineteenth century consisted of a number of independent provinces. In 1867 the United States purchased Alaska, and two possibilities seemed on the cards. Either western Canada would join the United States, or Canada would be united as a single entity. The western states were prepared to agree to joining a new Dominion of Canada, but only on one condition: they wanted to be joined to the rest of the country by rail. British Columbia seemed the most likely to look south, so a start was made on building inland up the Fraser River in 1880 under the direction of Andrew Onderdonf. He followed many American examples, and in particular he adopted the philosophy of 'Build quick, build cheap.' Once again, Chinese formed over half of the 15,000 strong workforce who laboured for seven years in covering less than 400 miles. If money could be saved, it was saved, regardless of any other consideration. Dynamite with a safety fuse was by now available for blasting, but instead the cheaper, but far less stable, nitroglycerine was employed. No one can be quite certain, but the most modest estimate suggests that at least 800 men died as a result of the drive to save money. It seemed that too many lessons had been learned in America, and the one that proved most persuasive was that the unscrupulous could make a fortune.

In its route through the mountains, the Central Pacific passed through a large number of tunnels and covered snow sheds, so that the crew were frequently enveloped in smoke. The ingenious answer was to move the cab to the front of the locomotive. This immense 4-8-8-2 locomotive was built by Baldwin in 1944, and now has a permanent home in the California State Railroad Museum, Sacramento.

The Canadians had, however, also learned one sensible lesson from their southern neighbours: there would only be one company, the Canadian Pacific. The problems faced by engineers were certainly no less than those of the American route, and there were some similarities. Part of the line would be easy going across the prairies, but the difficult sections offered monstrous challenges. The rocky shore of Lake Superior, where cliffs fall sheer to the water's edge, was the first big obstacle on the way west and beyond the wheatfields of the prairies lay the Rockies. When work finally got under way in the east, railroad construction no longer depended entirely on muscle power. The steam shovel took over a lot of the work that had once been left to the navvies; pneumatic drills were far more efficient than the old hand drills. It was difficult going, but there was worse to face in the mountains. There were places where the terrain was so difficult that construction costs rose to a staggering $500,000 a mile. Given such figures, it is not perhaps too surprising that where money was saved it was, even if the solution was less than satisfactory in terms of engineering. From Kicking Horse Pass, at a height of 5329ft, the lines swooped down the

Union Pacific No. 4019 storms across Devil's Gate with a freight train – a picture that seems to sum up both the endurance of the men who conquered a continent and the power of the big American steam locomotive.

The builders of the Canadian Pacific faced much the same construction problems as did the Union and Central Pacific further south. Here locomotive 5810 emerges from a snow shed at the foot of Mt. Stephen, hauling a freight train.

Yoho Valley on the startling gradient of 237ft in a mile. Going up required the services of four locomotives, two in front and two behind, but coming down was simply terrifying, with everything depending on the braking power of the locomotives. The company had to install a system of trap sidings to capture runaway trains. Inevitably the system could not last, and was rapidly replaced by tunnels which gained height by spiralling through the mountains at the more manageable grade of 1 in 45. Other improvements followed, including the replacement of many of the older trestle bridges with steel.

The CPR was very successful, later branching out into steamers on the Great Lakes and then into ocean-going liners. Branch lines were built and the railway network provided the wheatfields of the Prairie Provinces with a route to the eastern ports and valuable export markets. But it is a very long way from Winnipeg in Manitoba to the east coast, and there was a much shorter route giving access to the outside world, and one with a long history of trade: north to Hudson Bay. In 1886 the Hudson Bay Railway was born. It was to run from Winnipeg to Churchill, where ships could load up with wheat for Britain and, as the promoters pointed out, Liverpool was as near to Churchill as Churchill was to Montreal. The fact that the sea route was only open for three summer months every year was conveniently forgotten. The *Manitoba Daily Free Press* trumpeted the event as the dawn of a new age and declared that 'the grand obstacle of distance will be swept away at a single stroke'. The writer had probably never been to the far north and seen the terrain, which could hardly have been less suitable for railway construction. It was to need more than a single stroke to conquer the Canadian north. The line was not completed until 1929. By then, money did not run to paying for a gold spike for the final rail, nor even a silver one, so the men on the spot improvised and wrapped tinfoil round a common metal spike. At least it shone in the sun.

The work was arduous. Anyone who has spent any time in the countryside north of Winnipeg will know just how appalling the climate can be, and it is hard to say which is worse, the heat and flies of summer or the freezing cold of winter. Looking down on this wilderness from the air, a luxury denied to the surveyors, reveals a country of dense woodland, spattered with lakes varying from the immense tracts of Lake Winnipeg, around 250 miles long, to stagnant ponds and swamps. No one would choose to build a railway in such a location. Further north, new problems appear. There is a foundation of permanently frozen ground, the permafrost, and above that a moss-covered peat bog. Just how hostile this land could be was discovered when a construction train, running at night, was derailed and turned over on its side beside the track. The crew were unhurt, and set off to get the rescue train. By the time they returned, the locomotive had gone. The heat from the boiler had melted the permafrost and it had simply sunk away. It would be pleasant to record that all this labour was not in vain, but the Hudson Bay line was never a success and its future and that of the port of Churchill looks bleak.

North America developed a railroad system that has very much its own character, both in terms of civil and mechanical engineering. Huge problems were overcome and immense distances covered. Developments in other parts of the world were no less dramatic.

Attempts to construct railways across the tundra of Alaska were not a success. These three Forneys began their working life on the New York elevated railway and ended here in the northern wilderness.

CHAPTER 6

COAL WAGONS TO WAGON-LITS

RAILWAYS EXISTED LONG BEFORE the steam engine appeared on the scene, so rolling stock had a long development period, dating back at least as far as the mid-sixteenth century. A splendid book published in 1556, Agricola's *De Re Metallica*, shows mines of the period in beautifully detailed technical illustrations. The author

depicts pumps, water wheels, horse gins and all kinds of mechanical devices, in amongst which is a simple rail system. This consists of two planks set close together to act as the rails. On these, very basic four-wheeled wagons run, with the wheels set underneath the body of the truck, and the vehicle kept in place by a pin running in a groove. The earliest records of these systems are from Germany and Transylvania, but by the end of the sixteenth century, the railed track had reached Britain, and it developed steadily through two centuries of use. Eighteenth-century illustrations show horses pulling single wagons, some with solid and some with spoked wheels, but the system for keeping them on the rails had been greatly improved. In the most sophisticated versions the wheels have flanges, but an alternative appeared when wooden rails gave way to iron. The alternative was to have plain wheels on the wagons, running inside the verticals of L-shaped rails. The most common type of wagon was the design from north-eastern England with curved sides, which was designed to take one chaldron, an official measure equal to 2 ton 13cwt – confusingly, the wagon itself is also known as a chaldron. The other notable feature is the brake, operated by a long lever, an essential for a wagon that when loaded was sent on a downhill passage from mine to waterway. The horses were employed pulling the empties uphill and walked behind for the downhill journey. In 1828, Thomas Brandreth of the Stockton & Darlington Railway took pity on the horses, and provided them with a 'Dandy-Cart', which was fastened behind the train for downhill sections, allowing the horse to ride in style. It was not entirely a humanitarian thought: because the horse

ABOVE: **Agricola's *De Re Metallica* (1556) has some of the earliest representations of wagons running on rails.**

Early tramways were built with a slope from the colliery to a river, such as the Tyne. Loaded wagons travelled by gravity, controlled by the brakeman. The horse was used to haul back the empties.

had a rest it was able to do more work in a week, which was actually measured at an impressive 40 percent increase in efficiency. The other type of wagon in use was the flat truck, to which any bulky item could be strapped.

As the wagonways developed into tramways serving canals, so wagon construction became more sophisticated. Among the earliest to be moved by steam power were the wagons of the Penydarren tramway (p. 16). An example can be seen in the Deutsches Technikmuseum in Berlin. It has cast-iron wheels turning loose on the axles, fitted to an underframe of wood and iron. Sadly, the actual wagon top is missing, but it is a useful reminder of how comparatively crude wagons were, even at the beginning of the steam age. In essence it combines the features of both chaldron and flat truck, and was developed into what would be an early railway standard, the four-wheeled truck with straight sides, which came into use in the 1840s. The GWR with its broad gauge could take heavier loads so a six-wheeled truck was introduced, which could carry about nine tons compared to the six tons of the four-wheelers. Gooch described them as 'probably the most economical we have for carrying loads'. They remained, however, the oddities among the huge numbers of simple four-wheeled trucks.

In the early days, many railway companies owned no freight wagons of their own, but simply charged companies for hauling their own, privately owned stock. This was all very well as far as saving construction costs went, but it made running the railway very tricky. Trucks came in all shapes and sizes and in all sorts of conditions of repair. A train could be made up of a raggle-taggle of trucks, all loose coupled, clanking away down the track in a sometimes alarming manner. Within the first decades, closed wagons had been developed and specialist vehicles such as cattle trucks appeared. These were still, like the old colliery chaldrons, fitted with individual hand brakes. Stopping a train of these trucks on the move depended on the locomotive brakes at one end and the brake van at the other. It was not a system designed for high speeds, but it was to last for a very long time.

If wagons running on tracks were developed over centuries, there was no real precedent for railway carriages. The first example, on the Stockton & Darlington Railway, was simply a stagecoach with its conventional wheels removed and replaced by flanged wheels. It was still pulled by a horse, and that system was to last for some time. A German horse train was running as late as 1830 with a pair of horses, harnessed side by side, hauling a cumbersome coach down the tracks. The future of passenger travel on the railways lay elsewhere, but the coach pulled by horses was to develop in its own direction, as the urban tramway. A rare survivor, the horse tramway at Douglas on the Isle of Man, was first proposed by a Sheffield engineer, Thomas Lightfoot in 1870, and opened in 1876. It still runs today, having resisted all suggestions for modernisation.

The steam railway needed to develop a whole new system, and do so with some speed to meet a rapidly growing demand. An early decision was to divide passengers into three different classes, to be provided with a rapidly descending level of comfort. A famous set of

This iron wagon underframe is of great historical significance, since it started off on the Penydarren tramway, scene of Trevithick's famous locomotive trials. It is now on show in Berlin's museum of technology and transport.

plates appeared shortly after the opening of the Liverpool & Manchester Railway. The first class coaches look exactly like three stagecoach bodies rammed together, stuck on top of a four-wheeled flat truck. Baggage is piled up on top, secured it seems by nothing more substantial than low rails round the edge of the carriage. The stagecoach effect is completed by a pair of nonchalant-looking gentlemen perched on rooftop seats, and presumably in charge of braking. Not all the first-class passengers liked the notion of being crammed into the coaches with their three cramped compartments, and there was an alternative: they could rent a flat car and have their personal carriage secured on top. There they could stay for the entire journey, with the benefit of springs, which on road carriages of the time were better than anything available on the railway. They had the added advantage that they could adapt their environment to the climate, riding with the top down and enjoying the breeze on a good day or retreating behind the hooded canopy in the wet. This was a luxury not enjoyed by second- or third-class passengers.

The second-class passengers were squashed together into what was really no more than a truck with a canopy on top, but with open unglazed sides. The seats were wooden benches. The third class was no more than a truck, with little or no embellishments of any kind. Some railways provided wooden benches, but others simply made everyone stand up in the open wagon. The Liverpool & Manchester was one line that provided seats, and even those who followed their example did not always stay with it. The directors of the Glasgow, Paisley, Kilmarnock & Ayr Railway originally put seats in the third class, but when

they discovered how many more passengers could be crowded in if they all stood, they decreed that henceforth no seats would be provided – and seats would be removed from the existing stock. The Great Western showed their contempt for the poorer passengers by deciding that they should not even have the luxury of the fast journey times enjoyed by those in first and second class. They were to be allocated to slow goods trains instead, human cattle to join the other cattle being shuffled along the track. This is not an example of author's hyperbole. When the Sheffield, Ashton & Manchester Railway ordered their first cattle trucks, they told the makers to fit sprung buffers, so that if there was a shortage of cows they could also be used for passengers.

No one was much concerned about the obvious risks of crowding people into open trucks until 1842. On Christmas Eve the 4.30 a.m. goods train from Paddington to Bristol also had two third-class vehicles attached. Heavy overnight rain had led to a landfall in the deep cutting at Sonning, and the locomotive ploughed straight into it. The loose-coupled goods wagons pushed the passenger compartment into the engine tender, with the result that eight passengers died and seventeen were seriously injured. The accident had a particularly strong impact on Parliament, as most of the men on the train had been working on building the new House of Commons and were heading home for the holiday. There was an immediate uproar, and the Board of Trade began an enquiry into the conditions facing third-class passengers. One result appeared in the Act of 1844, promoted by Gladstone. This decreed that all new companies should provide one train a day in each direction, running at

Travel on the Liverpool & Manchester Railway in the 1830s: the first-class carriages (above) show the strong influence of stagecoach design, including luggage piled on the roof and the guard perched at the rear. Second and third class (below) are little better than cattle trucks. The most comfortable ride is being enjoyed by the family in their own coach, where they can enjoy the benefit of its springs.

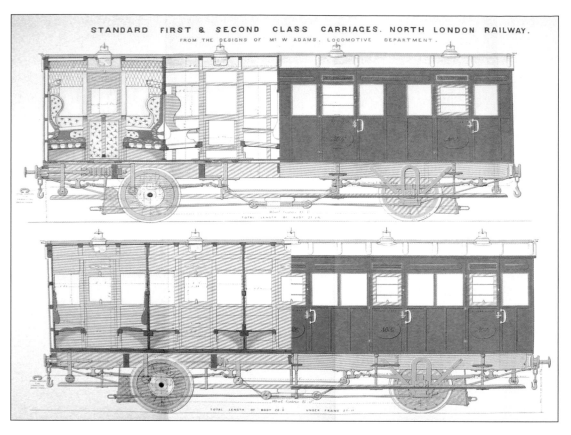

A cut-away diagram of a North London Railway coach, suggesting that commuters in the first half of the 20th century might have enjoyed rather more comfort than their successors today.

a minimum speed of 12mph, in which the third-class passengers could enjoy carriages with seats and an overhead cover for a rate of not more than one penny per mile. The companies at once prophesied their immediate ruin, and proceeded to try and find ways round the rules. One method was to start the Parliamentary trains, as they came to be called, at unreasonable times, while others tried to get back to the good old days when the lower orders knew their place by bringing back the open trucks for a new fourth class of passenger. That people put up with such appalling conditions at all is at least a mark of the huge improvement offered by rail travel. Before this, even a seat on the top of a stage would have been well beyond the means of most of the community. If they wanted to go long distances, they walked. Even twelve miles an hour represented a huge improvement in journey times.

The changes to third-class coaches had a beneficial effect on the second class as well. No one was prepared to pay a higher fare unless they got something extra for their money. So they got padding on the seats and other small luxuries. The essentials of these early coaches were much the same, all built on the same basic chassis and carried on four-spoked wheels. On some lines first and second class appeared in the same vehicles. An Eastern Counties coach of the 1840s had three compartments. The central, widest portion was the first class, with upholstered seats and headrests and pairs of windows to either side of the door. The second class areas at the ends were narrower, with padded seats but no headrests, and windows only in the upper parts of the doors. In the earliest coaches there was no lighting of any kind, but passengers could rent lanterns at the stations to be hung on hooks in the carriages.

Not only passengers began to see improvements as the years passed by. In the early years, the guard or brakesman was usually given a perch on top of the brake van, totally unprotected from the weather, but by the 1850s he had been brought under cover and given an eyrie at one end of a carriage, popularly known as a bird cage. Internal steps took him to his high seat and windows looking out over the top of the coach roof. In later versions, windows bulging out from the side of the van provided a forward view down the train. Technical improvements also made rides somewhat smoother. The old spoked wheels gradually gave way to solid wheels, and the six-wheeler gradually ousted the little four-wheelers.

A variation on the standard first-class carriage was the bed-carriage, first introduced onto the London & Birmingham Railway in 1837. It was a standard coach, but by supplying poles fastened together with webbing, rather like stretchers, and covered with firm cushions, beds could be made up. As the carriages were none too wide, passengers' feet stuck out into a hollowed area known as 'the boot'. A version of this carriage was adapted for use by Queen Adelaide, the widow of William IV. Made like all early carriages of wood, the bodywork was not left to railway engineers but entrusted to Hooper's, one of the leading coach-makers of the day. It was given a suitably glamorous finish with gold-plated handles and hand-painted crests on the doors. Grand as it was, it was quite eclipsed by the London & North Western Railway saloon built for Queen Victoria in 1869. Originally this consisted of two six-wheeled carriages joined by a flexible gangway, the first time this useful device appeared on a British train. It was later modified by mounting the two coaches on a twelve-wheel bogie, as the Queen expressed a dislike for the flexible connection. This was not a railway coach as other passengers understood the term, but a gorgeously ornate apartment on wheels, with richly upholstered chairs and sofas, silk hangings and a very practical addition – a toilet. One curious feature was a semaphore on the roof, which could be used to communicate to the driver that he was travelling too fast for Her Majesty's comfort; he was never, it seems, going too slow.

Perhaps the most remarkable aspect of railway travel in the early years is the complete absence of what would now seem essential features. Gangways between coaches, toilets and reasonable comfort for all passengers were rarities. The Midland Railway broke the mould in 1874 when they introduced heating for everyone by means of a stove and hot-water pipes,

Gas lighting for carriages was a boon in many ways, but could also be extremely dangerous. In the accident at Quintshill on the Caledonian Railway in 1915, a troop train was in a collision as a result of which the gas reservoirs caught fire and 227 lost their lives in the inferno.

gas lighting in place of dim oil lamps and toilets. The biggest change was the abolition of the second class, and the upgrading of the old third class. For the first time, the cheapest seats were to be padded; and where the Midland led, others were forced to follow. One reason that the changes were slow to arrive was that journeys were generally comparatively short. In other countries, circumstances demanded a different approach to carriage construction, and nowhere was this more true than in North America.

American railroads with their extravagant bends and rough track were not suitable for the rigid six-bodied coaches being developed in Britain. As early as the 1840s, carriages were being built with eight wheels, arranged on two pairs of bogies, so that front and rear wheels could swivel independently. The first sleeping car was introduced on the Cumberland Valley Railway as early as 1836. Travel in the nineteenth century in America was something of a lottery, standards varying greatly from line to line. In 1879, Robert Louis Stevenson joined emigrants from Scotland making their way to California. He took the Union Pacific from Council Bluffs and was unimpressed. The coaches had hard wooden seats on either side of a central gangway, and there was a stove at one end and a toilet at the other. The conditions were cramped, sleeping arrangements were primitive, and any chance of comfort depended on how crowded the train happened to be. The conductors looked after the arrangements.

> They prevail on every two to chum together. To each of the chums they sell a board and three square cushions stuffed with straw, and covered with thin cotton. The benches can be made to face each other in pairs for the backs are reversible. On the approach of night the boards are laid from bench to bench, making a couch wide enough for two, and long enough for a man of the middle height; and the chums lie down side by side upon the cushions with the head to the conductor's van and the feet to the engine. When the train is full, of course this plan is impossible, for there must not be more than one to every bench, neither can it be carried out unless the chums agree.

For this spartan set-up, Stevenson paid the conductor two dollars. He then discovered, to his chagrin, that once the gullible had paid up the conductor sold off the rest at an ever-decreasing rate.

When the time came to change onto the Central Pacific, Stevenson found a huge improvement. The cars were higher and airier, the seats freshly varnished, and arranged so that they could be drawn out to make up bed boards. Extra accommodation was supplied by upper berths that were pulled out at night. He also noted that, spartan though his sleeping arrangement were, others made do with worse – but they were not paying. They were the hobos, riding through the night beneath the cars. Stevenson was not, on the whole, hugely impressed by American railroad travel across the entire continent. Nor was he alone. In the 1850s a young man took his bride on honeymoon by train and was equally depressed by the experience. His name was George Mortimer Pullman. He tried to interest various companies in his ideas for an improved service, but when no one would listen he went into business for himself. He bought an ordinary day coach from the Chicago & Alton Railroad, and converted it so that it was a parlour car by day and a sleeping car by night. In all, he built twelve of these cars but they were not a great success, and his venture was brought to a temporary halt by the outbreak of the Civil War in 1861.

When the war was over, Pullman was in funds, having made money trading with the gold mines of Colorado, and he set out to build an entirely new coach of revolutionary design, called *Pioneer*. It was of wooden construction on an iron frame, carried on two four-wheeled bogies, with springs and rubber shock-absorbers. It was fitted out with comfortable chairs that could be converted into beds, and had upper berths that folded away during the day. The standards of fittings tended to the luxurious, with thick-pile carpets, embroidered seat covers, panelled walls and brass light fittings. It looked grand and was grand, too grand for many railway companies who baulked at the weight of the coach as much as anything. Pullman's *Pioneer* seemed in danger of becoming Pullman's white elephant. Then, in 1865, Abraham Lincoln was assassinated, and it was agreed that the President's body should be sent from Washington, back to his birthplace in Illinois. Pullman offered *Pioneer* for the journey and the offer was accepted. Companies who had previously complained that the coach was too large for the system rushed to remove obstacles that might impede the funeral car. Thousands lined the route to see the car pass and pay their respects. For Pullman it was a public relations triumph, and his name was to find an honoured place in railway history.

This was not the end of Pullman's inventiveness. He also designed a 'hotel car', which doubled up as dining car and sleeper. Once again, the beds were neatly stowed away in the day, and there were tables between the chairs and a kitchen at one end of the car. Among those who came to see the Pullman cars was Georges Nagelmackers, who came from a powerful Belgian banking family. Back in 1835, the Nagelmackers had been prominent among the financiers who had provided backing for the introduction of the country's rail service, and it was railways not banking that fascinated Georges. He was also fascinated by a young lady who failed to succumb to his wooings, so he took himself and his bruised heart off to America in 1869. Investigating the exciting new world of American railroads was to be his solace. He was very impressed, particularly by the Pullman cars, and quizzed the inventor at some length. But Nagelmackers realized that what was suitable for democratic America would be frowned upon in aristocratic Europe. The rich in Europe travelled with their own entourage, and were deeply conscious about who could and could not share their space. The open carriages would have to go, and be replaced by separate compartments that could be reserved.

There were technical problems involved with the introduction of the new, heavier coaches that had serious safety implications. The existing trains had brake vans at the rear, where the guard or brakeman operated a hand brake. The only other means of stopping was the steam brake that had recently been added to the locomotives. Increased train size made this system dangerously obsolete, particularly with the heavy coaches Nagelmackers was proposing to build. Luckily for him, the answer appeared during his visit, when George Westinghouse invented the compressed-air brake. At its simplest, a steam-powered pump on the locomotive compresses air in a reservoir. The steam is taken to each of the carriages in turn through flexible connectors. Secondary air reservoirs are attached, so that when the brake is applied by the engine driver, the pressure in the main reservoir is reduced and the excess pressure in the secondary reservoirs forces a piston down to activate the brakes. As a result every element on the train is braked at the same time. With this system, there was no obstacle to the introduction of heavy coaches. Nagelmackers now began to dream of a train that would run across national frontiers, and which would unite Europe as the transcontinental lines had united America.

Just as Pullman had used the publicity surrounding Lincoln's funeral to promote his cars, Nagelmackers turned to King Leopold II to forward his ideas. All Leopold had to do was lend his name to the enterprise, heading the list of subscribers without actually having to pay a penny. The first coaches were technologically simple, six-wheelers on the common European pattern. All the differences were on the inside. The American cars had rather shocked Nagelmackers. People climbed into their upper bunks, with nothing between them and the other passengers but drawn curtains. His coaches had separate compartments with bench seats that could be made into beds, with a second layer of let-down bunks above. These compartments were joined to the toilet facilities by a separate corridor down one side of the carriage, instead of along the middle as in the American version. He first planned to run his cars across France, Austria, Switzerland and on into Italy, but his timing was less than perfect. Completion of work on the first set of cars coincided with the outbreak of the Franco-Prussian war in 1870. Undeterred Nagelmackers planned even bolder ventures, and gave his company a new name, La Compagnie Internationale des Wagons-Lits. The company still survives into the present day.

Nagelmackers entered into a brief partnership with an American, William Mann, an entrepreneur who dallied on the fringes of legality. Mann had designed a boudoir car, which sounded rather French and frivolous, and indeed one of his cars was used by Leopold II to entertain his mistress, Cléo de Merode, earning it the popular name of the 'Cléopold'. The partnership was short lived, and Nagelmackers began the long process of persuading companies to add his high-fare cars to their regular trains throughout Europe. In 1882 he added a dining car, complete with kitchen, pantry, wine cellar and coal-burning stove and two dining saloons, so that the men could retire to the second car for their evening cigars. His great ambition was to traverse Europe, and establish a route all the way to Constantinople, modern Istanbul, the gateway to Asia. It was to become perhaps the most famous train of all time, the Orient Express.

The very first journey of the Orient Express set off from Paris on 4 October 1883. Nagelmackers was always something of a showman. The invited passengers arrived at the station to find an old six-wheeler carriage standing at the platform, when they had been led to expect something quite different. It was Nagelmackers' joke. Soon one of France's finest locomotives, a 2-4-0 Class 500, with its two pairs of 1.5-metre driving wheels, chuffed into the station with the actual train. The train consisted of two fourgons or baggage cars, one for mail and the other to hold passengers' luggage and the all-important reserve stocks of fine wines. Then came the two sleeping-car saloons and the dining car. The saloons were built with two four-wheeled bogies and the interior was as luxurious as a first-class hotel. The chairs were upholstered in embossed leather, panelling was in teak and mahogany inlaid with elaborate marquetry and gilt, and the whole baroque interior of the dining car was lit by gas chandeliers. As the train left the Gare d'Est, the guests were ushered in for what was to be the first of many gourmet meals, which passed the test of even the exacting French critics. At 50mph the tables were as steady as if the diners had been enjoying a meal in a boulevard restaurant. As the train rushed through the night to Strasbourg, the stationmaster was on hand to show off the latest technological miracle. His station was lit by electricity, the first of its kind in Europe. Sadly for him, the replete guests were all snoring between silk sheets.

La Compagnie Internationale des Wagons-Lits embellished their coaches with beautiful paintwork and their ornate insignia.

Nagelmackers had not been entirely honest. The train did not exactly reach Constantinople. The passengers had to cross the Danube on a ferry and join an altogether less luxurious train that took them on to the Black Sea port of Varna. From there a somewhat aged steamer carried them on the last lap to Constantinople, where they enjoyed a break before returning to Paris right on time, eleven days after they had set off. It was a huge success. Over the years, the rails were to be advanced all the way to Constantinople and beyond. The Orient Express could take passengers to marvel at the great archaeological sites of Egypt, and important new European routes were also added. A major event was the opening of the Simplon tunnel, which allowed trains to run to Venice and Trieste: the Simplon Express was born. By 1912, a boat train connection made it possible to extend the working of the famous train via the South Eastern & Chatham Railway to London.

The glory days of the Orient Express came in the 1920s and '30s, when it was probably the most exotic train in the world. New all-metal coaches were introduced, painted a rich deep blue, and such famous interior designers as René Lalique were brought in to decorate the carriages. Even more impressive was the service supplied by the *conducteurs* who were not only supremely adept at their work but also famously discreet, an important factor given the reputedly large numbers of illicit liaisons for which the Orient Express became famous. The Orient Express lives on, running special excursion trains rather than a scheduled service, but still using some of the famous luxury carriages.

Nagelmackers had begun by borrowing ideas from Pullman, and ended as his rival. Pullman, however, was not greatly harmed by the competition. The company was kept busy in America and was soon exporting to other countries, notably Britain. The first Pullman car on the Midland Railway went into service in 1874. The cars were prefabricated in America and assembled in England, where they remained the epitome of luxury. Trains made up with Pullman cars were named, and when I worked as a porter on Harrogate station as a student the arrival of the Yorkshire Pullman was a major event. It was a novelty to have a car with a continuous central aisle, with tables between the seats, each with a little elegant brass lamp. They seemed very grand, but by then far more luxurious trains were operating in other parts of the world. There were areas where long-distance travel made comfort an essential rather than a luxury. As early as 1856, the Grand Trunk Railway in Canada had introduced a sleeping car service between Toronto and Montreal. The Montreal paper was filled with enthusiasm.

> Perhaps in no respect had science achieved such results conferring more comfort on the traveler than are to be found on the night cars of the Grand Trunk Railway. Literally, we are embodying the dreams of youth, when we read of the dreams of Sinbad and of the Flying Horse. Who 20 years ago could have thought it possible that a party of Gentlemen would enter a comfortable saloon and after an hour's chat and a well-served supper each would take a rest upon a lounge and find himself next morning before breakfast 300 and 400 miles from whence he started, with untired energy and fit for exertion?

The reporter makes it sound as if he had joined a gentleman's club that just happened to be on the move. As more long-distance routes were added around the world, so the need for the same degree of ease and comfort spread. The first trans-Australian train did not run until 1917, when the final link was made between Port Augusta, north of Adelaide and Kalgoorlie to the east of Perth. Comfort was essential, not least because there was nothing to distract the traveller as the train made its way for over 300 miles across the flat monotony of the

The south-bound Golden Arrow leaving Sevenoaks tunnel, hauled by one of Bulleid's slab-sided locomotives, affectionately known as 'Spam Cans'. The journey would be continued across the Channel by its French equivalent, the Flèche d'Or.

Nullarbor Plain. The early carriages combined the openness of an American car with the stained glass and plush upholstery of Europe. Some later carriages even boasted a piano to amuse the passengers on the journey. The twentieth century also saw the arrival of the buffet car, altogether more informal than the restaurant car and considerably cheaper. It was no longer necessary to sit down to a full formal dinner provided by a first-rate chef as one did on the Orient Express. There nothing was too much trouble. When the hugely wealthy Maharajah of Cooch Behar used the train in 1907, catastrophe struck the kitchen. The Maharajah declared a preference for spiced lamb, but there was no lamb on board. In such an emergency there was only one option. Contrary to the rulebook, an unauthorised stop was made at the next station and an employee scurried off to the nearest butcher to buy the meat. The day was saved. Less demanding customers in the New World simply wanted a coffee, a doughnut, a soft drink or maybe something a little stronger; and they wanted it when they felt in the mood for it. Not surprisingly, the buffet bar was an American innovation.

European developments often seem quite modest compared with those in other countries, particularly North America. Dining cars, for example, were not introduced into Britain until the 1880s and were only available to first-class passengers. The Great Eastern was the first to offer third-class passengers the service on the York-Harwich boat train in 1891. They realized, however, that there was a problem with the British dining car. If you wanted food, you had to sit there throughout the journey, whereas in the Pullman coaches the small tables could be separately set at mealtimes. The answer was to put coaches with side corridors to either end of the dining car, and link them together. The notion of the corridor coach was comparatively novel and removed some interesting dilemmas. The Midland had long coaches divided up between different specialist compartments, but not linked together. The ladies had the advantage of a ladies-only compartment, and the gentlemen could opt for a smoking compartment. The ladies had access to the toilet but were barred from smoking; the gentlemen could enjoy their cigars, but might have to sit cross-legged for a long time. It was only in 1892 that the through corridor train was introduced onto the Great Western Railway: which was also, amazingly, the date when heating the train by steam also became common.

The dining car of the Blue Train, South Africa's most famous luxury train.

The British developed a system of carriage design that was to remain standard throughout the steam age. Trains had through side corridors, with individual compartments fitted out with facing bench seats, and toilets at the ends of the carriages. Carriages were linked together by flexible gangways, so that it was possible to walk from one end of the train to the other. There were exceptions, apart from the Pullmans. The London & North-Eastern Railway introduced streamlined trains in the 1930s, with such famous names as *Silver Jubilee* and *Coronation Scot*. The locomotives, which included world record-breaker *Mallard*, looked as if they belonged to a new era, and it seemed absurd to continue a carriage type intro-

Coaches such as this Southern Railways third class represented the norm for most travellers in the years before steam gave way to diesel.

duced in the Victorian era. Out went brass, plush and wood veneers, and in came aluminium and steel. The style was very much Art Deco, and in place of the bench seats there were now a series of alcoves to either side of a central gangway, each with a table for two and individual chairs. It was a style and arrangement that never became widely accepted in Britain, which remained very conservative. Other countries were more open to new ideas.

The LNER trains were comparatively short lived, but the great American classics survived in name for decades, so that one can trace the evolution of style over the years. Perhaps the most famous of them all was the Twentieth Century Limited, which first ran between New York and Chicago in 1902. The man behind the scheme had an unlikely career. George H. Daniels began his working life selling patent medicines before ending up in charge of passenger services for the New York Central in 1889. He set out to sell the railroad with all the enthusiasm with which he had once pedalled dubious remedies. One of his first actions had been to introduce the famous 'redcap' service of free baggage-handling, but his dream was of something far grander, a luxury service on the line's most important route. He got his chance to try the idea with the opening of the splendid Columbian exhibition in Chicago in 1897. He laid on a special train for New Yorkers, the 'Exposition Flyer', which covered the 980-mile journey in just twenty hours. It was a huge success, and Daniels was immediately authorised to introduce a regular luxury service.

The first version was known as the 'Lake Shore Limited'. There were seven cars and they all came with the full nineteenth-century opulence of heavy wood-carving and ornate finishes. What set the train apart from its competitors was not the standard of accommodation provided in the three sleeping cars, but the range of services supplied in the four special cars. Commercially the most important was the club car, where businessmen could enjoy a drink and a cigar and, very importantly, get a regular update on market prices on Wall Street, supplied by telegraph to each station along the way. Another very modern innovation was the provision of a stenographer who could help turn the train into a mobile office. To ensure that they arrived spruce and neat ready for the meeting at the other end of the journey, the executives could make use of the on-board barber's shop. Ladies had their own parlour car, with a buffet and library. Everyone had the choice of buffet or formal dining car and an observation car with individual armchairs and an open balcony completed the set. Those who were prepared to pay for extra privacy and still more luxurious accommodation could book state rooms.

The service was expected to match the quality of the coaches. Men were required to have white linen shirts: the cheap option of celluloid cuffs and collars was strictly prohibited. They were not to put their hands in their pockets as, apart from giving 'a decidedly loafing appearance', it resulted in 'spreading the tail of the coats and getting them out of shape'. The list of items maids were expected to carry has a real period feel: 'bottle of smelling salts, liquid camphor, black and white thread, package of needles and box of assorted pins for

Birmingham Snow Hill station in its heyday. The central, freight line is occupied by a typical mixed assortment of wagons of all kinds. Note that Pullman travellers were given special signs telling them where to wait for their particular carriage.

The ornate private stateroom of a Canadian Pacific first-class sleeper of 1898 (RIGHT) makes a striking contrast with the Art Deco freshness of the Union Pacific Hollywood Lounge (BELOW).

ladies' use'. The rules about fraternisation with the passengers were very strict. The train offered speed and luxury, but Daniels was not yet satisfied. The journey time on the regular service was twenty-four hours, and he saw huge publicity value in having a run of twenty hours to meet the demands of the dawn of the twentieth century. So the Lake Shore Limited gave way to the Twentieth Century Limited, and in time running time was reduced to sixteen hours. Other Limiteds were run, offering all kinds of special cars, including the Pennsylvania Limited which boasted a bridal car with a suitably wedding cake decor, all twiddles, twirls, gilt and lacquer. But the Twentieth Century Limited was offering standards that others could only strive to meet, and were unlikely ever to surpass.

The first Twentieth Century only had room for forty-two passengers, so that it was indeed Limited, and even then sceptics doubted whether the gruelling schedule could be maintained. It was, in fact, only achieved by a standing instruction that the train was to be given precedence over all other traffic. It was not just speed, however, that attracted passengers, but the high standards throughout the train. Passengers in the diner could enjoy a meal that began with oysters and went on through soup, fish, meat, salad, dessert and cheese to coffee, with nibbles between courses in case anyone was feeling hungry. And the whole meal came at the incredibly low price of just one dollar, though no doubt the canny Daniels had built the extra cost into the ticket price in order to present this bargain feast.

This, however, is not the image that comes to mind when the phrase 'Twentieth Century Limited' appears, for its true glory days came in the 1930s. This was the age of the streamlined train, and the arrival of a new character in the railway drama, the industrial designer. These men were not necessarily, or even mainly, employed on the railways. One of the best known of the American designers was Raymond Loewy, who over the years turned his hand to everything from car bodies for Studebaker to the Lucky Strike cigarette packet. But the steam locomotive was his first and greatest love. In his own book *Locomotive*, he wrote:

Raymond Loewy, looking very dapper, poses beside one of the magnificent streamlined locomotives built to his own design.

Unable to control an irresistible craving to sketch and dream locomotives at the oddest moments, it was a constant source of trouble during my college days, and the despair of my professors. Later, as a young man, it led to my complete oblivion as a dancing partner, for I spent long, enchanting hours at the locomotive depot instead of taking scheduled dance lessons. I have no regrets. In recent years it has been my privilege to design all sorts of things, such as streamlined ships, transcontinental motor buses, automobiles and electric engines. Never did I dream that my career as an artist-engineer would lead me some day to that glorious adventure, the designing of a steam engine. And still the day has arrived.

Loewy's engine took to the tracks on the Pennsylvania Railroad in March 1936. This was to appear at the head of an all-modern, streamlined train, in direct competition with the Twentieth Century Limited – the 'Broadway Limited', which went into operation in 1938.

This Union Pacific Railroad observation car, photographed in the 1930s, has something of the air of a fashionable café of the day that just happens to be running on wheels.

The equivalent role for the New York Central went to Henry Dreyfuss. In that same year, the new Twentieth Century Limited appeared, also headed by a magnificent semi-streamlined locomotive, which was in fact the familiar powerful Hudson 4-6-4, to which Dreyfuss had added a bullet-like nosepiece. It looked the part, and set the style for the coaches, which offered passengers the very latest in modern design. Out went the old-style sleeping cars, with upper and lower berths, and in came individual rooms. In its heyday, the Twentieth Century Limited epitomised sophistication, from the Club Car, with settees and easy chairs in pigskin, subtle colours and textured walls using materials such as cork, to the dining car converted at night into a club, where the latest hits from the swing bands were set on the turntables for the passengers.

One other spectacular form of car had its origins in an idea tried rather tentatively in the 1890s, when Canadian Pacific introduced glazed cupolas in the roof of some coaches to enable passengers to enjoy the spectacular scenery of the Rockies. When the coaches ended their useful life, they were not replaced and the idea only re-emerged in 1944. It

An irresistible invitation to enjoy a scenic ride through Banff National Park in the Canadian Rockies

was an executive of General Motors, riding a freight train on the magnificent Rio Grande line, who realized that passengers would pay extra to enjoy the view he was getting from the driver's cab. He drew out a rough sketch of a standard carriage, with not a modest cupola on top, but an immense glazed dome standing above the regular compartments. His idea was put into practice with the help of Pullman, and the first domed car was built, promoted as the 'Train of Tomorrow' and sent around the country on exhibition. The idea was also taken up by the Burlington Railroad, who introduced the Vista-Dome, which went into service in July 1945. Perhaps the grandest of all the domed cars were those of the Santa Fe Super Chief, which ran between Los Angeles and Chicago. Here one could step up to the observation saloon, and watch the world go by from the comfort of a swivel chair, or go below to the cocktail bar: it was aptly named by the company 'The Pleasure Dome'. Even Coleridge would have been impressed. Trains such as this set the standard, but it is as well to remember that throughout the world, many passenger trains at this time offered standards of comfort little improved from the previous century.

Not everyone travelled for pleasure on the railways. They also played a vital role in the transport of men and munitions in wartime. The outbreak of the First World War in 1914 brought regular passenger services between Britain and the Continent to a halt, but the value of a boat train connection to France was recognized by the military authorities, who saw the advantages of being able to run equipment and ordnance without the need to load and unload the trains at the ports. A brand-new ferry port was created on the Kent coast at Richborough – brand new that is in terms of railways. This was the natural harbour where Claudius's army had landed in AD 43. For a while Richborough had one of the busiest railway scenes of anywhere in Britain, with boat trains regularly crossing between there and Dunkirk. In 1918, Richborough lost its train-ferry terminal, but other ports developed to deal with the boom in civilian traffic of the post-war years.

The improvements in passenger traffic created problems for freight, and vice versa. The slow trundling goods trains were apt to get in the way of passenger trains dashing onwards to a destination, with drivers determined to keep to their schedule, however ambitious it might be. There was one solution, which was to provide main lines with four sets of tracks, two reserved for passenger traffic, the other two for freight, but that in itself created problems in track allocation. The long-term answer was to increase the speed of freight trains, and there the problem became acute. The rail system had grown up with the idea of privately owned wagons loose linked together to form a train. This provided an inescapable limitation on speeds. When the locomotive braked, the trucks cannoned into each other all the way down the train from first to last, and at high speed there were dangers of damage and even derailment. This had been solved on passenger trains by continuous braking, but the small owners of private wagons could not afford the expense. The problem was particularly acute in Britain, where continuous braking was introduced onto the GWR only in 1903, and even then not onto every train. Other companies were slow to follow. As late as 1955, Britain had to introduce a modernisation plan that set out the whole unsatisfactory situation. In 1959 no more than a third of the million wagons on the British network were equipped for through braking. The plan pointed out that Great Britain was then the only major industrial nation

still to persist in the old ways, and spelled out the implications. Not only were passenger trains held up, but the goods trains themselves often had to be held back in sidings, so that both sides suffered. Things were made far worse by the continuation of the old pick-up system, whereby a train could be stopped and shunted into a siding at some remote station simply to pick up a single privately owned wagon.

Modernisation did come, and specialised wagons were introduced to carry the important bulk cargoes such as oil. But in many cases change came too late to halt the move from a slow, antiquated rail system to road vehicles offering door-to-door delivery. It remains to be seen whether or not, in this age of increasingly congested roads, the rail system can recover the business lost in recent years. It is not an easy option. In America, huge freight trains trundle across the country, covering immense distances. Anyone who has ever driven long distances in America has waited at a level crossing while the flashing lights go on, a barrier drops and a seemingly endless freight train goes past. It is a good solution, as far as clearing the roads are concerned, but these trains also hold back passenger services, so that travelling by train in America has become something of a lottery. The result has been inevitable, with passenger trains finding it increasingly difficult to compete with the private car on one hand and the busy network of internal flights on the other. The rail system is by no means dead, and all around the world, improvements are being pushed forward. After two hundred years of development, it would be a brave soul who prophesied what the next two decades might bring, let alone the next two centuries.

The advances in all aspects of railway technology in the nineteenth and early twentieth centuries were immense, but the differences made to the social life of communities were even greater. The railways made long-distance travel possible not just for the rich, but for all classes of society. It would never have happened, however, unless the public could be convinced that travel by rail was as safe as it was cheap and convenient.

There was a time, not very long ago, when little Hunslets such as this could be seen scuttling all over the intricate network of lines linking the collieries of north-east England. Now the collieries have gone and their trains with them.

Steam still lives on, for a while at least, in China.
Here a pair of mighty QJ 2-10-0s are leaving
Harbin with a long-distance freight.

CHAPTER 7

MASTERING THE IMPOSSIBLE

O N THE EARLIEST RAILWAYS, line construction may have involved a good deal of engineering work, with cuttings and banks, tunnels and viaducts, but at the end a reasonable line was built with manageable gradients. Even in the mountains of North America, though the high passes contained gradients that taxed the power of the locomotives of the day, no special measures were required. The time was bound to come, however, when conventional methods were simply not able to cope with a fierce terrain. That time first came in India. Reading accounts of the early years in India, it seems a miracle that anything got built at all. The great power in the land was still the East India Company, who allowed two companies to make experimental lines, on the understanding that if they failed to show a profit then the builders would be reimbursed. The East Indian Railway was to build a 100-mile stretch of what it was hoped would eventually be a 900-mile route linking Calcutta to Delhi. The Great Indian Peninsula Railway had just 30 miles to construct, northward from Bombay to Kalyan.

The East India Company proved nervous promoters, and did what the nervous always do – they tried to put as many checks in place as possible to ensure nothing would go wrong. They proposed having two engineers, one appointed by the railway company and another by the government. The first would draw up plans and proposals and submit them to the second. If there was any disagreement, the matter would be passed on to the government, and if there was still no successful outcome, the final decision would be taken by government officials in London. Quite apart from the delays built into such a system, the sheer folly of having an engineering decision regarding, say, the position of a bridge over a river, being settled by someone who knew nothing about railways and had never visited India is beyond belief. Fortunately, the scheme was scrapped. When the work was getting under way, a new Governor General was appointed in India, who impressed the locals by having not one but two titles: the first Marquess and tenth Earl of Dalhousie. He actually knew something about railways and was an enthusiastic supporter of their construction. But he soon found himself faced with the pettiness of bureaucracy. The cost of construction had been badly underestimated: the cost per mile was set at a figure far below that for any other railway being built anywhere else in the world. The rules laid down at the start called for the East Indian engineer Simms to construct double track. He reported that at the price, the double track would only reach half way but he could build single track to the important coal mines of Raneegunge. Officials were adamant that the agreement called for a double track, and a

OPPOSITE: **The Durango & Silverton Railroad is one of the few surviving narrow-gauge sections of the once mighty Denver & Rio Grande system. It has survived largely because of the irresistibly appealing combination of steam engines and magnificent scenery. Here the train is making its tortuous way down Animas Canyon.**

double track was what they would have, even if it did come to a halt in the middle of nowhere. An angry Dalhousie stepped in to ridicule the double track notion.

If, as I have assumed, the object in view is to prove the profitableness as well as the practicability of a railway in India, I regard this proposal as totally useless. The Government might as well contract a railway from the Gaol to the General Hospital.

The single track was built.

Over in the west, the great day arrived in 1853 when a steam locomotive hauled a train from the Bori Bunde station in Bombay to Thana just twenty miles away. The local press hailed it as a triumph, and the opening was a big occasion, with large crowds, a 21-gun salute and patriotic airs played by the military band. For the British hierarchy, railways were rather unpleasantly noisy and dirty affairs. It was the habit of the officers of the Raj to leave for hill stations when the summer heat became uncomfortable, and the arrival of the country's first railway was not going to make them change their plans. The Governor of Bombay, the Commander-in-Chief and the Bishop of Bombay duly set off, just hours before the ceremony.

It was a modest beginning, but the main objective of the line was to link the increasingly important seaport of Bombay to the interior. That was where the troubles began. Between the two lay the Western Ghats, a line of cliffs separating the central plateau from the coastal plain, with no gaps. If the two were to be joined, then somehow a way had to be found to get the trains from sea level to the top of the Ghats, a height of about 2500 feet. There were no precedents for anything like this.

The inaugural train of 1853, running on the line from Bombay to Thana, the first railway to be completed in India.

Robert Stephenson was called upon for a consultation, but the real work was done under the leadership of the chief engineer, James Berkley, and the supervising engineer, Robert Graham. There were and are roads up the Ghats, and very frightening they are too. They wind in a series of hairpin bends, and the ubiquitous Indian trucks wheeze and grunt during the painfully slow climb. Roadside wrecks show that many fail to make it. But the Indian trains could not go round corners as trucks can. The engineers introduced an ingenious system for two routes, one up Thul Ghat and the other up Bhore Ghat. This involved the construction of long steep inclines, at gradients between 1 in 37 and 1 in 48, and solved the problem of getting round corners by adding in reversing stations. The train would make its slow progress up one long incline until it levelled out at the reversing station. It would then stop and carry on in the opposite direction up the next slope. The inclines were taxing – the longest was over 15 miles – but at least the Ghats were conquered, and there was a respite when the plateau was finally reached.

The amount of work involved in construction was immense, with the Bhore Ghat requiring twenty-five tunnels and twenty-two bridges. The work force was a mix of British navvies and locals, and the British who came over with the contractors behaved just as they did anywhere else in the world. When two native policemen tried to calm everyone down as things seemed to be getting too rowdy, a navvy picked them both up, one under each arm, and threw them out over the fence. It all sounds very amusing, but there was not much to cause amusement in the workings. Disease was rampant. A British contractor, Solomon Tredwell, arrived at Bombay in 1855 and within two weeks he had died from some unspecified fever. With no other source of income, his widow, Alice, took over the contract and saw it through. The real sufferers were the local labourers. No one ever produced an accurate estimate, but it was said that tens of thousands died of cholera. If official reports sound callous, that is because they were.

In order to move inland, India's railway engineers had to conquer the Western Ghats, a range of hills rising up from the coastal plain. This was achieved by building the line as a zigzag route, with frequent reverses.

ABOVE: **Railway construction in Australia involved building across vast areas of open, inhospitable land. This is 'The Gahn' approaching Alice Springs at the heart of the continent.**

The fine season of eight months is favourable for Indian railway operations, but on the other hand, fatal epidemics, such as cholera and fever, often break out and the labourers are, generally, of such a feeble constitution, and so badly provided with shelter and clothing, that they speedily succumb to those diseases, and the benefits of the fine weather are, thereby, temporarily lost.

The notion that lives – and the inconvenient loss of working time – could be saved by providing proper shelter and decent conditions does not seem to have been considered.

Berkley gradually came to realize that he could not get the best out of the workers by imposing European methods. At first he had regarded Indian working methods as 'barbarous and clumsy', but he eventually decided that they were 'the cheapest and quickest means that could be employed'. Bridge construction involved the erection of a 'forest of jungle wood', apparently flimsy and held together by faith. But these men were using the technology that had created the great monuments of India, and it was a system that worked. Indeed, one can still see forests of bamboo scaffolding surrounding building sites today. The conquest of the Ghats was a triumph, but one that came at a terrible cost.

India was not the only country to face this kind of problem. In Australia, the rails were slowly extending westward from Sydney, heading for the interior of New South Wales. The engineer, John Whitton, arrived from England in 1857 to take over the work, and was to stay on to supervise some 2000 miles of track construction. But first he had to conquer the Blue Mountains, which spread out as a daunting barrier. The population was too small to provide the necessary workforce, so Whitton went to the one man who could solve that problem, Thomas Brassey. The contractor recruited a work force in Scotland and fitted them out at a cost of £5 per man, and the government paid £12 to cover the cost of the passage. Brassey's man in Australia was Samuel Wilcox, who soon had 2000 Scots in his labour force. He needed them all.

OPPOSITE: **Over the years India has acquired a number of different gauges, the narrowest being used for purely industrial lines, such as this 2ft-gauge line at the Ledo Brickworks in Assam, seen here with a hard-working 0-4-0 Bagnell saddle tank.**

The Australian Blue Mountains represented an immense obstacle to early railway builders, who had to cross a 3336ft-high ridge. The answer was the Great Lithgow zigzag, photographed here in the 1870s.

The ridge that confronted Whitton and Wilcox was 3336ft high, and an early proposal had been for a line that went straight up at a gradient of 1 in 20, though there was no locomotive then available that could have tackled such a climb. Whitton settled for zigzags to a point halfway up the mountains, where a two-mile-long tunnel was cut through the rock. There was a huge amount of rock to blast away to create the route, and it all caused a great deal of excitement. One great chunk, estimated at over 40,000 tons, was dispatched in a single explosion. This was such a spectacular event that the honour of setting it off went to the Countess of Belmore, the wife of the governor-general. The climb up the eastern face was accomplished with just two reverses, but kept the gradient to a reasonable 1 in 60. The Lithgow zigzag was even more spectacular, the lines doubling back on each other over a series of viaducts.

There was one line on which the need to build zigzags seems to have been almost the least of the problems. The Kenya and Uganda Railway was built from the coast at Mombasa, across Kenya to Lake Victoria. It was backed by the British Government, ostensibly with the laudable aim of reaching into the heartland of the slave trade to put an end to the traffic. The real reason was the familiar colonial story: they wanted a railhead by the lake to prevent further German expansion into East Africa. Decisions were taken in London, where no one had a clear, or indeed any, idea of what the engineering problems might be. Major J. R. L. Macdonald was appointed chief engineer and took a gloomy view. The scenery he declared was 'wonderfully beautiful' but 'far from cheerful from the standpoint of a railway survey'. It turned out to be even more gloomy than he expected. A hundred and twenty donkeys had been supplied as pack animals for the expedition into what was then largely unknown territory. By the time Macdonald saw them half were dead and the rest were 'evidently desirous of following the bad example'. The survivors proved useless anyway, and the work of carrying equipment relied on human porters. The survey party found the jungle almost impenetrable. It rained on average twice a day, they found few points where they could see ahead for more than fifty yards and they kept falling into pools of water, hidden in the long, wet grass. As Macdonald dryly noted, 'survey work in the interior could not be classed as altogether amusing!'

Things got steadily worse. First they were attacked by vicious ants, which clung to their flesh and had to be removed by pulling off the bodies and digging out the heads with a knife point. They were followed by swarms of violent bees and, even more frighteningly, Macdonald was pursued by an angry rhino. The latter might be said to have had justice on its side, since Macdonald had been potting away at the local wildlife throughout the expedition. They had the occasional brush with the Masai, who had attacked a previous expedition, but this time matters were settled more amicably. In the end, a route was chosen and Macdonald returned to active service, which probably seemed quite peaceful by comparison.

The engineers were unable to recruit any local labour when work got under way, so they went to India, and between 1897 and 1901, when the line was completed, over 30,000 people were employed. In those imperial days, they were known indiscriminately as coolies, whether they were navvies or skilled surveyors and draughtsmen. The conditions they faced were appalling. Drinking water was a constant problem, with water holes often choked with

In order to build a railway across Kenya to the border with Uganda, an immense workforce was recruited in India. Here the Indian platelayers are striking camp to move onto a new site, taking all their belongings with them – probably including the kitchen sink.

vegetation. One engineer was recommended to try his servant's technique of filtering the water through his turban, but he preferred his own method – adding Eno's Fruit Salts, which produced 'hundreds of green bubbles' and brought a green scum to the surface which he scooped off to reach the clear water underneath. The route lay across desert where the tsetse fly inflicted terrible damage on the pack animals: out of 1800 that were sent to do the job, 1500 died of disease. This part of the line ended at what should have been a welcome sight, the river at Tsavo. Here a large force would be encamped for the building of the viaduct. It was to prove the most terrifying location on the line.

The nightmare began when a lion broke into a tent, grabbed one of the workmen, Ungan Singh, and dragged him away. It was not long before the local lion population discovered that men in flimsy tents were far easier prey than fast-moving gazelles and antelopes. They became ever bolder, making nightly raids. Lt.-Col. J. H. Patterson, one of the engineers, declared war on the lions. A keen hunter, he found that the men who were dragooned into helping him were less enthusiastic. One bright idea was to build an immense trap with a closed compartment at the far end. This was to be occupied by two coolies who were armed with rifles, and ordered to shoot the lion when it entered. In the event the terrified men fired at almost everything except the lion, and almost shot Patterson – and one could not have blamed them if they had. At times the story of the Tsavo lions reads as if it had come out of the pages of a Victorian adventure yarn. Patterson was expecting a visit from the District Officer, and when he met him later he expressed his annoyance at his non-appearance.

In order to complete the Uganda Railway, the engineers had to conquer the Great Rift Valley. Tracks were laid up the steep sides, and special wagons were constructed on triangular frames, so that they remained level on their journeys up and down the slopes.

'Where on earth have you come from?' I exclaimed. 'Why didn't you turn up to dinner last night?'
'A nice reception you give a fellow when you invite him to dinner,' was his only reply.
'Why, what's up?' I asked.
'That infernal lion of yours nearly did for me last night,' said Whitehead.
'Nonsense you must have dreamed it!' I cried in astonishment.
For answer he turned round and showed me his back.
'That's not much of a dream is it?' he asked.
His clothing was rent by one huge tear from the nape of the neck downwards, and on the flesh were four great claw marks, showing red and angry through the torn cloth.

But this was not from the Boy's Own Paper, in spite of the language, but a genuinely terrifying experience. In time, the hunters won the battle with the lions and the work was completed. The final obstacle was the Great Rift Valley, with a 2000ft fall from the edge of the escarpment. Special trucks with a triangular frame were used to carry material up and down the fearsome slopes.

This was not the last of the really difficult lines to be built in Africa. The greatest challenge of all was the completion of a route from the Cape to Cairo, a dream never to be fulfilled. By the beginning of the twentieth century, a route had been completed all the way to the Zambesi, and it was decided to make the crossing right by the famous Victoria Falls, so close that passengers would see the spray hit the windows. It was to be a major tourist attraction as much as a useful railway link, and the bridge was to soar 420ft above the low-water mark. The start of work involved slinging a cable across the gorge, and a young engineer, C. Beresford Cox, made one of the first crossings on a bosun's chair, no more than a piece of wood hung from four ropes with a strip of canvas as a back rest. He found that looking down from his fragile chair had 'real charm'. The bridge was built as two sections cantilevered out from the sides of the gorge, eventually meeting in the middle in April 1905. The Zambesi bridge was an engineering triumph, as were the other ways of coping with mountains and ravines, but some of them were undeniably inconvenient. Zigzags in particular proved troublesome, requiring constant stops as the train changed direction. There were other solutions available.

The first answer to coping with mountainous routes had been that of the tramways of the eighteenth century. As these were almost without exception designed so that loaded trucks went downhill, and only the short trains of empties had to be hauled back by horses, they could be built with steep gradients and tight curves. In North Wales, William Madocks acquired land to the south of the mountains of Snowdonia. He carried out a series of land reclamation projects, which included building a huge embankment right across the Traeth Mawr estuary. At the western end, he created a new port, Port Madoc, now Porthmadog. Up

The Ffestiniog Railway was originally built as a gravity line, with loaded slate wagons going downhill and the empty wagons hauled back up by horse power. It ran to the newly created harbour at Porthmadog, crossing the estuary on the artificial embankment, The Cob.

in the hills were slate quarries and mines, providing a steady cargo for the sailing vessels of the new port. At first, pack animals were used, but by 1832 the engineer James Spooner had constructed a tramway up to the slate town of Blaenau Ffestiniog. No great thought was given to the gauge of the line, which was simply a continuation of that already in use at the quarries, an arbitrary $23^{1}/_{2}$ inches. Certainly there was no consideration given to the idea of using steam locomotives, so the loaded trucks ran down by gravity, with the horse enjoying the downhill ride in its own special 'dandy cart'.

The system worked well enough, but as the quarries prospered and the demand for slate to roof the new industrial towns of Britain grew it came to seem increasingly primitive. In 1856, James Spooner's son Charles took over the control of the line. In 1862 he took the bold decision to order steam locomotives and the following year George England & Co. of London sent the first two locomotives to the line, *Princess* and *Mountaineer*. The *Princess* got her *Prince* the following year, and the happy couple remain on the railway to this day, though they have been greatly modified over the years. Today they are modest 0-4-0 saddle tank engines. In 1864, the little railway was authorised to carry passengers, so that the line was now the first narrow-gauge railway in the world to carry both passengers and freight. Not all the problems had been solved, and the biggest difficulty lay in the fact that this was a single-track line. Given the nature of the terrain, with the tracks often running on narrow ledges carved out of the steep hillside, the obvious answer of supplying double track would have been hugely expensive. The alternative was to run longer trains, but the tiny 0-4-0s were simply not up to the job.

The Ffestiniog was the first narrow-gauge line to be worked by steam locomotives, and Robert Fairlie designed special double-ended locomotives for the job. The 1879 Fairlie *Merddyn Emrys* is still in steam, and can be seen fighting its way up one of the narrow mountain ledges.

The nature of the line with its tight curves seemed to make it impossible to build bigger engines, as they would simply not get round the bends. The solution was found by the ingenious Robert Fairlie. The Fairlie engines are unlike anything seen on the railways before or since. At first sight they look like the result of an unfortunate accident in which two engines have been reversed into each other and stuck solid. In effect what Fairlie had designed was an engine with a long boiler, with a central driving position and two fireboxes. The boiler was mounted on a continuous frame. Under each end of the frame was a four-wheeled bogie, each with its own steam cylinders and two pairs of coupled wheels, giving an 0-4-4-0 arrangement. The bogies pivoted independently, enabling the locomotive to cope with the bends. They were an immediate success.

In time, the slate trade died away, and less and less traffic passed through Porthmadog. It might have been the end of the story, but before the line was closed it was taken over by

The Fairlie appears to be the push-me-pull-you of the railway world, looking like two engines that have collided and stuck together. In fact, the engine has two power units and two bogies, enabling it to cope with the steep gradients and the sharp curves. This example was built for New Zealand.

a charitable trust, the Ffestiniog Railway Trust. They had their own problems, not least when permission was given to build a reservoir right across the line, cutting off the route to Blaenau Ffestiniog. The Trust was not to be defeated. If the original line could not be reopened, then a new one would be built. They faced a dilemma: how to gain height to reach the summit without creating an impossible gradient. The answer was to create a spiral, with the line looping round over itself. It was not an original solution. There is, however, a certain pleasing symmetry in that the world's first narrow-gauge steam line was to borrow an idea from its own most famous successor, which we shall be meeting shortly.

The delights of the Ffestiniog today come in large measure from a combination of factors: the hugely important history of the route, the magnificent scenery through which it passes, and, by no means least, the chance to ride in vintage carriages behind locomotives that have been with the line since its inception. Riding on the footplate with rock walls seemingly only inches from your nose is exhilarating, and there is still something of the same experience as there was in the horse days. Travelling uphill is hard work, and the engine puffs and pants with the effort. Going down, the crew are rather like the horse in the dandy cart; the main requirement is for the engine to act as a brake. The success of the Ffestiniog experiment was followed by other narrow-gauge lines in Wales, a number of which also served the slate industry. Prominent among these lines is the Talyllyn Railway, which owed its existence to the American Civil War. The north had set up an effective blockade around southern ports, effectively cutting off cotton supplies for the mills of Lancashire. As a result, a group of Manchester businessmen purchased quarries at Bryn Eglwys which were to be joined to a new port at Tywyn by rail. The first six and three-quarter miles from Tywyn was to be worked by locomotives, and was to carry passengers as well as freight. Above that was an old-style tramway, with horses and cable haulage on the inclines.

Construction costs were kept to a minimum, but economy went too far. When the railway inspector arrived to approve the line, he declared that the gaps between bridge abutments and carriages were too narrow for safety. No one wanted to rebuild all the bridges, but they hit on an ingenious answer. Instead of running down the centre of the arch, the rails were moved sideways, giving good clearance on one side. On the other side, doors and windows were bolted shut, resulting in an odd one-sided train. In spite of the concerns for safety, the railway indulged in some very dodgy practices. Passengers were allowed to hire trucks by the day for a picnic up in the hills. If they missed the last locomotive home, all they had to do was jump in the truck, shove it off and enjoy a dash down the hill, relying only on the handbrake and providence. The locomotives had their own quirks. No. 1 *Talyllyn* tended to bounce up and down, while No. 2 *Dolgoch* swayed from side to side. The problem with No. 1 was solved by adding a pair of trailing wheels, converting it from an 0-4-0 to an 0-4-2. The problems with No. 2 were more difficult to resolve, as they resulted from a fundamental design problem, a long crank. Nothing seemed to happen, apart from the wobble, and everyone got used to that. Both engines have survived, as has the railway. It has a special place in railway history.

In 1946 the quarries closed and the owner, Sir Henry Haydn Jones, kept the passenger service going, more from sentiment than for any practical purpose. His widow did not share his enthusiasm and it might have gone the way of so many old industrial lines, had not author and engineer L. T. C. Rolt gone walking in the hills. He saw behind the rust and the badly maintained track to appreciate that this was a beautiful line, with aged but historic locomotives. He and friends got together and the Talyllyn Railway Preservation Society was formed,

In many parts of the world the little industrial lines have continued with steam, simply because there is no money available for replacements – and the old engines still work. This Baldwin 2-8-0 was built in 1914 and is seen at the Rafael Freyre sugar mill in Cuba.

not just saving this one line but setting in motion the whole idea that amateurs could take over and run steam railways. Thanks to their efforts, steam travel was saved to be enjoyed by generations who might otherwise never have had a chance to enjoy its unique pleasures.

The idea of narrow-gauge lines spread right across the world. New Zealand was one of the latecomers to the railway world, and only arrived at all after a few false starts. There were three railways proposed in the early days – each one with a different gauge. Some strange ideas were also tried: an American engineer proposed saving money by doing without metal rails altogether, and using native hardwoods. It was an interesting experiment: the little locomotive literally blazed down the track, leaving the rails aflame behind it. Fortunately common sense prevailed before chaos was born. Julius Vogel had arrived in New Zealand from the Victoria gold fields in Australia and rapidly rose to the position of government treasurer. He persuaded the government to pump money into construction on the grounds that railways were the way to open up the country and to encourage immigration. Unlike many politicians Vogel was aware of his own ignorance on technical matters and asked for and (even more remarkably) acted on expert advice. So a gauge was set which, while not as narrow as the Ffestiniog, was still modest, at 3ft 6in. The first line to be completed was on South Island, between Dunedin and Port Chalmers. The new company decided to take advantage of the latest technology available for narrow-gauge lines and ordered a double-ended Fairlie, which arrived in 1873, just four years after the prototype had puffed its way up to Blaenau Ffestiniog.

New Zealand's mountainous landscape presented severe problems to railway builders. Here a J-Class locomotive *Gloria* is heading a special excursion train on the North Island route between Gisborne and Napier.

Probably the most spectacular narrow-gauge railway in the world: this picture of the Darjeeling Himalaya Railway was taken shortly after the opening in 1879, and shows the track zigzagging up the hillside.

The awareness that narrow-gauge lines offered unique advantages in hilly and mountainous country soon spread. In America, the citizens of Denver, Colorado had two rail connections by 1870, but one man was an enthusiast for a third line that would follow the old Santa Fe Trail, south through the mountains to Mexico. The pioneer was a former Union general, William Jackson Palmer. In 1870 he got married, and went off to Europe for his honeymoon, where he combined pleasure with business. He went to see the Ffestiniog Railway and met Robert Fairlie. What he saw convinced him that this was just the system that was needed to conquer the Rockies. Fairlie recommended a rather wider gauge than that of the modest Ffestiniog. The two men agreed that 3ft would be ideal, and Fairlie provided one of his double-ended engines for the line. Just one year after his visit to Wales, Palmer had the pleasure of seeing the first train on what was now the Denver & Rio Grande Railroad make its way from Denver to Colorado Springs. But it was not hauled by the Fairlie, which had failed to impress the Americans when it was shipped over. Instead the honour went to a native locomotive, a 2-4-0 called *Montezuma* in anticipation of the growth of the system into Latin America. Thanks to the coming of the railway, Colorado Springs began its career as a major holiday resort.

It is rather appropriate that, as the D&RG network had grown out of the ideas first tried on the Ffestiniog, in its latter days a part of the American network would follow the Welsh example once again. As commercial traffic declined, a new source of revenue was found among rail enthusiasts. Silverton was just what its name suggests, a town that grew up around its silver mines. What it needed in order to thrive was good transport, which was provided in 1882 with the arrival of a branch line from the Durango. It was an ambitious line even by narrow-gauge standards, with cuttings blasted through the rocks and a number of daunting grades. The line carried passengers as well as freight, and even boasted sleeping cars, a rarity in the narrow-gauge world. As freight declined, there was a small but notable increase in passenger traffic. People just wanted to travel the line for its own sake, and it is easy to see why. The scenery is breathtaking, surrounded by high mountain peaks and having as its climax the journey down Animas Canyon. The canyon has been carved hundreds of feet down through the mountains, by a rushing mountain river, and the little line spends part of its time hugging the cliffs on a narrow ledge before eventually coming down to the waterside. The combination of this scenery and the historic steam engines and vintage rolling stock is irresistible. Today the line is privately owned, running a tourist service just like its Welsh cousins.

There can be few arguments over which is the most remarkable narrow-gauge railway of them all. It is one thing to conquer the Rockies, quite another to build a railway in the Himalayas. The Darjeeling Himalaya runs from New Jalpaiguri down on the plain to Darjeeling spread out along a ridge, 7000ft above sea level. The town grew up on this unlikely site because it proved an ideal place to grow tea that had been smuggled in from China. The problem once again was the lack of decent communications, with just a long tortuous road winding up through the hills, suitable for little more than the crudest bullock cart. Nothing but a narrow-gauge line could bring the benefits of the steam train to Darjeeling, and even then it had to be built to the modest gauge of just two foot. Work was put in hand in 1879 and completed just two years later. Every possible device was needed to keep gradients manageable, including the zigzags, which called for five reverses along the way, and four loops where the line curves over itself. The first locomotives came from Britain, and a Sharp, Stewart built in Glasgow in 1889 is preserved at the railway museum in Delhi. It was largely rebuilt in 1917, but still managed to carry on working this extraordinary line right up to 1952. Another familiar name from the railway story also put in an appearance when Baldwin began to supply engines. The engines are so small that the largest item of equipment on view is generally the headlamp. They were just about capable of doing the job, but were often hard pressed and progress up to Darjeeling was so slow that young lads would jump off the train at the start of one of the loops, run across the middle and rejoin the train at the far side. What was needed was a better way of bringing extra power to the narrow gauge without losing the essential ability to cope with the bends: something that would be an improvement on the old Fairlies.

One of the last vertical boiler Shays is at work on the Philippine island of Negros. The bulbous, spark-arresting chimney does not appear to be entirely successful.

Some narrow-gauge lines were required to carry very heavy traffic. This was certainly true in South Africa, where major trunk routes were built to a 3ft 6in gauge. A combination of power and manoeuvrability was provided by articulated Garratts. This magnificent 4-8-2+2-8-4 was photographed in Natal.

Tasmania has as difficult a terrain for railway construction as anywhere in the world, and although a standard gauge was set at 3ft 6in, there were sections where that had to be dropped right down to 2ft. Hauling heavy trains on such lines was taxing, and an inspecting engineer from New South Wales called William Garratt came up with a solution. Instead of the rigid frame of the Fairlies, he proposed an articulated locomotive. There would be just one boiler, but it would feed two quite separate power units. The first part of the engine would be a more or less conventional locomotive, apart from the positioning of the cylinders either behind or under the cab. In front of that was a second smaller assemblage, without a cab, but with a further set of cylinders. He sent his ideas to Beyer, Peacock back in England, and they sent their first locomotive out from their Manchester works in 1909. It was built for the 2ft gauge, and had a novel 2-4-0+0-4-2 wheel arrangement. It proved a huge success, and the Beyer Garratts were soon being sent around the world. They proved particularly popular in Africa and even bigger locomotives were built, culminating in the mighty 4-8-4+4-8-4s. By 1921, back in Tasmania, the new generation of Garratts were working the 3ft 6in line at speeds of 55mph, which for a mountainous narrow gauge puts them in the express category. Even so, there remained areas where normal traction alone was not quite enough.

The Alps presented a major obstacle to the extension of a rail network across Europe. The mountain passes are generally high and steep, but they offered the best possibility of making connections. The Mont Cenis Pass links Switzerland to Italy, and was to provide the basis for two rail links. The conventional answer was to build a tunnel, an immense undertaking but one that was within the capabilities of the technology of the late nineteenth century. The less likely alternative was to go over the top, following the existing road route. The latter was the option taken by John Barraclough Fell. The route was 48 miles long, with a maximum gradient of 1 in 12. No locomotive could tackle such a slope without assistance, so wherever the gradient was greater than 1 in 25, Fell laid a central rail between the two conventional rails. On the locomotive was a pair of horizontal wheels which could be moved inward by a screw operated from the footplate to engage with the central rail. The addition of these two gripping wheels effectively doubled the adhesion. The line opened in 1868, but was destined to have a short life. Three years later the Mont Cenis tunnel was completed. A locomotive that was limited to hauling a twenty-ton load at a stately 10mph simply could not compete and the mountain line closed down.

The Fell system was adopted elsewhere in the world, with a notable example in New Zealand, where the route between Wellington and Masterton was blocked by the Rimutaka Mountains. Various ideas were tried, including a tramway, and a zigzag such as that used on South Island seemed the only solution. The chief engineer, John Blackett, was not keen, so he suggested a more direct, steeper route using the Fell system. It worked, but at a high price. The line climbed the 1 in 15 grade for $2\frac{1}{2}$ miles, and in that distance the engine consumed as much fuel as it did on the whole of the rest of the line, all 63 miles of it. The engines had cast-iron shoes that could be used on the central rail to brake the train, but even that was not considered safe, so a special brake van, also braking on the centre rail, was added at the end. The system did work after a fashion, but the locomotive was limited to hauling 60 tons on passenger trains and 65 on freight. As this was clearly inadequate, the railway saw a complex marshalling manoeuvre at the foot of the bank. There might be a locomotive at the head, followed by a couple of coaches, then a second locomotive, more coaches and so on. By the time the train was made up it might have as many as four engines spread down its length and a whole string of brake vans hanging on at the end. This way loads of over 250 tons could be moved at the pace of a not over-energetic jogger. The disadvantages of the Fell system are obvious, but it did have the advantage that the Fell locomotive could work conventionally on level sections, where there was no need to go to the expense of adding the third rail.

The Fell system was a solution to a particular problem of extending rail links through difficult country. In the late nineteenth century a new challenge appeared. The Romantic movement had helped to develop a taste for wild scenery, and mountains previously considered barren wildernesses now became tourist attractions. The new sport of mountaineering enabled the daring to reach Alpine summits, but how were the more timid or less fit to enjoy the best of the scenery? The answer was the mountain railway, provided a means could be found of conquering gradients where even the Fell system would fail. The answer was there right at the beginning of the railway age: the rack and pinion. This was to become a feature of Alpine travel, but the Europeans did not get there first.

As early as 1852, an American businessman, Sylvester Marsh, was on holiday in New Hampshire and admired the scenery around Mount Washington. It would, he thought, be a good idea to build a railway to the summit, but his idea was met with mockery. It took him several years before he found two local engineers who were prepared to make that dream a reality: a father and son, Herrick and Walter Aiken. They devised what they called a cog system, which was a pair of rack rails set between the conventional rails. Constructing the track was a major problem, since all the materials had to be brought by ox cart through dense woodland and forest. The track was carried for much of the way on wooden trestles to a summit at 6288 feet, and was finally opened in 1869. The little locomotive, colourfully named *Old Pepperass*, has all the look of a prototype. The simple iron frame carries two pairs of wheels, the front smaller than the rear, so that the platform would remain horizontal even when the locomotive was on the slope. Power came from a vertical boiler and no form of cover was supplied for driver or fireman. The line still operates, but now with more conventional locomotives, though they still need to compensate for the slope by having inclined boilers to prevent the water uncovering the firebox crown. As is normal with mountain railways, carriages are pushed instead of pulled, so that the locomotive is always on the downhill side. The engine remains in forward gear during the descent to act as a brake.

Niklaus Riggenbach was one of the pioneering engineers of the Swiss railway system, who drove the country's first locomotive in 1847. As an executive of the Swiss Central Railway, he began to dream of a railway that could take visitors to enjoy the finest scenery that the mountains could offer. Quite independently of the American inventors he developed his own rack-and-pinion system in 1863. The Vitznau Rigi railway was originally run, like the Mount Washington, with a vertical boilered locomotive, and the first successful trial took place on Riggenbach's birthday on 21 May 1870, over a 300m length of track. The following year the whole line was open. Riggenbach had predicted it would attract 50,000 visitors a year: there were 60,000, and the numbers went on growing. The only problem was one of rather rough running, which was soon solved by another engineer, Roman Abt. He patented his system in 1882. He used two racks next to each other, but out of phase, so that a tooth on one would be opposite a gap on the other, engaging with a pair of stepped pinions resulting in a much smoother ride. It can be seen on the Brienz-Rothorn Railway in Switzerland, which still runs with steam locomotives, from the earliest, built in 1888, to new engines no more than two or three years old. The Abt system soon became very popular, even being used across the Channel on the Snowdon Mountain Railway in Wales.

The Alps were to see many mountain railways over the years, and the technology was steadily improved. By 1889 the mountain railway using the locomotive had, it seemed, been pushed as far as it would go. The Mt. Pilatus Railway was designed to climb this very steep mountain, rising above Lake Lucerne, and the engineers were actually proposing a railway with a gradient of 1 in 2. For this a quite new method of working was devised, the Locher system, which could be thought of as combining the features of the Fell and the Abt. There is a central rail and horizontal wheels at either side as in the former, but the centre rail and the wheels are cogged as in the latter. The line ends at an altitude of 7000ft, just over 100ft below the summit – enabling passengers to claim that they have walked to

There was a limit to the terrain that even the best narrow-gauge railway could conquer. To overcome steeper slopes a new system was needed – the rack-and-pinion mountain railway. The very first was the Mount Washington Cog Railway, built in 1869 and still running. The locomotive has not taken a nose-dive, but is built this way to keep the boiler level, even though the engine is climbing a steep slope.

the summit of the mountain. It was and is the steepest cog railway in the world, and in early days it must have been an extraordinary sight, with the little engine, its rear end stuck up in the air like a duck's tail, pushing the sloping carriage with its stepped compartments. Steam haulage came to an end in 1937 when the line was electrified. It now runs far more efficiently, but has lost a little of its quirky charm.

When one thinks of constructing railways under the most difficult conditions imaginable, the mind turns to mountains and deserts, wide rivers and deep ravines. But there is another form of obstacle every bit as demanding which is man-made: the city. Cities arrived long before the railways, and in the nineteenth century they were spreading out to cover ever more ground. Given the likely opposition to demolishing huge tracts of buildings, let alone the expense of purchasing valuable city freeholds, railway builders who wanted to provide services inside the city itself had only two options: they could go under or over. The notion of building a railway under the streets of London was first proposed as early as 1830, but the world was not yet ready for such a startling innovation. However, by the middle of the century, the value of railways was so universally acknowledged that the idea was brought out again. In 1854, Parliament approved the formation of the Metropolitan Railway and John Fowler was appointed chief engineer. Investment funds were unavailable during the Crimean War, but by 1860 work had begun.

The Metropolitan was not a very long line, originally planned to go no further than from King's Cross to Farringdon Street, but by the time construction started an extension westward to link with Paddington had been agreed. This is still only a modest four miles, but on the way it had to cross some of the city's busiest streets. Fowler's answer was the

A problem every bit as difficult for railway engineers as conquering mountains was presented by the need to build a line through crowded cities. One answer was to go under the streets and the world's first underground railway, the Metropolitan, was opened in London in 1863 (RIGHT). Unlike the later tube systems it was built as a series of deep cuttings, which were then covered over (BELOW).

technique known as 'cut and cover'. He dug deep cuttings, covered them over again with brick and iron arches, and then relaid the road back on top. The line was hidden from view, apart from the ventilation shafts which were liable to erupt without warning, giving modest Victorian ladies the sort of experience that delighted Marilyn Monroe in *The Seven Year Itch*. During construction, the line was a monumental nuisance, and pedestrians often found themselves wobbling precariously across muddy planks with a chasm beneath their feet. The inaugural run on 24 May 1862 was over a short length of track, and dignitaries including Gladstone, and at least one brave lady, made the trip in contractors' wagons with bench seats. They looked a somewhat incongruous group, their top hats and frock coats not altogether in keeping with the rough trucks. Once the line was officially open for business it was an immense success, with 30,000 passengers being carried on the first day.

Conditions were not altogether ideal, with underground haulage in the care of 4-4-0 tank engines by Beyer, Peacock. Lighting was essential, and relied on gas lamps fed by gas bags in the carriages, though many passengers brought their own candles. The line soon spread, and in the process produced one of London's curiosities. On its extension westward, the line passed through fashionable Leinster Gardens, a typical symmetrical terrace in Bayswater. Go there today and the terrace seems undisturbed, but numbers 23 and 25 are no more than a facade. The original houses were knocked down to make way for the tracks and false fronts stuck up, as in a Hollywood set. The underground railway proved to be an answer to a major transport problem, not just for London but for cities throughout the world. It was obvious, however, that the cut and fill technique could not be applied throughout the city, and the eventual answer for London was to build lines in deep tunnels, the familiar Tube.

London's underground railway system was initially worked by steam locomotives, and in time it spread out to the suburbs. This modest 0-4-4 tank engine is typical of the engines that worked the Metropolitan line in the early days.

The alternative to going under city streets was to go over them. This is a part of New York's elevated railway on its way through the Bronx.

The original Metropolitan still has much of its old character, with the brick arches a prominent feature at the stations. London's underground has expanded hugely, and station design has changed with the years, from the very Victorian character of the early lines through the clean modernism of Arnos Grove, with its distinctive rotunda, built in 1932, to the very latest, such as Canary Wharf, which can stand proudly with its forerunners. Elsewhere, all kinds of styles were developed, from the famous Art Nouveau signs of the Paris Metro to the Baroque splendours of Moscow. The system is always developing as demand grows, and the biggest change came with the introduction of electrification, removing the soot and smoke of the steam age.

The alternative to diving underground is to build a line above the city streets, an elevated railway. The best-known examples are in America, particularly New York and Chicago. The New York Elevated was developed from the 1870s onwards. As in London, steam was used up to the end of the nineteenth century, when it was banned from the central city areas. The line was opened using stubby little 0-4-0s, with a cab like a greenhouse stuck on the back. Later versions had a totally enclosed engine, which looked from the outside very much like a passenger carriage in which all the passengers were smoking heavily. In time, the most popular locomotive was the 0-4-4, plainer than its predecessors, with a small bunker at the back.

Chicago acquired its elevated railway in the 1890s and the Union Loop is a magnificent example of just what can be done with riveted steel girders. Mostly the steel is left bold and bare, but stations are generally given a jaunty classical facade. Quincy Street, for example, strides across the road on its steel frame, but right at the top, like a curious afterthought, is the station itself, complete with fluted pilasters topped by floral capitals and a decorated frieze. The contrast between the entrance at street level with its massive girders and the classical lodge at track level could scarcely be greater.

Engineers were always on the look out for systems that would use space more economically and so reduce the cost of acquiring land, particularly in expensive urban areas. One solution was the monorail. Charles Francois Marie-Therese Lartigue introduced his system into Ireland in the 1920s on the Listowel and Ballybunion Railway. The line boasted what was probably the world's first 0-3-0 locomotive. Quite why the company adopted this bizarre system is unknown. The track was built up on a triangular frame, and the locomotive was in effect doubled, half of

One of the grandest of all mountain railways, still worked by steam, is the Brienz Rothorn in the Swiss Alps. Here one of the trains is seen at the summit station, with its astonishing mountain panorama.

the engine hanging down on either side of the central rail with a cab in the middle. It was incredibly inconvenient. Where roads would have been supplied with level crossings, they had to build drawbridges, and rail crossings were effected by manually pushing a pivoted junction rail from one line to the other. It was a glorious failure, but the monorail idea was sound. It worked when it was realized that the real advantage was to be gained by raising the rail on high, and, instead of running the train precariously on top, suspending it underneath. The pioneering Barmen-Elderfeld line in Germany was built over a public road, and to cause minimum disturbance to traffic the line was carried on U-shaped arches. Modern versions, such as the Shonan Monorail in Japan, built in 1970, have more than proved their worth.

Overhead and underground city railways have developed side by side, co-existing in many places, such as the U-bahn and S-bahn of Berlin. To this, in recent years, has been added a light railway system, occupying a sort of halfway position between the conventional railway and the tram. Sometimes, as in Manchester, for example, a disused railway that once served mainline trains has been brought back into use for the new generation of light railways. It seems possible that as city streets get ever more congested, there will be more and more ingenious ideas employed.

CHAPTER 8

SAFETY FIRST

RAILWAYS ARE UNLIKE every other transport system in that vehicles cannot get out of each other's way if any form of collision looks possible – except by derailing, itself a disaster. The former was never very likely in the early years of tramways, but the latter was all too possible if anything went wrong with trucks descending an incline. The Duke of Rutland visited Wales in the first decade of the nineteenth century, and went to see the tramways of the Brecon & Abergavenny Canal. He described the primitive braking system, which was simply a man running behind the wagon, operating the long lever brake. If that broke, which (according to the Duke) it often did, the truck would dash off, gathering momentum as it went. He related the experience of the proprietor of a local iron works, Mr Frere, who was coming down the road in a post chaise when he looked up and saw a wagon hurtling out of control down the hill towards him:

> He could not possibly get out of the way, and must have been crushed to pieces, if fortunately the wagon had not broken over the iron groove, which had hitherto kept it in the track, and run forcibly up an ash-tree by the side of the road, in the branches of which it literally stuck, and thus saved him from imminent destruction.

Such accidents may have been rare, but they were potentially lethal. It was the speed of the wagon that terrified the unfortunate Mr Frere and froze him in his tracks. People were not used to seeing wagons moving at any speed beyond that of the plodding carthorse that was pulling them. The same problem was magnified when the horse gave way to the steam locomotive.

The first, and probably most famous, passenger fatality of the steam age took place on what should have been a date of triumphant celebration, the official opening of the Liverpool & Manchester Railway. Seven locomotives were put through their paces that day, and a grandstand had been erected at Parkside for the many distinguished guests to enjoy the show. Among the most important were the local MP William Huskisson, who had been a prominent supporter of the line, and the Duke of Wellington, who had been notably less enthusiastic. When the train with the ducal carriage stopped at Parkside, everyone got out and strolled around as if they had just left their own personal carriages on a quiet country lane. The Duke and Huskisson were not on the best of terms, but the Duke made a friendly gesture and Huskisson walked across to shake his hand. At that point, one of the meandering guests spotted a locomotive in the distance, and there was a general uproar as people returned to their coaches. Huskisson seemed uncertain what to do, and after dithering

OPPOSITE: **This signal box on the preserved Bluebell steam railway is typical of hundreds that were once found throughout the British rail network. The levers are coloured to show which operations they perform, the track diagram indicates train positions, and there is even an electric telegraph.**

tried to join the Duke in his carriage. He was too late. *Rocket* was sweeping towards him, hit the carriage door and flung Huskisson onto the track where a wheel ran over his leg.

Northumbrian was on hand, with a flat car which had held a band of musicians. Huskisson was lifted on board and the locomotive with George Stephenson himself at the controls dashed off to the nearest town, Eccles. It was too late: Huskisson had died. The locomotive had done its best, travelling at an average speed of over 30mph, but it was the speed that might have saved the unhappy Huskisson that had resulted in the accident in the first place. He had been frozen like a rabbit in headlights by *Rocket*'s terrifying advance. If the accident did nothing else it pointed up the necessity of keeping trains and pedestrians apart, except at recognized station stops. One possible danger point occurred where road and rail met at the same level. The simple solution was to have crossing gates, and many were built with a tiny cottage alongside for the gatekeeper. In the modern world, the automatic barrier has largely taken over, but on a few little-used lines the crossing gates have gone together with the keeper, and improvisation has taken over. There is a delightful tourist line running from Thury-Harcourt along the Orne valley in Normandy. As the train leaves the station, two men set off down the road in a small car. Their job is to get to each crossing before the train arrives, leap out with red flags and stop any other cars on the road until after the train has passed.

One obvious way to avoid a repetition of the Huskisson tragedy would have been to have had some sort of warning that the locomotive was on its way towards the busy scene. No one seems to have thought of that idea until a far less serious accident occurred on the Leicester & Swannington Railway in 1833. A horse and cart, carrying milk and eggs, was crossing the line and was hit by a train. No one was hurt, though the resulting omelette was probably very expensive. Ashlin Bagster, the railway manager, suggested to George Stephenson that it would be a good idea to fit locomotives with some sort of whistle blown by steam. Stephenson took the idea to a musical-instrument maker in Leicester, and the first whistle, known as a 'steam trumpet', was fitted to the locomotive *Samson*. It was to become a familiar feature on generations of steam locomotives.

It was all very well warning pedestrians and carters of the approach of a train, but who was to warn the locomotive driver of trouble ahead? The problem was neatly put in an early treatise, *The Practical Railway Engineer*, in 1855.

> Without a system of well-arranged, well-understood and faithfully-worked signals, it would be utterly impossible to conduct the traffic of any railway with safety and regularity. The 'all right' and 'hold hard' of the stage coach, the 'go on', 'ease her', 'stop her' and 'half-turn astern' of the steamboat are sufficient for the proper progress of those conveyances; but against the puff, whirr, the chatter of the Vulcan, the Rocket, the Ajax, the Thunderer, or the Hurricane, what human voice, even if pitched in the key of a Stentor, could possibly prevail?

The first and most obvious requirement of any signalling system is that it tells the driver that he can safely go ahead without encountering another train on the line, or to stop if it is not clear. Less obvious, but no less important, is the need to warn a driver to slow down,

Hand signals from a 19th-century manual for engine drivers. From top to bottom, they show All Clear, Caution and Stop.

for example if he is about to be switched to another track or if there is a stop signal a short way ahead. On the opening of the Liverpool & Manchester Railway, train control was primitive. The rules stipulated that there must be a minimum ten-minute gap between trains, but obviously that in itself was not sufficient. One train might be faster than another, or there could be some unexpected delay, so that in the course of a journey the time gap could shorten or even disappear altogether. The job of maintaining the time gap went to the railway policemen, who gave hand signals to the drivers. 'Carry on' (arms kept to the side), 'slow down' (arm held up at 45°), and 'stop' (arm held straight out) were the full repertoire. Other railway companies developed slightly different hand signals. Apart from keeping the time, they could also stop a train if they spotted anything amiss. The trouble was that policemen had other duties, from spotting baggage thieves to chasing off trespassers. They could not be relied on to keep an accurate check on train times, and the drivers were never quite sure where they would appear along the track. Something better was clearly needed, something fixed and reliable. The railways needed signals.

The first signals were installed on the Liverpool & Manchester in 1834 to cope with the special problem caused by running trains at night. These consisted of lanterns hung on posts: a clear light to give the go ahead, and a red light for stop. The system still depended on someone being on hand to note the passage of a train, at which point he would climb a ladder to the top of the post, change the white light for red, wait ten minutes and then put the white light back again. The first daytime signals were simple. The earliest type consisted of a swivelling red plate on top of a tall pole. When the disc was at right angles to the line, it indicated stop, and when it was turned through ninety degrees the driver could not see it, so knew he was free to carry on. A rather less satisfactory system used coloured flags, which were fine on a windy day, but difficult to see when they hung limply from their flagposts. Sir John Hawkshaw introduced the first really significant improvement: a signal consisting of a disc on top of the signal post with a bar at right angles to it. When the bar was turned to the driver, he was to stop, while (just as importantly) the disc gave him the all clear. It was fortunate that, in this area at least, the different railway companies saw the need for uniformity, particularly in the form of colour codes, which were essential for night running. The first system used red for danger, green for caution and white for the all clear. This would become unacceptable with the spread of street lighting, when a railway white light would be indistinguishable from a host of others, but it served well enough in the early years. Other countries developed their own versions, including a quarter rotating chequer board that was used in France.

As the railways developed, the building of junctions where different lines crossed or converged created a special problem. A system was needed to give right of way on one track or another. An early example was at Normanton, where the York & North Midland Railway from York met the North Midland Railway from Derby. A signalman had the job of stopping one of the trains on one of the lines by operating the stop signals, and a trackside brazier gave advance warning of the problem up ahead at night. On the outskirts of London, a branch line was built from the main line from Greenwich to Croydon, with a junction at Corbett's Lane. In order to keep a lookout over the lines, an odd little structure like a miniature lighthouse was constructed – the world's first signal box. That solved one

An early Great Western signal at Didcot. The disc acts as the Clear signal, the bar as the Stop.

of the problems, but there was still a considerable area of confusion. Was the same person to be responsible both for switching the points from one line to the other and for operating the appropriate signals, or were the different jobs to be handed over to different railwaymen? It was to take some time for that to be resolved.

Another problem lay in communicating information over a distance, which was particularly important when trains were entering long tunnels. The solution already existed in the form of the semaphore telegraph, developed in France by Claude Chappe in the 1790s. The system consisted of a pivoted wooden beam, with movable arms added at the end. By using a combination of different positions of the arms and the main beam, individual letters could be represented and messages transmitted over long distances. In 1793 Chappe was given the official post of Ingénieur-Télégraphe and the job of installing a telegraph system between Paris and Lille, 144 miles apart. He built fifteen stations and on 15 August 1794 the government received the news of a successful battle at Le Quesnoy via the very first telegram. The idea of having tall poles to provide visual information was adopted at Box Tunnel, where the signal could be read by both the driver and the tunnel-keepers at either end. More importantly, the hinged semaphore arm was recognized as a very satisfactory method for supplying information to train drivers. The system first used was to let the semaphore arms represent the equivalent hand gestures; horizontal for stop, inclined for caution and out of sight in a slot in the post for clear. The advantage over the policeman was that a semaphore signal could carry a number of different arms, covering different tracks, all attached to the same post or on separate posts for junctions. The signals could be used at night by installing lanterns with different coloured glasses. A more sophisticated system used a white light in conjunction with

ABOVE: **Claude Chappe's semaphore telegraph system illustrated in 1794. It shows the movable arms being manipulated by ropes to send a message, while the man on the roof looks through his telescope to the next telegraph station. This was the basis for the semaphore signal.**

RIGHT: **This illustration by Bourne shows Box tunnel, and is full of interest. The emerging train is being given the 'All Clear' hand signal. The bar and disc signal is set so that it can be read at trackside and can also be relayed to the far end by the repeated signals at the top of the post. In the background a coach and pedestrians can be seen crossing the hill, presumably passengers too nervous to travel through the hill by train.**

coloured glass 'spectacles' in the semaphore arm, so that when it moved a different colour appeared in front of the light. Even as late as the 1950s one of the jobs of porters on the early shifts was to trudge off down the line from the station to check the signal lamps.

Chappe was also interested in using the latest developments in science to improve the telegraph system, and he began experimenting with using electricity to send his signals. He did not have a great deal of success, though the idea was sound. Others were to take up the challenge, and a better understanding of the underlying science led to a breakthrough. It was the discovery by a Danish physicist that current flowing in an electric wire would deflect a magnetic needle placed below it that first showed the connection between magnetism and electricity. This was used as the basis for the development of the galvanometer, which in turn gave way to the electric telegraph, in which the flow of electricity caused a precise movement of a needle. William Fothergill Cooke, whose military career had ended when he was invalided out of the East India Army, saw an early version of such a device and devoted the rest of his life to its improvement. He tried to interest the Liverpool & Manchester in his experiments in 1836, but he had problems with the electromagnets. At about the same time he met a scientific experimenter in the field, Professor Charles Wheatstone of King's College, London. They agreed to pool their ideas and formed a partnership, taking out a patent for an electric telegraph in 1837. This used five needles, which could point to different lines on a grid to indicate which letters were to be read. They gave a demonstration to the directors of the London & Birmingham Railway, sending messages between Euston and Camden Town, but it was the Great Western Railway that took up the idea. The first telegraph was installed between Paddington and West Drayton in 1838 and later extended to Slough. The system recorded a notable success in 1845, when a woman was murdered in Slough and the suspect was seen boarding a train for Paddington. His description was telegraphed ahead and on his arrival in London he was arrested, later tried and executed. It is surprising that this case is not as well known as Doctor Crippen's capture as a result of the use of the radio, for it is just as striking an example of a new use for technology. The real advantage of the electric telegraph on the railways, however, was not for police chasing after murderers, but as a means of passing on up-to-the-minute information about train movements.

The signalling system gradually became more sophisticated, thanks to the use of the telegraph. An important advance came with the introduction of a whole new system of train control on the Yarmouth & Norwich line in 1844. Instead of separating trains by a fixed time interval, they were separated spatially. The line was divided up into a series of 'blocks', and only one train at a time was allowed into a block when travelling in the same direction. Once a train had entered a block, the next signalman down the line was telegraphed and nothing else could enter until he had passed back the message to the first man that the train had left the block. The other potential source of danger was the way in which signals and points were operated quite independently. Hutton Gregory, who was one of the first people to try semaphore signals, was also the first person to provide a system of linking them together so that all gave the right message. It was first tried at Bricklayers' Arms in the 1840s. The real break-

Cooke and Wheatstone's five-needle electric telegraph enabled signalmen to communicate with each other, a huge improvement in safety. When the operator pressed a key, two needles would move indicating two lines, which intersect at the appropriate letter.

through, however, was the introduction of a system in which both signals and points were completely interlocked. In 1856 its originator, John Saxby, took out a patent that made the highest claims for the advance in safety.

The semaphore signals, the coloured glasses of the signal lamps, and the 'points' are all activated by a single motion of the lever, thus rendering the duties of the signalman of the most simple character and making it impossible for an accident to arise from the signals and the points differing.

This was true as far as it went, and was undoubtedly a huge move forward, but no safety system is ever perfect. Surprisingly, the interlocked system spread comparatively slowly, only reaching American railroads when it was installed at Spuyten Duyvil, New York, in 1874.

The early signalling devices were quite satisfactory for a time, when speeds were modest and junctions comparatively uncommon. The semaphore signals still had the disadvantage that the signal for road clear was still, in effect, the absence of a visible signal instead of a positive sign. If a driver saw no signal, because the semaphore arm was tucked away in its slot, then he could assume the way ahead was open. That this assumption was not always justified was proved to devastating effect on the Great Northern Railway on 21 January 1876. On a foul day, with snowstorms reducing visibility, a slow goods train with thirty-seven coal wagons was trundling south from Peterborough. The signalman was supposed to stop it and shunt it off into a siding to allow through the *Flying Scotsman,* also on its way south. What he did not know was that the signal arm was frozen into its slot, so that as far as the goods train driver was concerned he had a clear road. By the time the express driver had seen the goods train it was too late, and he ran into the back of it, spewing trucks across both tracks. It was a serious situation about to become tragic, as the next express train from London was steaming at full speed on the down line and flew straight into the wreckage. In the resulting mayhem, fourteen people were killed and twenty-four seriously injured. The only good thing to come out of the disaster was an improvement in safety regulations.

There were special problems associated with single line working, where there was a possibility of two trains not only appearing on the same length of track but heading straight for each other. The simplest answer was to use a simple baton, known as a staff. The line would be declared open for traffic in one direction, say north, and trains could move freely up that length of track. When it was time for traffic to start moving in the opposite direction, the driver of the last train authorised to go north was given the staff, which was handed in at the far end. Only when it was received there could any train enter the section heading south. In more sophisticated systems, the staff was needed to move points, ensuring that one-way working was maintained.

The basic system of semaphore signals and points operated through levers set in a frame in the signal box and working through mechanical links remained in use for a very long time.

FAR LEFT: **Points can be changed at the trackside by ground frames. This example is part of a wonderful range of equipment on display at the little railway museum at Winchcombe.**

CENTRE AND LEFT: **This signal beside the Ffestiniog railway is not in use, but it is a rare example of the type where if no signal was visible the way was clear. Here the signal is shown at Stop (left) and at Clear with the arm out of sight (right). The shortcomings of this system became all too apparent in 1876 when the signal froze in its slot and the** *Flying Scotsman* **sped past, reading the signal as clear, and ran straight into a coal train.**

There were variations. In France, signals came in a motley array of diamonds and chequer-boards, which probably only the French ever understood. In America, signals scarcely existed over long stretches of track passing through thinly populated areas. Drivers were simply sent telegraphic instructions telling them to continue as far as such and such a junction or loop, and then wait until a certain train came through before proceeding. On more crowded networks, however, the signals ruled. The physical work was made easier by pneumatic systems, electro-magnetic systems and ultimately all-electric systems for moving points and signals. The biggest change came as early as 1872 with the introduction of the track circuit in the signal box, showing which way the different points were set at any one time. It became popular in America, but it was in Britain that the biggest improvement appeared. In 1905, the London Metropolitan District line was electrified, and a young engineer, Bernard H. Peter, installed an illuminated track circuit board. Electric connections were activated by a passing train and the information was relayed to the board, where lights went on and off. The signalman could see from the board just where every train was, without even needing to look out of the window. It has to be said that although it was a huge advance in safety, it was a sad day for many signalmen. Many had joined the railways because they actually liked trains, and a long-distance comradeship had developed between them and the passing footplate crews and guards. Now they were lucky to see a train at all.

The other major change was the gradual replacement of mechanical signals by signal lights. The system was mainly developed in America in the early years of the twentieth century. In Britain and Europe the lights were generally colour coded, in the familiar red, yellow and green that we see on the roads. The alternative was to use white light clusters that could show horizontal, sloping or vertical lines, replicating the information from sema-phore signals. Soon the signal box was transformed. Control of main lines was divided up

BELOW: **The Westinghouse automatic braking system used compressed air to activate the brakes. Air from the central reservoir was passed down pipes along the length of the train. When the brake was applied, the air forced down a piston in a cylinder, (shown between the two wheels) pressing the brake shoes against them.**

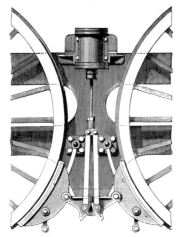

between a small number of large boxes, with track circuits and switches on panels in place of windows and rows of heavy levers. There still remained, and remains, the possibility of human error. A train will only stop at a stop signal if the driver (or, in steam days, the fireman) sees the signal. A better system, using electricity, was introduced as long ago as 1905. A ramp between 40 and 60ft long was placed between the rails near a signal. On top of the ramp was a T-shaped bar which was electrically charged if the next distant signal was at caution, but dead if all was clear. This connected with a plunger on the train, which was pushed up whether the ramp was active or live, so that there was always an audible signal in the cab. A bell rang if all was clear, a suitably alarming siren wailed if it was not. If there was a faulty contact, then the plunger would pick up the danger signal, whatever the state of the road ahead. The final refinement came when this was fully automated. If the driver failed to react appropriately to the sound warning, then the brakes would be applied automatically. The GWR pressed ahead with installing the system throughout their network, but others were less enthusiastic about going to all the trouble and expense. As so often in the past, it took a tragedy to prove the point that safety mattered, and that the adoption of improved technology could save lives.

In December 1937 there was a heavy snowstorm in Scotland. The conditions made signals all but invisible, and the express from Dundee to Glasgow went past a danger signal at Castlecary. Up ahead it was brought to a halt by a goods train, unable to clear the line because the points had been blocked by snow. The local signalman knew nothing about this problem; as far as he was concerned the express had gone past and was safely on its way, and he accepted the next express, from Edinburgh to Glasgow, onto his section.

Again, the danger signals were invisible, and the Edinburgh train ploughed straight into the back of the Dundee train. There were 35 deaths and 179 injuries, and the total would have been much higher if the trains had not been using modern steel coaches which did not telescope. Would the GWR's Automatic Train Control system have prevented the accident? Officers from the London & North-Eastern Railway were invited to a special demonstration on the line between Paddington and Reading. A ten-coach train, hauled by one of the heavy Castle class locomotives, *Earl of Eldon*, was used for the experiment. The train reached a speed of 69mph when the cab warning announced that the distant signal was at caution. The driver was under instructions to ignore it, and with the steam full on the train was automatically brought to a halt in 900 yards, a quarter of a mile short of the supposed danger point. It was a hugely impressive demonstration, but before the system could be widely adopted, Europe went to war and the chance was missed. Unlike some other European countries, Britain still has to adopt automatic train control for the rail network.

Signals are needed throughout the system, no matter how inhospitable the terrain, and there can be few more remote spots than here at Rannoch Moor station on the line from Glasgow to Fort William.

In the twenty-first century signalling and traffic control have moved a long way, and nowhere can this be seen more dramatically than in France's famous fast express service, the TGV. Once the decision had been taken that the TGVs would not be able to operate at their top speeds if they had to follow the old track lines laid down a century earlier, it was possible to rethink the whole question of train control. In the Paris control room, the entire 390-kilometre stretch of the line between Paris and Lyons is laid out on a track circuit, consisting of three curved panels which can be taken in at a glance by the operator. Everything is, of course, computerised. There is a constant check being made between actual journey times and the ideal times of the timetable, and all necessary information is passed to the driver by radio through his headset and by visual display. This is not train control in the old sense, but much closer to air traffic control, where the controller passes on a stream of information for the driver to act upon. It is all a very long way from a uniformed policeman holding out an arm to wave a train to a stop.

Problems of traffic control were not limited to trains dashing down the track. Before they set out on their journeys, the trains had to be assembled with everything in the correct order. This was a particular problem with freight, since a train might have to be made up from an array of different wagons provided by different companies. The movement of freight often seemed chaotic as wagons were shunted around the yard, and the slow trains

Signal systems vary throughout the world and French railways developed their own version based on coloured patterns, as seen here at La Buisson.

made regular stops, perhaps picking up no more than a single wagon from a siding at a lonely station. As traffic increased, so the need developed for major distribution centres, the marshalling yards. There are two distinct operations involved. The first is the reception area, the other the despatch. For example, a colliery may have sent a trainload of coal trucks, which arrive at the reception tracks, but then have to be divided between a number of different destinations. This can be a tiresome business, involving breaking up the train into its separate parts, which in the early days meant uncoupling by hand, recoupling to a shunting engine, taking them off to the appropriate siding and coupling on to the steadily lengthening train destined for one particular line. It all involved a good deal of to-ing and fro-ing, with constant switching of points. It took some time before the system was rationalised, and the breakthrough came with the realization that the railways had access to a free, never-ending source of power: gravity.

As well as traffic movement on the running lines, there has to be internal movement within the yards. At Didcot, locomotives and rolling stock can be moved out of the sheds and onto the line by means of this traverser.

The reception roads and the sorting sidings were separated by a hump. Once wagons had been allocated and sorted, they were taken over the hump to run down the other side, where they could be switched to the appropriate road. As the trucks could pick up a considerable speed, hand operation of the points became all but impossible and power points, which could be controlled from a central tower, were installed early in the twentieth century. It was an improvement, but there were still scores of men rushing around, slowing the trucks down to stop them crashing into the set already in the sidings. That problem was solved in American marshalling yards in the 1920s, with the introduction of the 'car retarder' or 'rail brake'. Metal beams were set at the foot of the hump, one pair to each rail. The controller could activate these so that they moved inwards to grip the wheels and slow the trucks down to the appropriate speed which, if judged correctly, would see them rolling gently to a stop precisely where they were needed. It was a highly skilled job gauging the right speed and applying just the right amount of braking, and the controller in his eyrie was not ideally placed to make the right assessment. There was nothing much that could be done about that until the arrival of the computer age.

A big marshalling yard when rail traffic was at its peak was an extraordinary sight. Carlisle, for example, was the main interchange between the London, Midland and Scottish rail networks. The yard was divided into two parts, the Up Yard and the Down Yard. Altogether the yard was built with eighty-five classification sidings and eighteen retarders, all centrally controlled, and thanks to floodlighting work could carry on day and night. Perhaps nowhere in the rail systems of the world was there a more complex control system than in the great marshalling yards.

CHAPTER 9

SPEED AND POWER

T HE TITLE OF THIS CHAPTER might just as easily have been 'efficiency', since it was only by increasing efficiency that performance could be improved, and this applied to every single component of the locomotive. To put it at its simplest, the first objective of the system is to extract as much heat as possible from the fuel being burned, and then to use that heat as efficiently as possible to create steam at the appropriate pressure. Having got the steam, the next aim is to make the maximum use of it in driving pistons in cylinders, and then to translate that motion to the turning wheels. This is by no means a comprehensive list, but it gives us a starting point.

The fireboxes of early engines were comparatively small and designed for burning coke, which was a requirement forced on the railways by Parliament to avoid the nuisance created by smoke from coal fires. It was not quite the ideal solution, for even if the smoke problem was largely solved, another took its place. Sparks flew from the fire, and it was not unknown for the unfortunate passengers in the cheap, open carriages to find their clothes set alight by flying cinders. There is a solution, a way of minimising the amount of smoke caused by coal. Given a hot enough fire, and enough time for the fumes from that fire to be in contact with hot air, then the carbon that causes the black smoke will be burned away as carbon dioxide. The locomotive firebox was developed throughout the nineteenth century, and although there were to be later improvements, the fundamentals were established. One thing you do not want to do is lose any of the precious heat that the fireman has worked so hard to obtain, and the quickest and easiest way to waste heat is to let it escape into the atmosphere. If your firebox is out in the open air, then heat will be lost through the outer case, so the firebox has two basic components. The outer box is essentially a part of the boiler. Inside this an inner box is installed, generally made of copper in Britain, joined to the outer by stays. Instead of being surrounded by air, it is now surrounded by water, and it is water that requires heating.

The fire is set in the grate of the inner box and needs to reach a high temperature. Just as the extra air provided by a blacksmith's bellows increases the heat in his hearth, so plenty of air needs to be drawn through the fire. As in a domestic fire, some air can be drawn through the grate and controlled by dampers. The locomotive, however, has another source available, which was employed right back at the beginning of the railway age by Trevithick. If the exhaust steam, instead of simply passing straight out to the atmosphere, is turned up the chimney, then it can have a very beneficial effect. At the opposite end of the boiler from the firebox is the smoke box. The gases from the fire collect here and pass up the chimney. The

OPPOSITE: **Gresley's streamlined A4 Pacifics for the LNER are famous as the fastest steam trains in the world. One of the class, *Union of South Africa*, is seen here on a rare mainline outing, heading a special excursion from a 'foreign' station, Waterloo, in 1995.**

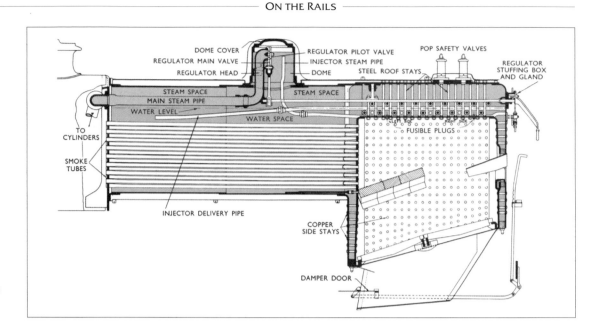

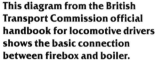

This diagram from the British Transport Commission official handbook for locomotive drivers shows the basic connection between firebox and boiler.

The innards of locomotives are rarely on view when running, but can generally be seen in workshops. Here at the Bluebell it is possible to inspect the construction of both a firebox (TOP) and a boiler (BOTTOM).

steam exhaust pipe also arrives here, through the blast pipe, which is narrowed to a nozzle. The jet of steam carries the firebox gases with it up the chimney, drawing more gases down the boiler pipes and at the same time pulling air in through the grate and firehole door.

A good supply of air ensures a hot fire, but the heat must be properly used, so the hot gases are sent on a long journey inside the firebox by mean of a deflector plate and brick arch. This allows the necessary time for the carbon to be burned off. How well this is achieved depends on proper firing. The ideal is a good even surface, with no holes or dead patches. The control of air to the fire is crucial: too little and you fail to burn off the carbon and the result is billowing black smoke; too much air and heat is wasted, and there will be no smoke at all coming from the chimney. A good fireman will have a shallow bed of coal, just deep enough to ensure regular combustion, and a well-regulated air supply, so that when he looks out of the cab he will see grey smoke drifting down the train. The golden rule for firing is 'little and often', sometimes also known as 'light and bright'.

The other essential feature of any boiler is that it should contain water. It may seem obvious, but ensuring that there is just the right quantity of water in the boiler is not as easy as it sounds. The first thing the fireman needs to know is how much water there is to begin with, for he has no way of seeing through the metal case. The first, primitive method was to use a set of test taps, but that was replaced by the water gauge, in which the water level is always the same as in the boiler itself. If water levels drop, there is a danger that the crown of the firebox could become uncovered, with disastrous results. There is a fall-back position for safety. Fusible lead plugs are set in the roof of the firebox which, if they get too hot, melt and allow water and steam onto the fire, dowsing it. This is not something any fireman wants to see happen. So water levels have to be kept up. Again, in the early days, the only solution was to stop, wait for the boiler to cool down, top it up and carry on again. In large locomotives, a water tank is carried in the tender, and in smaller locomotives it is either bent over the boiler top like a saddle – the saddle tank engine – or set on either side of the boiler. The problem then is how to get the water from the tank to the boiler. The answer was eventually found: the steam ejector. Steam under pressure is allowed to escape through a cone, inserted inside another cone connected to the water supply. As the steam shoots out of the nozzle, it collects water as it goes, and both are passed across a short gap to a delivery cone connected to the boiler. In this way, the fireman can ensure that water levels in the boiler are always exactly as they should be.

It is not enough just to use heat to turn water into steam. The locomotive needs high-pressure steam. The more heat added to the steam, the more it will try to expand, but as the boiler is a closed unit that is impossible and the pressure inexorably rises. At boiling point, the steam will be at atmospheric pressure and the pressure gauge will read zero, but as the temperature climbs so too does the pressure shown on the gauge. At a temperature of about 200°C (400°F), the pressure gauge will have a reading of 250 pounds per square inch. That need not be the end of the matter. If the steam is heated again without any contact with water, its temperature will rise – it will be superheated. This has the advantage that any water still trapped in the steam will be evaporated, further increasing the pressure and, just as importantly, ensuring that no water droplets make their way to the cylinders. Really efficient superheaters were first designed by Wilhelm Schmidt in Germany at the very end of the nineteenth century. There is, of course, always the possibility of having more high-pressure steam than is actually needed to work the engine at any one time, for example when the engine is stopped. Safety valves lift when the pressure gets too high and blow the excess away with clouds of vapour and high-pitched shrieks to advertise the fact that calculations have gone a little astray on the footplate, or that the train has been unexpectedly stopped when it was hoping to steam on. When I used to fire a small ship's boiler, the penalty for blowing the safety was to stand a drink for everyone else on board – a great encouragement not to waste steam and expensive fuel!

The next stage in the process of making an engine work is to supply the steam to the working parts. A familiar feature of steam locomotives is the dome on top of the boiler, between the chimney and the cab. This contains steam, the steam pipe and the regulator

The Walschaerts valve gear was first introduced in Belgium in 1844. It spread rapidly throughout Europe, but was not used in Britain until 1878. Being set outside the frame it proved much easier to maintain than Stephenson's inside gear.

valve, opened and closed by the regulator in the cab. Starting a locomotive is one of the more skilled operations for a driver: it should be smooth and regular. Get it wrong, and there is either an embarrassing wheel spin or a jerky motion. There has to be enough steam power to overcome inertia, but not too much. One adaptation that made this task easier was the vertical slide regulator. On starting, the regulator uncovers two small ports to allow steam into the steam pipe, and then, in normal running, two larger ports are uncovered and the smaller covered up again. There was also a steady improvement in the valve gear that controls the movement of steam into and out of the cylinder. The Stephenson gear was popular in Britain, but was challenged by the gear invented by the Belgian engineer Eugene Walschaerts in 1844. This was able to provide a longer travelling valve than the Stephenson, which improved control of the cut off, a particular advantage when superheating was introduced and the steam needed to work expansively in the cylinder for as long as possible. In the Stephenson valve, too much steam entered into the cylinder before cut off at high pressures, making for less efficient working.

A variety of cylinder positions were tried over the years, inside and outside the frame, towards the front or at the back, and attempts were made to make even better use of the steam. One idea developed first for stationary engines and then widely adapted for marine engines was compounding. Steam leaving the cylinder is still under pressure, and could be passed on to a second cylinder with a larger diameter than the first. The change in size from small to large cylinder was necessary to compensate for the reduced pressure. Compounding was no problem for stationary engines in their roomy engine houses, and space could be found in a ship's engine room for an extra cylinder. Finding space on a locomotive was more problematic. In France, Anatole Mallet designed a compound engine for the Bayonne and Biarritz Railway in 1876, with just one high-pressure cylinder exhausting into a low-pressure cylinder. In Germany, the Hanover State Railways introduced a compound with two high-pressure cylinders in 1880. Over the years, variations included three-cylinder engines, with one low-pressure and two high-pressure cylinders, and four-cylinder engines. There was even a locomotive which used triple expansion, the steam going successively into three cylinders: high, middle and low pressure. Compounding was said to increase fuel efficiency, and French railways remained the most enthusiastic users of the technique. One of the most important engineers to develop compounds was André Chapelon working in France in the 1920s, though the increased efficiency of his locomotives was less due to compounding than his realization that power was being wasted in the transfer of steam from boiler to cylinders. He was a pioneer in undertaking a scientific investigation of steam flow, and when his results were applied to a four-cylinder compound on the Paris-Orleans Railway, he was able to report an outstanding 50 percent improvement in output. His redesigned steam passages and other improvements were seized on just as eagerly by designers of simple, uncompounded locomotives.

Making changes in design is the most obvious way in which performance of locomotives was improved, but that alone is not sufficient. The technology for translating design into working parts also has to exist. The biggest change came with the introduction of accurate machine tools. In the early nineteenth century, for example, producing a flat surface had been done by hand; by mid-century machines could do the same work faster, more accurately and considerably more cheaply. Joseph Whitworth, one of the key figures in the revolution in machine tools, calculated in 1856 that the cost of producing a plane surface had been over a hundred times greater thirty years earlier than it was in his day. It was Whitworth who introduced standard screw threads so that nuts and bolts could be mass produced and would be interchangeable, a huge advantage in complex machines such as locomotives. James Nasmyth's steam hammer made metal-forging far more precise, and so the list goes on. It seems remarkable today just how crude some parts of a locomotive were in the early days. To ensure a steam-tight fit for the piston in the cylinder, it was packed with hemp just as it had been a century before in the early beam engines. In 1854 John Ramsbottom from the Grand Junction Railway Works at Crewe read a paper to the Institution of Mechanical Engineers describing his successful experiments with brass piston rings to replace the hemp. Brass was soon replaced by iron rings set in slots at the edge of the piston. Being springy, they automatically pushed outward against the cylinder wall to create a seal. This is a classic example of a very simple device making a very big difference. And it was not just the way in which materials were used that made a difference; the materials themselves changed. The changes in the metal industry made available mild steel, which combined the best qualities of cast and wrought iron. It could be cast like the one and rolled into bars and sheets like the other, and was more hard wearing than either of them. Steel was also to provide an essential component for all later locomotives, with the introduction of the steel tyre. The steady improvement in the steam locomotive was the result of a whole range of interconnecting factors.

Although development was continuous from the days of the first steam locomotive right through to the present day, the best way to get some idea of the rich variety of locomotives is to look at a few examples from around the world. Surveys such as this tend to concentrate on the glamorous expresses, dashing along at high speed with carriageloads of delighted passengers. They are certainly not going to be ignored here, but it is also worth pointing out that some of the most powerful locomotives ever built were designed for freight and that arguably the most successful engines in terms of numbers and work load are the little tank engines and other industrial locomotives.

In Britain, the search for the perfect passenger locomotive took many forms. Speed was an attraction certainly, but passengers were not going to be impressed if they were shaken until their teeth rattled just to save a minute or two on the journey. The most popular wheel arrangement in the mid-nineteenth century was the 2-4-0, but a new invention inspired one engineer, Patrick Stirling, to try something different. This new invention was the steam sander, which shot a stream of sand in front of the drive wheels for good adhesion, making it much easier to start a locomotive when the rails were wet or icy. Engineers had known for some time that bigger wheels meant higher possible speeds but poorer adhesion, hence a popular arrangement was to have two sets of comparatively small wheels coupled together.

In 1866 Stirling took charge of locomotive design for the Great Northern Railway, and he realized that, thanks to the sander, this limitation had become less important. His most famous locomotive was the 4-2-2 Stirling Single, so called because of its single pair of drive wheels, but what drive wheels they were! They were 8ft in diameter and helped make the Single one of the fastest, if not the fastest, engines of the day. It was not just fast, it was supremely elegant, and one can still admire Number 1 at the National Railway Museum in York. The huge circles of the driving wheels set the pattern for a series of curves carried throughout the engine. Even when seen front on, the effect is equally graceful, with the front cover for the outside cylinders set in a sweeping curve. Add to that a dashing livery, with every one of those sinuous curves emphasized by bold red and yellow lining and the Single looks the racer that it was. It is also, for some, including the author, one of the most beautiful locomotives ever built. Stirling remained at the GNR until his death in 1895 in his seventy-fifth year, and for his memorial he was paid the greatest compliment any engineer could ask for. A fountain was erected at the Doncaster works, paid for not by the directors or the shareholders but by the men who really knew how good his engines were – the drivers and firemen.

Patrick Stirling's famous Single, so called because of its large single set of driving wheels, was one of the fastest locomotives of the 19th century. It is seen here on the Great Central Railway.

The Great Northern Railway was engaged in fierce competition with the London & North Western Railway for the profitable passenger trade between London and Scotland. The GNR's trains ran out of King's Cross up the east coast and the L&NWR ran up the west coast from Euston. The Stirling Singles were involved in 1895 in a record-breaking run, the first covering the leg from London to Grantham, the second taking over to continue the next leg to York. The average speed for the whole 188-mile journey was a remarkable 64mph. But the finest run in what became known as the Races to the North went to the other side, in a gallop to Aberdeen on 22 August 1895, when the entire 540-mile journey took just 512 minutes, or eight and a half hours. The fastest leg of all, from Crewe to Carlisle, which included the ascent of the notorious Shap bank, went to a train headed by another star of the York collection, *Hardwicke*. With driver Robinson's hand on the regulator, the engine charged along at a good speed, never dropping below 65mph before Shap slowed progress down to a speed of 58mph at the summit. That was more than matched by the times on the other side where the leg from Penrith to Carlisle was recorded at nearly 75mph. *Hardwicke* is more conventional, with the familiar 2-4-0 arrangement, but although it is heavy it gives little away in elegance to the Single. Edward Fletcher, the designer, could claim a long and excellent railway pedigree. He actually worked with the Stephensons on the construction of *Rocket*, and at the age of 23 he had the honour of driving another famous, and preserved, locomotive, *Invicta*, at the opening of the Canterbury & Whitstable Railway in 1830.

The English engineer Thomas Russell Crampton did a great deal of his work for French and German railways. His express singles could scarcely be less like those of Stirling as far as appearance was concerned, but proved their worth both in terms of speed and durability, though the early versions look alarmingly flimsy. *Die Pfalz*, built for the Palatinate Railway, is a 4-2-0, with the driving wheels set right alongside the cab. Cylinders, cranks and gear are all outside the frame, which makes for very easy access, even if the engine does not have the

The Crompton-style locomotive *Pfalz*, with big single drive wheels set right at the back of the frame, was built for the Bavarian Palatine Railway in 1853.

almost streamlined elegance of a Stirling. The tall thin chimney gives the engine a very distinctive air, and a replica is now on show in the Transport Museum at Nuremberg.

Speed was not only desirable in itself but a valuable selling point for competing railways, and as the nineteenth century drew to a close it was obvious that the first 100-mile-an-hour run could not be far away. William Dean moved to the GWR Swindon works as superintendent in 1877 and designed his own elegant 4-2-2 singles, though it was his 0-6-0 goods engine for which the company had most cause to be grateful. This sturdy class did stalwart work for many decades. He was also aware of the need for fast passenger expresses, and he was joined in the 1890s by an enthusiastic assistant, George Churchward. Together they planned a new series of 4-4-0s with 6ft 8in coupled wheels. A new and revolutionary feature was the tapered boiler, which increased the water space at the firebox end of the barrel. The new engines were known as the City Class, because they were given names derived from the various cathedral cities served by the GWR. By the time they came into service, Dean had retired and Churchward was in charge. On 9 May 1904, the Ocean Mail left Plymouth for Bristol, with *City of Truro* at the head. Descending Wellington Bank, the speed was recorded at 102.3 miles an hour. The magic number had been reached at last, and the speed record was to stay intact until 1935.

A problem faced by all builders of fast locomotives was that of increasing size while still maintaining smooth running. The answer was to provide more wheels, which could be coupled to drive the engine as well as to distribute the load. The problem was particularly acute in America, with its long runs and often difficult terrain. A start was made with the 4-4-2s, which became known as Atlantics. They still only had two pairs of coupled wheels, but were well balanced and ideal for hauling comparatively short trains at high speeds. When extra power was needed, an extra pair of driving wheels could be added but still only on five axles,

A fine array of GWR locomotives on display at Didcot; they are, from left to right, *Pendennis Castle, Earl Bathurst, King Edward I, Hinderton Hall* and *Burton Agnes Hall*.

A basic footplate with the robust regulator in the centre, flanked by water gauges, steam pressure and vacuum gauges above and reverser to the right.

hence the 2-6-2 'Prairies'. In time it was recognized that with the extra power there was now a need for more stability and at the beginning of the twentieth century the famous 4-6-2 'Pacifics' were introduced. Among the best of these were the two-cylinder K-class engines built for the Pennsylvania Railroad. The first experimental model was delivered by the locomotive manufacturers in 1907, and by 1914 improvements led to the K4s, mainly built by Baldwin or in the company's own workshops. These were magnificent engines, capable of speeds of 75mph, and over the years more than four hundred were built, the last being retired from service as late as 1957. That is a quite extraordinary record for one class of locomotive on one railway. One of the few survivors from this class is preserved at the Railroad Museum of Pennsylvania at Strasburg, together with other superb locomotives. Pacifics soon ousted the Atlantics for high-speed, and high-prestige, runs.

Pacifics were extremely popular not only for American expresses, but also for export. Even countries that did not buy Pacifics from America soon set about designing their own. Perhaps the most famous of all the engineers who turned their talents to designing Pacifics was the engineer of the Great Northern Railway in Britain, Sir Nigel Gresley. His first effort was the *Great Northern* of 1922. It was big and powerful but looked beautifully neat and tidy, with two outside cylinders on view, and a third tucked away beneath the boiler. Other engineers, notably Churchward on the GWR, were using pressures as high as 225 psi and cylinders up to 18 1/2 inches diameter coupled with 10-inch piston valves, while Gresley's new locomotive was more modest. It worked at 180 psi, and although cylinders were 20 inches in diameter, the valves were a comparatively small eight inches, which must have limited the steam flow to some extent. One new feature made the locomotive particularly appealing to footplate crew: it had a big cab, with side windows and a previously unimaginable luxury – not just a seat for the driver, but a padded seat.

The new locomotive went through its tests with ease, proving itself capable of handling heavy trains at high speeds. The Pacifics had arrived, and Gresley was soon busy making improvements. In the 1930s, a new class of A1 Pacifics appeared, including the famous *Flying Scotsman*, and the succession culminated with the A4s. Never has a more mundane name been applied to a more romantic set of locomotives, but most passengers were not interested in letters and numbers. The very first which went into service in September 1935 had more than just a name, it had a name to fire the imagination. This was *Silver Link,* and it was a sensation. In essence this was a development of earlier Gresley Pacifics, though with any number of technical improvements, such as the use of a double blast pipe and double chimney, all adding together to create a more efficient engine. But it looked entirely new. For over a hundred years, locomotives had appeared with everything on show, so that the physical reality of a vast boiler providing steam through pipes and gears to cylinders was easily apparent. Not any more: now everything was encased in a sleek, metallic shell, carefully shaped to reduce air resistance. It looked startlingly modern, yet the idea was not entirely original. Gresley had visited France and seen a sleek new diesel rail car designed by a man better known for cars on the road than for cars on rails, Ettore Bugatti. In fact, Bugatti had taken out his first patent for a rail car as early as 1911, but the design for French railways was sketched out in 1931. It inspired Gresley and the result was to be seen on his new engine. *Silver Link* was streamlined. The engine was not merely capable of high speeds, but even more importantly it proved capable of maintaining high speeds over long distances. Speeds of over 100mph were recorded not just on downhill runs, but over several miles of undulating track. This was particularly notable on the big experimental run of 27 September 1935, when *Silver Link* maintained an average speed of almost 108mph on the far from level track

A busy scene at Derby locomotive shed in 1929. Originally this was the heart of the Midland Railway empire, but by that time it had been absorbed into the LMS.

One of the great workhorses of the steam age, an LMS Black 5 is seen here in a cloud of spray as it picks up water from the trough set between the rails.

between Biggleswade and Huntingdon. The search for speed famously culminated in the run of 3 July 1938, when the streamlined A4 *Mallard* reached a top speed of 126mph, a record for steam locomotives that has never been surpassed.

Mallard is safely preserved at the National Railway Museum in York, but other A4s have also been preserved and are occasionally allowed out to show a new generation just how beautiful a steam locomotive could be. Sadly, the chance of opening the regulator and letting the old engines fly has gone, but even so there is still a thrill in seeing the engines out on the rails, or better still riding behind one on a steam special. There is something about the steady, throaty beat of the double exhaust that seems to speak of contained power, and few modern engines can offer a smoother ride.

In moving freight, speed is less of a concern than power. What makes the money is the ability to haul really heavy loads. In America, while the Pacifics were dashing around the country at speed, freight trains trundled along at a more stately pace, seldom topping the 30mph mark, and often being held up as passenger trains were given priority. The result was that, even at the beginning of the twentieth century, average speeds over long journeys were scarcely more than 10mph – no more than they had been at the start of the railway age. But by then a new competitor was starting to make a mark on the world of transport: the motor truck, which offered door-to-door deliveries. This became particularly important at the end of the First World War, when a lot of cheap, army surplus vehicles became available. One line that responded intelligently was the New York Central, anxious to protect its most important route between New York and Chicago. They doubled the tracks, so that there were now two tracks for passenger traffic and another two for freight. Now that freight would no longer have to be held up for hours waiting for the aristocrats of the railway world to sail by, there was an incentive to improve performance. Freight locomotives would become bigger, faster and more powerful.

LEFT: *Mallard*, photographed in 1938, the year that it broke the world speed record for steam locomotives

BELOW: The streamlined American locomotives of the 1930s seemed to epitomise power and modernity, as seen here in Union Pacific locomotive 7002.

The difficulty engineers faced was in reconciling the needs of power for big loads with speed. The expresses had large-diameter drive wheels, but these were not able to deliver the power. So improvement meant adding more coupled drive wheels. Various large engines were already in use in the late nineteenth century on the New York Central, including 2-6-6-2 Mallets and immense 2-10-2s, the Santa Fes, but these were ponderous beasts. The Mallets had a maximum speed of around 20mph and the Santa Fes were little better. An enormous effort was needed just to move the heavy rods that were required to turn five pairs of drive wheels, and that meant a lot of steam from a big, efficient boiler. It was time for a rethink. The American manufacturer Lima had prospered during the First World War and was anxious to compete with the big names such as Baldwin. The latter had manufactured a new type of 2-8-2 locomotive for Japan in 1897, and after that engines with this new wheel arrangement were known as Mikados. The first success was the H-10 class which had a huge boiler capacity, making it the most powerful freight locomotive of its day. The engineer, Will Woodward, set about making improvements, including the installation of a boiler feed water heater and a much bigger firebox. To add support at the rear end, an extra pair of wheels was added to turn the Mikado into a 2-8-4. Woodward arranged a demonstration on the Boston & Albany line to which the directors of the New York Central were invited. An H-10 Mikado set off with a heavy load, and one hour later the new 2-8-4 set off in pursuit with an even heavier load – and overtook the H-10. It even used less fuel. The new engine had beaten what was then regarded as the finest freight locomotive in America on every count – power, speed and economy.

Two American 4-8-2s head a Union Pacific train through Granite Canyon, Wyoming in 1935. It is a passenger train, not a heavy goods, but still required to be double headed to overcome the steep grades.

This process of steady enlargement was to culminate in the Woodward 2-10-4s, designed for the Texas & Pacific, which combined huge boilers with very high pressure. Locomotive engineers went on experimenting with different wheel arrangements to meet different requirements. The Chesapeake & Ohio, for example, had to cope with crossings of the Allegheny Mountains, and in 1910 they introduced 4-8-2s, known appropriately as Mountain Class. These monsters were remarkably successful and were capable of long runs at good speeds. The coast-to-coast specials were equipped with particularly large tenders, able to hold 31½ tons of coal and over 22,000 gallons of water. Locomotives, it seemed, were destined to go on increasing in size forever, but there comes a point when things get too big, and that point was certainly reached in Russia, where they experimented with startlingly huge 4-14-4 locomotives. That was just too much for any conventional locomotive cylinder arrangement to cope with, and if there were to be any further advances a new approach was needed.

A Mallet type of compound had been built in America in 1904 for the Baltimore & Ohio by the American Locomotive Company, Alco, in 1904. This articulated locomotive started with steam pressure at 235 psi which went to the 20-inch-diameter high-pressure cylinders, and the exhaust steam was passed on to the 32-inch low-pressure cylinders. The wheel arrangement was 0-6-6-0 and it worked well on specialist freight lines where its snail-like progress caused no great inconvenience. The advantages of the articulated engine were clear, but a feeling was

In the 1940s, Union Pacific introduced a new articulated locomotive, a 4-8-8-4, specifically for the hard crossing of the mountains between Cheyenne and Salt Lake City, hauling freight trains up to a mile long. They became known simply as Big Boys, and the photograph shows the engine hard at work at Weber Canyon.

developing among engineers that the system could be more efficiently applied to simple engines, without the problems caused by compounding. These were to become the true giants of the steam age, and they came with all kinds of modern improvements, including super-heaters and mechanical stokers. The biggest preserved locomotive in the world is to be found at Steamtown, Scranton, Pennsylvania. The name 'Big Boy' scarcely seems adequate to describe this 4-8-8-4 engine, which saw out its working life with the Union Pacific.

America was by no means the only country in the world to opt for steam giants, though some were rather later arriving on the scene. China had a slow and far from trouble-free entry into the railway world. The first venture opened in 1876, thinly disguised as the work of the Woosung Road Company – a road which just happened to have rails and locomotives. The Chinese, who had not wanted it in the first place, declared that if it really was a road then anyone could use it. The inevitable accident soon occurred, and in 1877 the tracks were pulled up. The next railway was built to serve the coalfields of Northern China. To placate local feeling the first locomotive was built on the spot, more or less from scrapyard junk. There was a boiler from an old portable engine, wheels from no one could remember where and odd pipes and valves and pistons from all over the place. Duly christened *Rocket of China*, it emerged in all its unlikely glory on 9 June 1881, which just happened to be the centenary of George Stephenson's birth. It was a start, but for the next forty years progress was slowed by war and political upheaval.

In the 1930s, China was ready to move forward again and locomotives were needed to work the line under construction between Guangzhou and Wuhan, a difficult route that crossed a mountain range, rising to a height of over 7000ft. The result was a line with gradients of up to 1 in 80 and some sharp bends. The British had collected reparation money after the Boxer Rebellion of 1900, but were prepared to return it in 1931 provided the funds were invested in useful ventures to be overseen by British and Chinese Trustees. Some of the money went to completing the railway, and the job of supplying suitable locomotives went to Britain. All the latest technology was included, and Chapelon was consulted on the important matter of steam flow. Design work was completed in 1933 and the first locomotives were built at the Vulcan Foundry in England. They were 4-8-4s and when they were tested in China they proved more than adequate for normal passenger service, and could take larger freight loads, if at a more modest pace. In 1980 the Chinese government agreed to send one of these very imposing engines back to Britain for display at York.

That might be thought to mark a familiar end to the story, as the old steam workhorses were put out to pasture. But China had not yet finished with steam. Here was a country without oil, where electricity was expensive, but with abundant supplies of coal. While others were scrapping their steam engines, China was building new ones. In 1959 a new locomotive works was opened at Datong, high in the hills of Mongolia to the west of Beijing. It was to build steam locomotives, largely using designs based on engines in what was then the Soviet Union. The most successful was the Qianjin Class, universally known as QJs. These are 2-10-2 freight locomotives which first appeared in 1965 and have been going strong ever since. The Jitong Railway not only has over a hundred of these, but in 2003 even acquired ten more. Even more surprisingly, an announcement was made in the same year that the QJs were also

going to be brought back to the line for passenger services. China is now one of the few places left in the world where immense steam engines can still be seen, not as demonstration pieces to impress tourists, but working as they were always meant to work.

The locomotives of China can be seen as the very end of two centuries of steam development that began with Richard Trevithick. No machine has ever attracted such loving support as the steam locomotive. However complex individual parts may be, it has an elemental simplicity. Fuel is burned to heat water and the resulting steam expands to drive the machinery. Anyone can see just what is happening, unlike the modern motor car where the engine is normally hidden out of sight, at least until it goes wrong. And those who have had the opportunity to drive or fire an engine will know that there is real skill involved, an absolute necessity to be in tune with the mechanism. To give just one example: as a locomotive pulls away at the start of a run, it is not readings on dials that tell the driver how to control the regulator, but the sound of the beat. There is a moment when you feel that just the right time has arrived to lift the lever a touch higher and encourage the beast to ease its load into smooth motion. If sentiment ruled the world, we would probably have the steam locomotive still, but it does not. A sad truth has to be admitted: for all its many qualities, the steam engine is inefficient in terms of the percentage of energy produced by the fire in relation to work actually done. It takes a long time to get ready before it can do anything at all and a long time to bed down when the work is done. It consumes a great deal of energy in the course of a working day, even when it is not actually going anywhere. It may appeal to the enthusiasts, but to accountants and engineers it is a good deal less attractive. Even before the nineteenth century had come to an end, the hunt was on for other forms of motive power.

When railways reached China, it was obvious that big locomotives would be needed to cope with the huge distances and rugged terrain. This photograph taken at Hsu Chou Fou in the 1890s shows a locomotive built for the Tientsin Pukow Railway. British engineers came to supply their expertise, and their bungalow can be seen on the hill in the background.

CHAPTER 10

BEYOND THE STEAM AGE

MICHAEL FARADAY DISCOVERED how to make use of the fact that passing an electric current from a battery through a wire could make a magnet move, and – conversely – that rotating a magnet could create a current in a wire. The first was to lead to the electric motor, the second to the dynamo. Not everyone could see the use of electricity, other than as an amusing toy. William Gladstone questioned the scientist on the matter, and received just the answer to appeal to a politician: 'One day, Sir, you may tax it.' George Stephenson, however, was rather more perceptive than Gladstone and in his old age declared that one day electricity would be the most important power source in the world. He was right, but it was not to happen in his lifetime, nor even in that of his son. Even though Faraday had demonstrated a crude electric motor as early as 1821, over half a century was to pass before it became a reality that could be put to practical use. One man who did as much as anyone to develop the use of electrical power was the German scientist and engineer Werner von Siemens. In 1879, he demonstrated the world's first practical electric locomotive at the Berlin Trade Exhibition. The tiny little 3hp engine gave passenger rides, and the original is now preserved in Munich. Siemens' engine was brought over to Britain in 1881 and demonstrated at the Crystal Palace. The idea rapidly moved on from exhibitions to use in a regular public transport system.

Among the first to be attracted by the idea of the electric railway was Magnus Volk of Brighton. His father was a clockmaker from Germany who settled in Britain, where Magnus was born. He took an early interest in electricity, producing strange devices such as the 'Parlour Telegraph Set' and more mundane electric bells. When he married in 1870 he equipped his house with electric lights and telephones, the first in the town. Brighton Corporation was sufficiently impressed to give him the contract for lighting the Royal Pavilion. Volk then established himself as a supplier of telegraphic equipment, and in 1883, when an order fell through, he found himself with a few items of equipment for which he had no immediate use: a small electric motor, a dynamo and a Crossley

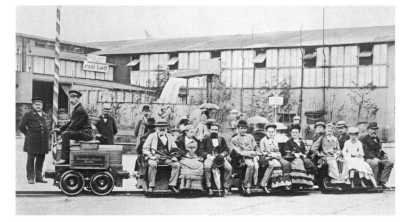

ABOVE: **The world's first electric locomotive was built by Werner Von Siemens and demonstrated at the Berlin Trade Exhibition in 1879. It is shown here, a diminutive engine, with its train full of passengers.**

OPPOSITE: **If *Mallard* came to epitomise speed in the first half of the 20th century, then the Japanese Bullet Trains did so in the second half. One can see how the train got its name, but this is more properly known as the Nozomi 500 *Shinkansen*.**

RIGHT: **Magnus Volk established the world's first public railway to be run by electricity at Brighton in 1883. Here it is at the start of what has proved a long career, for the line is still in use today.**

BELOW: **Volk's other great idea proved a lot less successful. What looks like a section of pier mysteriously cast adrift is in fact an electric train on stilts, the wheels resting on underwater tracks.**

gas engine. The latter had been used to generate electricity, but Brighton had just acquired its own main supply, so that was now superfluous. He realized, however, that putting this odd collection of pieces together would enable him both to build an electric railway and to generate the power to run it. In June 1883, Volk wrote to the town clerk to ask for permission to run a 2ft-gauge passenger railway along the seafront, and when this proved a success, he established a permanent line, Volk's Electric Railway. It still runs today, the oldest electric railway in the world.

The railway was built to a 2ft 8½in gauge. The gas engine worked a Siemens dynamo, to produce electricity at 40 amps and 60 volts, with power being supplied through the two rails to a 6hp Siemens engine. The drive was supplied through a belt to one axle, giving a very modest running speed of maximum 10mph. There were open carriages and a special non-smoking saloon. This was a very exotic creation, with an interior decorated by a young lady from the Brighton College of Art. It was not so much a saloon as a salon, with a painted ceiling, silk curtains, padded seats and gilt-framed mirrors. Sadly, the modern rolling stock is rather more spartan, but the little line has been steadily extended and improved over the years.

It is not quite the end of the Volk story. He would have liked to extend his electric railway round the coast to Rottingdean, but any conventional railway would have had to climb the cliffs separating the two, or be carried on embankments and viaducts round the base of the cliffs. The first alternative would have been wholly impractical, the second ruinously expensive, but Volk was not going to be defeated. His novel idea was to lay the railway on the seabed, so that it could easily go round the foot of the cliffs. There were a few difficulties to overcome, most notably how to run the service at high tide when the tracks would be submerged. Volk's solution was, in effect, to design a railway on stilts, with the wheels at the foot of the long legs and the carriage riding high above them. Again it was to be powered by electricity, but this time taking its power from overhead lines, like an electric tram. It must rank as one of the world's oddest railways. The saloon was even more elaborately decorated than that of the electric railway, looking like a Victorian conservatory, complete with stained-glass windows. It would not have looked out of place attached to a grand country house, but this conservatory was travelling above the waves on spidery metal legs. It was destined to last less than a decade, never more than a curiosity, though a delightful one. The next important application of electric power to the railways was not to come high above the sea, but deep underground.

The first underground railway had been worked by steam locomotives, but this was never a very satisfactory solution. When plans were going forward for the City & South London Railway, the original intention had been to use cables to haul the trains along the track. Clean, efficient electrical power provided a welcome alternative. The first plan was to put electric motors inside the coaches, but the Board of Trade showed no enthusiasm for the idea. Somehow, the idea of having a motor so close to the passengers seemed altogether too radical. So separate locomotives were constructed, fifty-two of them between 1889 and 1901. One of the less successful innovations came when the time arrived to design carriages. It was argued that as there were no views to enjoy, windows would be a pointless luxury. The only way passengers could tell when they had reached their stop was to listen out for the guard bawling out the station name. These claustrophobic coaches were known as 'padded cells'.

Electric traction provided a solution to the problem of running underground railways without all the difficulties caused by steam engines. It all began on the City & South London Railway, which opened in 1890.

The use of electricity for powering city transport had an obvious appeal, a great improvement on smoky steam locomotives. The Liverpool Overhead Railway followed hard on the heels of the rapidly developing underground system, with work starting in 1893. It offered a wonderful bird's eye view of what was once one of the country's biggest dock complexes, enabling passengers to look down on cargo ships or mighty Cunard liners. It closed in the 1950s, but the concept of high-level electrified lines for cities was to be reborn in the 1990s. Early in the twentieth century, however, the underground electric system seemed to offer the perfect solution to urban travel. The Paris Metro and the Berlin U-Bahn were built in 1900 and 1902 respectively, but not everyone was convinced by the electric tube train. The Glasgow subway system was very advanced in terms of civil engineering, with lines twice passing under the Clyde, but when it opened in 1896, the cars were hauled by cable. The system was only abandoned in 1935 when the cables were scrapped in favour of the familiar system of other underground railways, with power supplied through a live third rail.

The City & South London decided that because there was nothing to see in the tunnels, there was no need to put windows in the carriages. The result was these grim-looking coaches at Stockwell station.

The alternative method of providing power was via overhead cables. As with the underground, the system was first used for city transport in the electric tramway. Tramways themselves were already a familiar part of city life. The idea of adapting the horse omnibus by running it on a railed track was established in the Bowery, New York as early as 1832 and it was only a matter of time before some form of mechanisation came in. One of the pioneering lines in Britain was the Wantage Tramway. Wantage is a small market town in Oxfordshire, and although it was home to the Wantage Engineering Company, manufacturers of traction engines, the Great Western Railway declined to build a branch line. The best they could offer was Wantage Road Station, the name 'Road' attached to a station name being a sure indication that although it was on the road to somewhere, it was still some miles away from anywhere the passengers actually wanted to be. In the case of Wantage, it was a two-and-a-half-mile trip from the station to the town. A horse bus provided an inadequate and exorbitantly expensive service into Wantage itself. So plans were laid to open a tramway beside the road, still using horses, but, as a popular rhyme of the day pointed out, considerably cheaper than the bus on the road, which cost a full shilling ('bob').

From the station to Wantage an omnibus runs –
A small one – now pray do not laugh,
When I tell you the fare they charge over there
Is a 'bob' for two miles and a half.

They think bye and bye the rail will be nigh,
And then at the bus they will laugh;
They will ride in good style at a penny a mile
And no 'bobs' for two miles and a half.

Soon after the 1875 opening, the horse tram was replaced by a steam tram, based on a design by John Grantham. The steam tram itself looked like a conventional four-wheeled carriage, apart from the chimney it spouted at the centre, indicating the position of the little engine. The Wantage tram provided a good service, with the little trains chugging along beside the main road right through to 1946, steam-powered to the end. It kept going so long simply because the lines ran out in the country, causing very little inconvenience. A system that worked in the country could not necessarily be adapted to the town or city streets. The steam tramway suffered from exactly the same problem as the Metropolitan Railway: smoke. Electricity provided the answer. The power stations burned coal and created every bit as much smoke as an entire fleet of steam locomotives, but they could be built on the outskirts of towns, where no one was greatly concerned about this.

In 1884, a pair of four-wheeled tramcars, with what appears to be a very fragile overhead connection, were hooked together and set off on their inaugural run at Frankfurt-am-Main. The driver had an open compartment at the front with a simple lever for control and a hand bell. It was the start of a whole new system of urban transport. It does not look, and in that form certainly was not, a system that might find a place in the greater world of railways, a world of express passenger trains and heavy freights. But cleanliness was a factor to take into account in places other than just city streets. The Camden-Waverley tunnel carried four miles of Baltimore & Ohio tracks under the city of Baltimore. It was heavily used and fumes were becoming increasingly problematical. The decision was taken to elec-

ABOVE: **A new generation of tramways appeared in the 19th century, not serving industry but as light passenger services. The Wantage tram ran from the mainline station for two-and-a-half miles into the town.**

BELOW: **Just as electricity had provided the answer for underground railways, now it proved ideal for urban trams. The first electric trams taking their power from overhead lines ran between Frankfurt-am-Main and Offenbach in 1884 and the opening naturally attracted a great deal of interest.**

trify the route through the tunnel. The power supply system used on urban tramways was clearly inadequate for a mainline railway, so a new system was devised using a light, suspended conductor rail, connecting with a pantograph mounted on one of the two linked locomotives. It was a modest beginning, but it opened the way to the spread of electrification.

The electric locomotive is more efficient than the steam locomotive, but it has its own disadvantage: it requires an external power source. At the end of the nineteenth century, there were no national grid systems to tap into. If a railway wanted to use electricity, then it had to generate it. This was no great problem in the mountainous areas of Europe, such as the Alps, where hydro-electric power was comparatively easily and cheaply obtained. As early as 1901, Italy was experimenting with electrification between Milan and Varese and down the Valtellino Valley. Early motorised coaches on these lines were an interesting mixture of the old and the new. Outside, they were quite sleekly modern, but the interior was fussily Victorian. The first major mainline route in the Alps to be electrified was the Bern-Loetschberg-Simplon in 1910. Heavy 2-10-2 locomotives were introduced which were little more than square boxes on wheels, fitted with double pantographs. They were, however, considerably more attractive than some other electric locomotives, such as the 'crocodiles' brought into use in Austria and Switzerland in the early twentieth century. These got their name from the combination of the high cab with the double pantograph on the roof, and the long, low snout of the motor unit. They could probably count as the ugliest locomotives ever built.

The first main line to use electric traction was the Bern-Loetschberg-Simplon in 1910. The photograph shows typical box-shaped engines taking their power through pantographs, and also shows one of the many spectacular steel bridges that are a feature of the line.

Many countries were initially loath to turn away from steam to electricity: the capital expenditure was simply too high. There were other problems as well. When the railways were constructed in the nineteenth century nobody was thinking about installing overhead electric systems, so they left no space for them. The Woodhead tunnel was one of the engineering marvels of the Victorian age; built 1500 feet up in the Pennine hills, it ran for over three miles, in places 600ft below the surface. But when the decision was taken to electrify the lines in the region, the tunnel proved an insuperable obstacle so it and the entire line were closed, and the traffic diverted to other trans-Pennine routes. Long before that happened, however, steam faced another rival.

In 1892, Rudolf Diesel, a German engineer born in Paris, took out an English patent – a suitably international beginning for what was destined to be a transport revolution. He described an internal combustion engine in which the heat generated by compressing air was used to ignite oil pumped into the combustion chamber. The application of the diesel engine to trucks on the road was an enormous success, but it was not quite so obvious how the engine could be used on rails. The incentive was there. Diesel oil had been used instead of coal to fire steam locomotives very successfully, but when comparative tests were made between using oil in this way or more directly in an internal combustion engine, the results were more than impressive – they were startling. The internal combustion engine produced six times as much power for the same amount of fuel. No one disputed the figures, but there was still the difficult question of how to transmit the power. This was no problem with a truck, which could use a clutch and mechanical gearing; it was not so easy with a locomotive. One can imagine the effect of changing gear on an engine with a long, heavy train behind it.

One solution was to use the diesel engine with mechanical transmission, in small units or rail cars. These were excellent for high-speed runs with few passengers or for local services. The most spectacular example of the former was the two-car set built for German State Railways in the 1930s, which became known as the Flying Hamburger. If the name sounds comical today, with its image of a zooming bun packed with dubious meat products, there was nothing funny about it then. Its inter-city service out of Hamburg was notching up journey times to Berlin at average speeds of over 77mph. These compared with the very best speed available with British steam of 71mph on the Cheltenham Flyer. Britain did, however, boast a very elegant rail car service on the Great Western Railway, where the single cars had a modern, streamlined front. Elegant though they were, they could not claim to be anywhere near first in this field: rail cars were introduced into Sweden as early as 1913.

ABOVE: **Another new power source appeared on the railways with the introduction of diesel engines. They proved particularly successful in fast, light rail cars. This is the *Flying Hamburger*, which ran between Berlin and Hamburg in the 1930s at speeds averaging almost 80mph.**

LEFT: **British railways were slow to adopt diesels, with the exception of the GWR. This handsome rail car, seen at Didcot, was built in 1940.**

Other forms of transmission were tried, including hydraulics and compressed air, but the real future for most classes of locomotive lay with electric transmission. In this system, the diesel engine no longer drives the engine directly. Instead it is used as a generating plant, working a dynamo to produce electricity, and electric motors then take over the work of moving the locomotive. Subsidiary motors can also be run to provide everything from lighting to heating and even air conditioning. By installing a battery, the dynamo could be converted into a starting engine. Armstrong-Whitworth had developed an electric multiple-unit train for use on the Buenos Aires Great Southern Railway as early as 1929, but Britain with its cheap coal supplies was slow to follow up the idea. There was far more enthusiasm shown in Europe, where Denmark was among the pioneering countries, but the real impetus for change came from America.

The earliest successful American diesel-electric was a humdrum engine built for the important but unglamorous work of switching – moving trains at marshalling yards and termini. It was introduced onto the Central Railroad of New Jersey in 1925, a modest engine with an appropriately plain boxcab design and with an equally modest power of 300hp.

But by now the big players in the diesel game were turning their attention to the railroads. In 1935, General Motors introduced their new engines to the system. They had a rigorous programme of standardisation. They used V-type 2-stroke engines, with the cylinders set in two banks at an angle of 45° and driving a common crankshaft. They came in 6, 8, 12 and 16 cylinder versions, and that was it. The largest of these produced 1800hp and if extra power was needed they could be worked as a multiple unit. They proved particularly valuable when working at low speeds on steep gradients, which made them very attractive to customers such as Canadian Pacific with their demanding lines through the Rockies.

If the early electrics were comparatively ugly, the same could not be said of the new generation of diesels produced by the American companies. They started turning out passenger expresses, either as part of articulated train sets or as independent locomotives, which were immense, powerful and sleekly streamlined. With their bodies of stainless steel these locomotives epitomised the very best of design in the exciting years between the two world

American diesel-electrics were brought into passenger service in the 1930s as ultra-modern streamlined giants. This is the Burlington Zephyr, an elegant locomotive matched by new carriages in gleaming, unpainted stainless steel.

wars when modernism was sweeping through the world. Even the most blinkered steam enthusiast has to admit that there was something very special about these locomotives and, indeed, about the trains of which they were an integral part. The diesel-electric was proving itself in every department of railway work. The demise of the steam engine was delayed by war, but it was only putting off the inevitable. The diesel-electrics just went on getting more and more powerful by adding devices such as turbo-chargers. By 1965, General Motors was able to offer a 20-cylinder engine producing 3600hp. The electric railway and the diesel-electric locomotive represented the future of the railways across the world.

The story of what happened in Britain in the years following the end of the Second World War shows how battle was joined. Big steam locomotives were still being designed, notably by O. V. S. Bulleid of the Southern Railway. During the war he had introduced the Merchant Navy Class of three-cylinder Pacifics, and he then went on to adapt these as the Battle of Britain Class. These were among the last major developments of the private companies before they were taken over by the state in 1948. After nationalisation, engineers were given a brief to design standard locomotives that would meet a set of specific criteria. They were to be as simple as possible, with maximum steam-raising capacity, and the ability to handle a wide variety of traffic. Time saving was paramount, with mechanical lubricators, self-cleaning smoke boxes, rocking grates and self-emptying ash pans. The Britannia Class of 4-6-0s was developed to be used for mixed traffic, and the big 2-10-0

One of the most successful diesel classes in Britain was the Deltic, and the engines are now regarded with as much affection by many enthusiasts as the steam engines they replaced. Here Deltic D9000 *Royal Scots Grey* is seen on a rail tour, leaving Blea Moor tunnel on the Settle & Carlisle.

British Standard Class 9F No. 92220 was built at Swindon in 1960 and was to find a place in the history books as the last steam locomotive to be built for British Railways. In honour of the occasion it became the only one of its class to be given a name, *Evening Star*, and is seen here at the North Yorkshire Moors Railway.

Class 9s for heavy freight duties, and four other classes were also designed. Another four were planned but were destined never to leave the drawing board. The world of transport was inexorably changing. In 1959 Britain's first major motorway, the M1, opened and the following year the last steam locomotive to be built for the national rail system was rolled out of the Swindon Works. No. 92220 was a Class 9, but it was decided that it should be honoured with a name, and the general public was asked for suggestions. The final, appropriate choice was *Evening Star*. The locomotive is still to be seen regularly working on preserved steam lines all over the country.

Even before *Evening Star* took to the tracks, other engineers were thinking about the changes to come. Henry George Ivatt was the son of Henry Alfred Ivatt who, as chief engineer for the Great Northern, had pioneered the use of Atlantics in Britain at the end of the nineteenth century. The son was acting chief mechanical engineer at the Derby works in 1945, when he began to consider the diesel-electric as an alternative to steam. He went with his designs to English Electric and his first two engines, numbers 1000 and 1001, went into service in 1948. Their success speeded up the move away from steam. Engineers began to experiment in a variety of different areas, including the use of gas turbines, which were not very successful at first, and diesel hydraulics, which fared rather better. The most successful developments of the early years were the DMUs, the diesel mechanical units. There were four or eight cars in most sets of which half were powered and the other half were pulled. They worked local services successfully for many years. They were somewhat spartan in terms of passenger comfort, with bus-like seats, but they offered the passengers a novel experience – those sitting in the front could look out over the driver's shoulder to see the track up ahead. Perhaps the most famous of all the diesels built in the postwar period were the Deltics, which first appeared in 1961. They got their name from the arrangement of the banks of cylinders in a triangle, like the Greek letter delta printed upside down. They were powerful locomotives producing 3300hp, and they looked the part. They were pugnacious beasts, with the deep-set driver's window looking like a pair of eyes peering over a heavyweight boxer's jaw. They were capable of good speeds but usually limited to 100mph.

Style finally arrived on British tracks with the introduction of the High Speed Train in 1973, which was to run a new inter-city service at what was then the startling speed for regular running of 125mph. This was not a top speed reached by heading down a bank with the throttle wide open, but the speed at which the train was expected to work on a regular basis, so that in time they became known simply as the 125s. The power units and carriages were designed to work as a single unit, with a power car at each end. They soon became regular and welcome features on British rails, though the idea, borrowed from the airlines, of reducing leg room to cram in more passengers was less attractive. The 125s have worked well, establishing a diesel record of 143mph in 1974 and keeping up their regular high-speed schedules.

Railways everywhere were faced by growing competition. In America, the greatest challenge for passenger traffic came from the airlines, which offer fast inter-city connections at modest prices. Even the luxury trains looked unappealing when passengers were faced with a choice between the long overnight hauls and sleeper cars and the quick hop by jet. More and more the railways looked to freight to pay their way, and the passenger expresses which had once ruled the lines were reduced to the status of second-class citizens. Elsewhere the battle was joined. The problem faced by all railways, everywhere in the world, was that they relied on an infrastructure largely designed to meet the needs of nineteenth-century travel. Improvements could be made to locomotives and rolling stock; lines could be electrified; steam trains sent to the scrapheap to make way for diesels. But would that be enough? Some thought it would not. Japan showed a new way forward,

The Japanese rail system had been built to the comparatively narrow gauge of 3ft 6in. The authorities decided, quite rightly, that they would not be able to provide the service they wanted without radical changes. They chose to leave the old tracks in place, but built a brand new standard-gauge track alongside them, dedicated to fast trains with running speeds of 250km/h (155mph). The first route between Tokyo and Osaka was opened in 1964 to coincide with the staging of the Olympic Games in Japan. This was to be operated by the Shinkansen, the new super express, but when the electric train appeared before the public its revolutionary design gave it a popular name that it has never lost. It became the Japanese Bullet. Since the first line was opened the Shinkansen network has grown, and now the Bullets are a vital part of the whole rail system. Speeds have increased, with the fastest expresses, the 300-Series Nozomi trains, running at 270km/h, nearly 170mph. It is not only in speed terms that the service has been improved, and the conventional passenger trains have been joined by double-deckers, ideal for busy commuter lines.

The Europeans have also worked at developing faster trains, most famously in France, where there is a strong tradition of new thinking on the railways. An electric train had run as early as 1910 and engineers soon realized that the electric train would be particularly

effective in the mountains. One of the most spectacular lines in the Rhône-Alpes region was built to serve the giant anthracite mine of La Mure. It regularly disappears into mountain rock faces in tunnels, and at one point emerges on a narrow ledge a thousand feet above a lake. It opened in 1888 and in 1909 was converted to electricity. The mine has closed but the railway runs on, allowing tourists to enjoy the magnificent views. Other electric railways were developed in the Pyrenees, but the establishment of a countrywide network was hampered by the failure of the regional railways to agree with each other on standards, a problem that was only solved by the establishment of the national rail system, the Société Nationale des Chemins de Fer, SNCF. The new generation of fast trains, the TGVs, trains grande vitesse, have set a standard for modern rail travel. Like the Japanese, the French recognized the need for modern track to carry modern trains, and began building new track in the 1980s, continuing with more new lines, such as that from Paris to Avignon (p. 164). The TGVs are designed to work with different electrical systems across national boundaries. This process has been taken even further by the creation of Eurostar, and nothing shows more clearly the difference between thinking in Britain and French ideas.

The British contemplated the notion of replacing their Victorian infrastructure and discarded it. The preferred solution was to design a new type of locomotive that could travel at speed in spite of the track, the Advanced Passenger Train. It was to cope with curves by tilting, and speed would be ensured by the use of gas turbines. Work began in 1969 and the exercise proved far more complex than anyone had anticipated. The final result was highly sophisticated but not, it soon appeared, flawless. The more novel systems you introduce the more can go wrong. The first train entered service on 7 December and was withdrawn just two weeks later. The ATP has the unwanted record of having gone from operational use to museum exhibit in a fortnight. It was a sad affair, made doubly so by the fact that the tilting-train concept has been successfully introduced into Italy with the Pendolino. That is not quite the end of the story. In 2003 Virgin Trains introduced the Pendolino to Britain, but it was not as simple as putting the

train on the tracks and running a service. A considerable amount of track work had to be put in hand which involved closing an entire 40-mile section based on Stoke-on-Trent for four months. The result will be to cut journey times to London from two hours to ninety minutes.

The introduction of Pendolino is a step in the right direction, but Britain still has a long way to go if the system as a whole is to match the best of continental Europe. This might have passed largely unnoticed if the Channel Tunnel had not been built. The tunnel itself was an engineering triumph, even if the gap between the first proposals and the actual opening was rather longer than for most projects, at almost two hundred years. A wholly impractical plan for a tunnel for horse-drawn carriages appeared in 1802, with ventilation shafts poking up above the waves. Shipping interests soon put a stop to that! A more sensible selection for a rail link appeared in the 1870s, and some work was done. The scheme re-emerged a century later, and once again work started but was stopped because of political problems. The present system, with two rail tunnels and a service tunnel, was begun in 1987 and completed in 1991. It was an immediate success, carrying three million passengers in its first year. The tunnel is used by a shuttle service carrying cars, and by a brand-new passenger service, Eurostar, linking London to Paris and Brussels. The new train consists of an eighteen-coach set, offering real comfort with a smooth ride ensured by pneumatic suspension. The power unit by GEC Alsthom delivers a maximum speed of 300 km/h (187.5mph). For the first few years after the line opened, this beautiful train glided over the European network at high speed, only to emerge at Folkestone and be faced by a 100mph speed limit. The train was the same, but the track was incapable of carrying a high-speed link. The terminus at Waterloo International is as graceful as any station in Britain, and stands as proof that the architects and engineers are perfectly capable of providing structures that look at home in the twenty-first century. It only serves to make the failures elsewhere seem all the more lamentable. Happily, track improvements eventually got under way, with the first section of the high-speed rail link opened in September 2003.

Electric and diesel electric trains are at the forefront in most modern rail networks, but a new contender has appeared in recent years: maglev, an acronym for magnetic levitation. In this system the track consists of electromagnets with alternating polarities, so that when seen from the side a south pole is followed by a north pole and so on. The train contains super-conductive magnets, and the repulsive force between the magnets keeps the train hovering a little way above the track. It is driven forward by a linear motor. At trials in the 1970s in Japan, a train was found to be capable of reaching speeds of 500 km/h at an altitude of 10cm. There were a number of small-scale applications, such as in a subway at Osaka and in Britain on a monorail system at Birmingham Airport. Many countries have looked hard at the maglev option, but most have rejected it because of the very high capital costs. But in 2003 maglev was finally put into use on a line where its speed could be shown – if only very briefly.

The line runs from Shanghai to the airport at Pudong, just nineteen miles away. The track consists of a concrete monorail, with two sets of magnets, one for levitation and the other for guidance to ensure that the sides of the train remain free of the rail. Germany had earlier planned a maglev system between Berlin and Hamburg, but plans were dropped. Their expertise, however, was not wasted, for it was German engineering that produced the train. Hovering at a height of just 1cm, it reaches a speed of 430 km/h for a brief instant before it is time to slow down again for the end of the journey. Whether such an expensive system is justifiable over such a short distance is irrelevant. It has been an important proving ground for maglev, and now the talk is of extending the line to Beijing – and that, it has been calculated, would cut the journey time from Shanghai from fifteen hours to three. The maglev train has not broken any speed records yet. The Japanese Bullet scored 275mph in 1984 and this was passed under test conditions by a TGV five years later, pushing it up to 320mph. But passenger trains do not run under test conditions on a daily basis. The TGV has a maximum operating speed of 200mph but normally travels at around 155mph. The maglev maximum speed is currently less than the TGV, but it is expected to operate at an incredible speed of just under 250mph. History suggests that once a thing has been done and has been shown to work, it will be done again.

The world of railways has come a long way since Richard Trevithick first ran a little model locomotive over his kitchen table and went on to develop an engine that would run on rails. His was a world where steam seemed to offer almost unlimited opportunities for powering machines of all kinds, of which running trains down a track was just one out of many. He did not even see his locomotive as being entirely devoted to transport: it was a versatile machine that could be used as a stationary engine when power was needed at the works, and sent off down the tracks to pick up raw material or deliver finished goods. Others were to recognize that the steam locomotive could have more than purely local uses, and to take it out of the world of collieries and iron works and run it on a network of rails linking towns and cities throughout the world.

Steam itself has had a surprisingly long run. Just over twenty years ago, I visited the main-line passenger station at Delhi, where it seemed everything that moved in and out was still powered by steam. In the offices, enthusiastic officials showed me the plans for the electrification that was rapidly spreading throughout India. The old engines were destined for the scrapheap.

They were right to enthuse, for they were running a national rail network, and they wanted that network to be as efficient in terms of service and cost as they could make it. I congratulated them, but in my heart felt a sadness that in yet another country the steam years were ending. Logically, the steam engine's days should be over, but we are reluctant to let it go. There has probably never been a machine that has earned as much affection as the steam locomotive, with so many people prepared to spend a good deal of money and give up their spare time to preserve it. Even though it has not been possible to preserve examples of all the many varieties of locomotives produced over the last two hundred years, we have now begun building full-size working replicas. And there is even a proposal to take the process a stage beyond that – to build a steam locomotive that will capture the excitement of the great expresses of the last century. Known, unromantically, as the 5AT, this British design calls for a steam powered 4-6-0, inevitably conjuring up images of the Castles of GWR days. But the new engine, designed by David Wardale, draws on international expertise, borrowing from Wardale's work with South Africa steam in the 1980s, the American steam giants and the mighty QJs of China.

But, try as we might, we can never reproduce the real working days of the steam railway, nor should we want to do so. I am delighted that I can still enjoy the pleasure of travelling on preserved lines in many different countries; I am not so sure that I want the same conditions when I travel on business. One thing I can say with confidence: the last person to look back with nostalgia at the steam age would have been the man who started it all, Richard Trevithick. His eyes were always set on the future: given the choice between a ride behind an old steam engine and the chance to go and see maglev, he would have been on the first flight to China, inspecting and marvelling at the technology of superconductive magnets, and then he would be asking the question: 'What happens next?'

The railway systems of the world have faced immense competition from new transport systems, first on the roads and then in the air. Yet they have proved remarkably resilient. True, they no longer enjoy the position that they held in the nineteenth century, but they still play a vital role in both freight and passenger transport. More importantly, the spirit of innovation is as alive now as it was in the beginning. It seems likely as the airways become more congested and the road systems become clogged that the railways will have a vital role in the future. The man who began it all received little fame for his pioneering work and even less monetary reward, but he knew the importance of what he was doing, even if others doubted it. So the last word should go to the man who first set a steam locomotive running down an iron track, Richard Trevithick.

I have been branded with folly and madness for attempting what the world called impossibilities, and even from that great engineer, the late Mr. James Watt, who said to an eminent scientific character still living, that I deserved hanging for bringing into use the high-pressure engine. This so far has been my reward from the public; but should this be all, I shall be satisfied by the great secret pleasure and laudable pride that I feel in my own breast from having been the instrument of bringing forward and maturing new principles and new arrangements of boundless value to my country. However much I may be straitened in pecuniary circumstances, the great honour of being a useful subject can never be taken from me, which to me far exceeds riches.

THE WORKS OF THOMAS BRASSEY

Brassey was probably the busiest of all railway contractors, and he and his agents were responsible for construction throughout the world. The following list gives details of the lines on which he worked, but does not include a number of branch and mineral lines shorter than 10 miles. It is compiled from Sir Arthur Helps' book *The Life and Labours of Mr. Brassey*, published in 1872.

Year	Railway	Miles
1835	Grand Junction	10
1837	London & Southampton	36
1839	Chester & Crewe	11
1839	Glasgow, Paisley & Greenock	7
1839	Sheffield & Manchester	19
1841	Paris & Rouen	82
1842	Orleans & Bordeaux	294
1843	Rouen & Havre	58
1844	Lancashire & Carlisle	70
1844	Colchester & Ipswich	16
1844	Amiens & Boulogne	53
1845	Trent Valley	50
1845	Chester & Holyhead	31
1845	Ipswich & Bury	25
1845	Kendal & Windermere	12
1845	Caledonian	125
1845	Clydesdale Junction	15
1845	Scottish Midland Junction	33
1845	Scottish Central	46
1846	Ormskirk	30
1846	Shrewsbury & Chester	25
1847	Buckinghamshire	48
1847	Birkenhead & Chester Junction	18
1847	Haughley & Norwich	33
1847	Great Northern	76
1847	North Staffordshire	48
1847	Richmond & Windsor	17
1847	Rouen & Dieppe	31
1848	Glasgow & Barhead	11
1848	Barcelona & Mataro	18
1849	Royston & Hitchin	13
1850	Prato & Pistoja	10
1851	Norwegian	56
1852	Hereford, Ross & Gloucester	30
1852	London, Tilbury & Southend	50
1852	Warrington & Stockport	12
1852	North Devon	47
1852	Mantes & Caen	113
1852	Le Mans & Mezidon	84
1852	Lyons & Avignon	67
1852	Dutch Rhenish	43
1852	Grand Trunk (Canada)	539
1853	Sambre & Meuse	28
1853	Turin & Navara	60
1853	Royal Danish	75
1854	Central Italian	52
1854	Turin & Susa	34
1855	East Suffolk	63
1855	Inverness & Nairn	16
1855	Portsmouth Direct	33
1855	Caen & Cherbourg	94
1856	Elizabeth-Linz	49
1857	Leicester & Hitchin	63
1857	Leominster & Kington	14
1858	Worcester & Hereford	27
1858	Inverness & Aberdeen Junction	22
1858	Bilbao & Miranda	66
1858	Eastern Bengal	112
1859	Crewe & Shrewsbury	33
1859	Victor Emmanuel	73
1859	Ivrea	19
1859	New South Wales	54
1860	Salisbury & Yeovil	40
1860	Portpatrick	17
1860	Maremma, Leghorn	138
1860	Jutland	270
1861	Knighton	12
1861	Severn Valley	42
1862	Ashchurch & Evesham	11
1862	Nantwich & Market Drayton	11
1862	South Leicester	10
1862	Tenbury & Bewdley	12
1862	Wenlock & Craven Arms	14

Year	Railway	Miles	Year	Railway	Miles
1862	Mauritius	64	1864	Viersen-Venlo	11
1863	Epping & Ongar	13	1864	Delhi	304
1863	Sudbury, Bury St Edmunds & Cambridge	48	1865	Evesham & Redditch	18
1863	Meridionale	160	1865	Hull & Doncaster	16
1863	Queensland	78	1865	London & Bedford	37
1863	North Schleswig	70	1865	Llangollen & Corwen	10
1864	Epping	12	1865	Warsaw & Terespol	128
1864	Dunmow	18	1865	Chord (India)	147
1864	Corwen & Bala	14	1866	Moreton Hampstead	12
1864	Wellington & Market Drayton	16	1866	Bala & Dolgelly	18
1864	Enniskillen & Bundoran	36	1867	Czernowitz Suczawa	60
1864	Central Argentine	247	1868	Silverdale	14
1864	Lemberg Czernowitz	165	1870	Suczawa & Jassy	135

WHEEL ARRANGEMENTS

Throughout the book, steam locomotives have been described in terms of their wheel arrangements, generally using a three-digit system. The first digit refers to the number of leading wheels, the second to the driving wheels and the third to the trailing wheels. The example shown is a 2-4-2. Four-digit numbers are used to describe locomotives with two sets of cylinders, each driving different sets of wheels. An early example would be the articulated locomotive *Old Maud*, the first of the type to be built for the Baltimore & Ohio, which had an 0-6-6-0 arrangement. Many wheel arrangements were given names, and a few of the more popular and interesting classes are listed below.

2-6-0	Mogul
2-6-2	Prairie
2-8-2	Mikado
4-4-2	Atlantic
4-6-2	Pacific
4-8-2	Mountain
4-14-4	Andriev
4-8-8-4	Big Boy

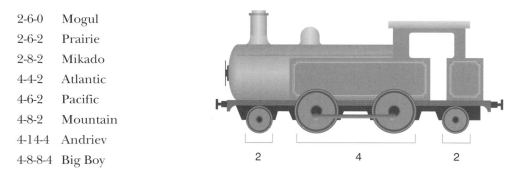

Many European countries use a different system, based on the wheels visible in a side view, which is why Honegger's musical salute to the steam locomotive is called *Pacific 231* and not *Pacific 462*.

CHRONOLOGY

c. 1550 Wooden rails used to help move trucks at mines.

1758 An Act of Parliament is passed for the Middleton Colliery Railway, the first to be authorised in Britain, originally designed to be worked by horses.

1769 James Watt takes out a patent for his improved steam engine, using a separate condenser.

1769 Nicolas Cugnot builds a steam-powered artillery tractor, which is tried unsuccessfully in Paris.

1801 Richard Trevithick builds the first of two steam carriages to run on the roads, first tried successfully at Camborne, Cornwall.

1804 Trevithick's first public demonstration of a steam locomotive running on iron rails, on the Penydarren tramway, South Wales.

1804 Oliver Evans builds a steam car for use on roads in America.

1812 Middleton Colliery Railway becomes the first railway to introduce a regular steam service. It uses a rack-and-pinion system.

1814 George Stephenson builds his first steam locomotive for Killingworth Colliery on Tyneside.

1816 An unsuccessful trial of a steam locomotive built in Germany on the Köningsgrube Tramway.

1820 John Birkinshaw patents a method for rolling, instead of casting, iron rails.

1825 The opening of the Stockton & Darlington Railway, the first public railway to use steam locomotives.

1827 The first railway in the Austrian Empire is opened using horse traction.

1828 The first railway in France is opened using horse traction.

1829 The Rainhill Trials are held to find a suitable locomotive to work the Liverpool & Manchester Railway. The winner is Robert Stephenson's *Rocket*.

1829 The first trial run of a steam locomotive in America by the *Stourbridge Lion*. It breaks the tracks and is withdrawn.

1829 Marc Seguin builds France's first steam locomotive for the Saint-Etienne & Lyons Railway.

1830 America's first public railway, the Baltimore & Ohio, opens in part with horse traction.

1830 Opening of the Liverpool & Manchester Railway, the first public railway to haul both passengers and goods by steam locomotive.

1831 The South Carolina Railroad opens with the American-built locomotive *Best Friend of Charleston*.

1834 The first steam railway in Ireland opens from Dublin to Kingstown.

1835 The first steam railway in Belgium opens between Brussels and Malines.

1835 The first steam railway in Germany opens between Nuremburg and Fürth.

1835 Joseph Locke designs a double-headed rail, forerunner of the bull-head rail.

1836 The opening of the Ffestiniog Railway, the first narrow-gauge line, run by steam locomotives from 1863.

1836 The first steam locomotive is built in Russia.

1836 The opening of the Champlain & St Lawrence Railroad, the first steam railway in Canada.

1838 The opening of the broad-gauge Great Western Railway between Paddington and Maidenhead.

1838 Electric telegraph is installed on a section of the GWR.

1839 The first steam railway in the Netherlands opens between Amsterdam and Haarlem.

1839 The first steam railway in Italy opens between Naples and Portici.

1839 The Bradshaw railway timetable is published.

1840 First experiment with atmospheric railway in London.

1841 Thomas Cook runs the first excursion train, and goes on to create a worldwide travel business.

1844 Block signalling system introduced between Yarmouth and Norwich.

1844 The first railway in Switzerland opens between Basle and St Ludwig.

1846 'Railway Mania' year in Britain, with 272 Acts of Parliament passed for new lines, most of which were never built.

1846 Introduction of an interlocking signal system at Bricklayers' Arms.

1848 The first steam railway in Spain opens between Barcelona and Mataro.

1851 The first steam railway in Africa opens between Alexandria and Cairo.

1852 A section of the Manua steam railway in Brazil opens, the first in South America.

1853 The Great India Peninsula Railway opens between Bombay and Thana, the first in Asia.

1854 The first steam railway in Australia opens between Melbourne and Port Melbourne.

1854 The first Scandinavian railway opens, between Oslo and Eidsvoll in Norway.

1856 John Saxby takes out a patent for a system for interlocking points and signals.

1857 The first steel rails are made in Britain.

1859 George Mortimer Pullman introduces the first sleeping-car service between Bloomington and Chicago.

1859 The Natal Railway opens, the first in South Africa.

1863 The first underground railway, the Metropolitan, opens in London.

1863 The first steam railway in New Zealand opens between Christchurch and Ferrymead.

1868 George Westinghouse demonstrates the automatic air brake on the Panhandle Railroad in America.

1869 The first American transcontinental rail link is completed at the Golden Spike ceremony at Promontory, Utah.

1869 The first mountain railway using a cog system opens at Mount Washington, USA.

1870 The first tube railway opens in London.

1872 The first Japanese railway is opened between Kyoto and Tokyo.

1879 A Siemens electric locomotive provides a passenger service for visitors to the Berlin Trades Exhibition.

1880 Opening of the Himalaya-Darjeeling Railway.

1882 The Swiss Gotthard Railway is opened, with a 15km tunnel through the Alps, the longest in the world at that time.

1883 The inaugural run of the Orient Express.

1884 Electric tramway opened at Frankfurt-am-Main

1885 The Canadian Pacific coast-to-coast line opens in Canada.

1890 The first electric underground railway opens in London.

1892 Rudolf Diesel patents his oil engine.

1893 The first electric elevated railway opens in Liverpool.

1895 Electric locomotives introduced onto the main line of the Baltimore & Ohio at Camden.

1904 *City of Truro* becomes the first locomotive to exceed 100mph in service between Plymouth and Bristol.

1906 Audible locomotive cab signalling introduced onto Great Western Railway, later developed into Automatic Train Control.

1907 Germany and Sweden linked by train ferry across the Baltic.

1909 Articulated locomotive, designed by Richard Garratt, built by Beyer, Peacock.

1913 The first diesel locomotive built in Switzerland.

1925 Automatic train coupling introduced in Japan.

1925 Diesel-electric shunting engines introduced into the USA.

1931 Railway speed record set in Germany of 143mph using a propeller driven railcar.

1938 *Mallard* sets a speed record for steam trains of 126mph.

1955 The French TGV reaches a speed of 331km/h (205mph).

1957 The Trans-Europe-Express service is inaugurated, involving six national rail authorities

1960 *Evening Star* becomes the last steam locomotive to be built by British Rail.

1964 A new dedicated high-speed line is inaugurated in Japan, with 'bullet' trains running at speeds of up to 220km/h (137mph).

1994 The Channel Tunnel opens, creating a direct rail link between Britain and France.

2003 The maglev train service opens in Shanghai and reaches a speed of 430km/h (267 mph).

INDEX

Numbers in *italics* refer to illustrations.

PICTURE CREDITS